SEVENTH CALIFORNIA EDITION

# How to Form Your Own
# CALIFORNIA
# CORPORATION

BY ATTORNEY ANTHONY MANCUSO

NOLO PRESS · BERKELEY

# Your Responsibility When Using a Self-Help Law Book

We've done our best to give you useful and accurate information in this book. But laws and procedures change frequently and are subject to differing interpretations. If you want legal advice backed by a guarantee, see a lawyer. If you use this book, it's your responsibility to make sure that the facts and general advice contained in it are applicable to your situation.

# Keeping Up-to-Date

To keep its books up-to-date, Nolo Press issues new printings and new editions periodically. New printings reflect minor legal changes and technical corrections. New editions contain major legal changes, major text additions or major reorganizations. To find out if a later printing or edition of any Nolo book is available, call Nolo Press at (510) 549-1976 or check the catalog in the Nolo News, our quarterly newspaper.

To stay current, follow the "Update" service in the Nolo News. You can get the paper free by sending us the registration card in the back of the book. In another effort to help you use Nolo's latest materials, we offer a 25% discount off the purchase of any new Nolo book if you turn in any earlier printing or edition. (See the "Recycle Offer" in the back of the book.)

This book was last revised in: FEBRUARY 1994.

| | |
|---|---|
| SEVENTH EDITION | MAY 1988 |
| Fourth Printing | September 1992 |
| Fifth Printing | February 1994 |
| ILLUSTRATIONS | Mari Stein |
| COVER DESIGN | Toni Ihara |
| BOOK DESIGN & PRODUCTION | Jackie Mancuso |
| INDEX | Mary Kidd |
| PRINTING | Delta Lithograph |

Library of Congress Catalog Card Number: 80-118046
ISBN 0-87337-069-4
Copyright © 1977-1994 by Anthony Mancuso
ALL RIGHTS RESERVED

by *Attorney Anthony Mancuso*
$29.95 BOOK WITH FORMS ON DISK

# ALL THE FORMS YOU NEED

# TO CONDUCT & DOCUMENT

# CORPORATE BUSINESS!

## *How to:*

- Stay out of trouble with the IRS and courts
- Comply with requirements for holding meetings
- Prepare minutes of annual and special meetings
- Pass board and shareholder resolutions
- Adopt employee fringe benefit plans
- Hire employees and independent contractors
- Borrow and lend money
- Make important tax resolutions
- Amend Articles and Bylaws

# INCLUDES FORMS ON DISK:

- Minutes of Annual and Special Meetings of Board of Directors and Shareholders
- Director and Shareholder Action by Written Consent
- Notice of Meeting and Waiver of Notice
- Yearly Meeting Summary Sheets
- Corporate Resolutions with the legal language necessary to accomplish numerous corporate tasks including:
  - Electing S corporation tax status
  - Adopting pension and profit-sharing plans
  - Adopting buy-sell restrictions on sale of shares
  - Amending your Articles and Bylaws
  - Borrowing or lending money from or to directors, shareholders or banks
  - Electing or re-electing your board of directors to another term
  - Approving the authorization and issuance of additional shares of stock
  - Hiring employees and contracting with outside firms and businesses
  - Approving the purchase or lease of commercial property
  - Declaring dividends

Plus **BACK-UP FORMS** necessary for important corporate transactions, including: corporate *promissory notes*, *employment contracts* and *independent contractor agreements*.

# TO ORDER

CALL **1-800-992-6656**
OR USE THE ORDER FORM IN
THE BACK OF THE BOOK.

**PREPARE A LEGAL PARTNERSHIP AGREEMENT FOR DOING BUSINESS IN ANY STATE**

# NOLO'S
# PARTNERSHIP
# MAKER ™

*from the publishers of WillMaker®*

• Get your business off to a good start
• Customize your agreement to fit your needs
• Avoid hefty legal fees

**DOS**

**N O L O   P R E S S   🔲   A C C E S S   T O   L A W**

# CREATE A LEGAL
# PARTNERSHIP
# AGREEMENT
# ON YOUR
# COMPUTER

*Nolo's Partnership Maker* allows you to quickly and easily prepare a legal partnership agreement on your computer. Using the step-by-step legal help, you can select and fill in clauses, print an agreement and show it to your partners for feedback. Repeat the process until you settle on a final agreement. Once you are satisfied, you can print out the agreement and have it signed by all the partners. And, you can change or revise your agreement at any time.

*Nolo's Partnership Maker* provides:

• 84 standard and alternative clauses
• on-line, step-by-step legal help for understanding each clause and filling in each blank
• an on-line editor that allows for customizing your agreement

Using *Nolo's Partnership Maker*, you and your partners decide:

• who contributes what to the venture
• what happens if a partner fails to contribute agreed upon money or services
• how profits and losses get divided
• how partners will be compensated
• how a partner can sell out or leave the partnership
• how to handle disputes without paying costly legal fees

### SYSTEM REQUIREMENTS

Dos 3.0 or higher, 512K Ram.

### FREE TECHNICAL SUPPORT

Nolo Press offers free technical support to all registered owners.

### UNCONDITIONAL GUARANTEE

All Nolo products have an unconditional guarantee. If for any reason you are unhappy with *Nolo's Partnership Maker*, simply return it to us for a refund.

# Acknowledgements

Special thanks to Ralph Warner for going over the technicalities of numerous corporate law and tax statutes and for helping me bring this material down to earth. Also to Jackie Mancuso and Toni Ihara for the production and design of this new edition, Ely Newman for proofreading, and Mari Stein for her imaginative illustrations. A heartfelt thanks to the hard-working people at Nolo Press for their help in making it all happen.

# Contents

## Introduction

CHAPTER 3

# Small Corporations and the Securities Laws

CHAPTER 4

# Corporate Taxation

CHAPTER 5

# Steps to Form Your Corporation

CHAPTER 6

# After Your Corporation Is Organized

CHAPTER 7

# Lawyers and Accountants

APPENDIX

# Tear-Out Forms

Request for Reservation of Corporate Name

Cover Letter for Filing Articles

Articles of Incorporation

Bylaws

Waiver of Notice and Consent to Holding of First Meeting of Board of Directors

Minutes of First Meeting of the Board of Directors

Notice of Transaction Pursuant to Corporations Code Section 25102(f)

Stock Certificates

# How to Form Your Own California Corporation

**D**espite the trend toward economic concentration of once specialized lines of business into multinational megacorporations, there are still many small businesses striving to compete successfully with large corporations which seek an inexpensive means of taking advantage of the formality and economic flexibility of the corporate form. This book is written for these California businesses and the people who are trying to make them work.

In this book, we provide you with all the forms and instructions necessary to organize a small California corporation. Specifically, you can use this book and its forms to organize a privately-held profit corporation (eligible to issue its initial shares under California's limited offering exemption—this state's securities law exemption, applicable to the majority of newly-formed smaller corporations, is explained in Chapter 3) that will engage in any business activity except the banking or trust business or the practice of certain professions. This is not just a book "about" how to incorporate. We show you how to accom-

plish this task step by step, form by form, and line by line. Also, since we did not want this book to be a simple "cookbook," forms book or corporate "kit," we have included chapters that provide in-depth discussions of the practical, legal and tax issues relevant to forming and operating a corporation.

Now a few words about professionals and their role in the incorporation process. Lawyers, generally, charge from $1,000 to $2,000 for an incorporation. The starting point, and basic premise, of this book is that it is usually not necessary for you to pay a lawyer to fill in the blanks on standard incorporation forms and to make routine filings with the state. This doesn't mean, of course, that you will never need, or wish, to consult a professional such as a lawyer or accountant. The incorporation of any business may pose complex legal or tax questions or unique problems related to the individual needs of your business. Consequently, throughout this book we have flagged areas of potential complexity or customization that you may want to discuss further with a professional. The lawyer's or accountant's job in the context of your incorporation will be to answer your specific, informed questions related to the individual facts of your incorporation, not to remake your decisions or rewrite your forms.

**Note on How to Use This Book**    Completing the Articles, Bylaws, Minute, and other documents necessary to form a small California corporation isn't difficult. But before you start filling in blanks, we have two favors to ask. First, read the material in the first four chapters carefully. It's designed both to give you background information about how corporations work and to warn you about potentially dangerous areas. You may find some of this material to be more technical than you need, especially if you are incorporating a small, relatively noncomplex business. Fine, you haven't lost much by reading it, and we are confident you will learn some things you need to know.

And now for the second favor. If you are confused by anything you read here, check it with an expert. Remember, if you form your own corporation the ultimate responsibility for making good decisions is yours.

**Please Note**    You cannot use this book to form a nonprofit or professional corporation (see Chapter 1), although organizers of these types of corporations will find much of the information contained in this book helpful. ■

**SPECIAL UPGRADE OFFER FOR COMPUTER USERS**

Nolo Press offers a special records binder with disk edition of this book. This special edition includes a disk containing computer files for each of the tear-out incorporation forms in the appendix of this book. These files have been prepared in the most popular wordprocessing formats, as well as text-only versions that can be read by all word processors. This special edition also contain tear-out and computer disk files to prepare minutes of ongoing director and shareholder meetings or to take action by written consent of directors or shareholders without a meeting. Separate stock register and transfer pages are also provided to help you keep track of share ownership in your corporation. Nolo Press offers a special upgrade offer to purchasers of this book—for the details, see the order pages at the front of the book.

# Advantages and Disadvantages
# of Forming a California Corporation

**T**his chapter provides you with general information on the advantages and disadvantages of incorporating. By way of a brief comparison, we will also look at the fundamental legal characteristics of other forms of doing business.

## A. Different Ways of Doing Business

As business owners, we know that there are many ways to run or operate a business. But the law, in its concern for the recognition and classification of form, places most businesses into one of three broad categories: sole proprietorship, partnership or corporation. Because this is a how-to-incorporate book, we won't spend a lot of time looking at the noncorporate forms of ownership.

### 1. Sole Proprietorship

A sole proprietor is the sole owner of a business. Employees may be hired and may even receive a percentage of the profits as wages. The owner, however, is personally liable for all the debts, taxes and liabilities of the business, including claims made against employees acting within the course and scope of their employment. The owner must report and pay taxes on the profits of the business on his individual income tax returns.

At death, a sole proprietorship simply ends. The assets of the business normally pass under the terms of the deceased owner's will, or by intestate succession (under the state's inheritance statutes) if there is no will. Unfortunately, in either case the probate process can take up to a year and can make it difficult for the inheritors to either operate or sell the business or its assets. Often, the best way to avoid this is to place the business assets into a living trust, a legal device which avoids probate and allows the business assets to be transferred to the inheritors promptly.[1] A good source of information on how to start and operate a small sole proprietorship is *Small Time Operator*, by Kamaroff (Bell Springs Press) (available through Nolo Press).

### 2. Partnership

A partnership is a business owned by two or more people. Although a simple oral agreement is enough to create a partnership, the owners normally prepare a written partnership agreement, specifying their respective rights and liabilities and the operating rules of the partnership (such as the manner of dividing profits and losses, what happens when a partner dies, or otherwise leaves the business, etc.). If no specific agreement is made to deal with these and many other central partnership issues, the statutory rules (contained in the Uniform Partnership Act) will apply to the operation and termination of the partnership. An excellent source of "how-to" information on doing business as a partnership and preparing a partnership agreement is *The Partnership Book,* by Clifford & Warner (Nolo Press).[2]

General partnership law principles include the following. Each partner is an agent for the partnership and can individually hire employees, borrow money and perform any act necessary to the operation of the business. Unless otherwise agreed, partners share equally in the profits. The partners themselves include their share of profits on their individual tax returns and pay taxes on them in the year in which they are earned at their individual income tax rates. Each partner is personally liable for the debts and taxes of the partnership. In other words, if the partnership assets are insufficient to satisfy a creditor's claim, the partners' personal assets are subject to attachment and liquidation to pay the business debts. Technically, a partnership terminates upon the death, disability or withdrawal of any one of the partners. However, commonly the partnership agreement provides in advance for these eventualities with the share of the departed partner being purchased by those who remain.

One final point about partnerships—the law also allows for the formation of a special kind of partnership, called a "limited" partnership. A limited partner, in conjunction with one or more general partners (the type discussed above), is allowed to invest in a partnership without the risk of incurring personal liability for the debts of the business. If the business fails, all that the limited partner can lose is her capital investment (the amount of money or the property she paid for an interest in the business). However, subject to some technical (and potentially tricky) exceptions provided for under California law, the limited partner is not allowed to participate in the management of the partnership. If she does, she loses her limited liability status.

A limited partnership cannot be established by verbal agreement alone. Under the California Revised Limited Partnership Act, setting up and operating a limited partnership is similar in many ways to the process of organizing and operating a small profit corporation. The Act requires the filing of a certificate with the Secretary of State, applies restrictions on the availability and use of partnership names, contains statutory requirements with respect to the manner of calling and holding meetings, and contains many corporation-like legal requirements which apply to the operation of the limited partnership unless alternative rules are clearly spelled out in the partnership agreement.

**Tax Note** Generally, under the federal tax law, expenses and losses from a limited partnership are considered "passive" (nonactive) items and cannot be used as deductions or offsets to regular active business income such as wages, salaries, profits from an active business, etc. These limited partnership items can, as a general rule, only be deducted against other passive income (e.g., only against the individual's share of any partnership income on his individual return). Exceptions to this rule have been carved out under IRS regulations. For more information, see the sidebar entitled "What Constitutes Material Participation?" in Chapter 4C and check with your accountant.

## 3. Summing Up

With the exception of the limited partnership, these noncorporate ways of doing business have the advantage of requiring little official red tape. However, doing business this way can be risky. This is because the owners (except in the case of a limited partner) are personally liable for the debts of the business. One unsuccessful business venture can wipe out most, or all, of their personal assets. In addition, noncorporate ways of doing business often result in reduced flexibility in tax planning. Any profits realized from the business are automatically passed along to the owners and fully taxed to them at the end of each year. By contrast, as discussed in Section B below, the corporate form of ownership allows for considerably more flexibility when it comes to tax planning.

The death of the owner or owners of a small business also raises problems for the sole proprietorship or partnership. It often means the end of a business that has been built up after years of hard work. While the death of a central figure also is likely to cause problems for the small corporation, the formal structure of the corporation often makes the continuance or sale of the business easier.

It is true, particularly with the partnership form, that some of the problems associated with noncorporate business forms can be solved by careful planning and by the use of custom-tailored, written business agreements (if you are interested in doing this, see *The Partnership Book*, by Clifford & Warner (Nolo Press) or *Nolo's Partnership Maker* software, a program that allows you to prepare a partnership agreement on your computer). Further, in some instances, the owners of newly-formed small business are not ready emotionally or from a tax perspective to incorporate their business. In these cases, starting off as a sole proprietorship or a partnership (backed up by a carefully considered partnership agreement) makes good sense.

## B.  The Corporation

Now, let's look at the basic attributes, advantages and disadvantages of the corporation. A corporation is a statutory creature, created and regulated by state laws. In short, if you want the "privilege" (that's what the courts call it) of turning your business enterprise into a California corporation, you must follow the requirements of the California Corporations Code (abbreviated as "Corp. Code" throughout this book).

What sets the corporation apart from all other types of businesses, and makes it special for legal, practical and tax purposes, is that it is a legal entity separate from any of the people who own, control, manage or operate it. It is a legal "person" capable of entering into contracts, incurring debts and paying taxes. It is this distinction between the business and the people who own the business (the shareholders) from which many of the advantages of the corporate entity flow.

Unlike sole proprietorships or partnerships, the corporation is a separate taxable entity. Business income can be sheltered in the corporation and reported and taxed at the business (corporate) level only. The decision as to how much money should be kept in the business and how much should be paid out to the owners is, of course, completely in the hands of the people who own the business. In addition, since the corporation is a separate taxable "person," the instant you incorporate your business, you become an employee of your own business, eligible for tax-deductible employee fringe benefits—in effect, once you incorporate, you are truly working for yourself.

And, best of all, while you enjoy this dual tax entity status, with the ability to place a respectable distance between your business income and the amount of individual income you must report on your individual tax return, you also enjoy the advantage of limited liability. By forming a corporation you substantially insulate your personal assets from lawsuits and claims made against your business.

Specifically, this means that normally the liabilities of the business are only those of the separate corporate "person," not of the real people behind the corporation. People with claims against the business can only reach as far as the corporate assets and can't take the personal assets of the people who own and operate the corporation. We discuss limited liability and the other unique advantages of doing business as a corporation in more detail below.

## 1. Limited Liability

An important reason for incorporating is to limit the personal liability of the business owners for the debts and liabilities of the business. A corporate director, officer or shareholder is usually not personally liable for the debts of the corporation. This means that a person who invests in the corporation only stands to lose the amount of money or the value of the property which he or she has contributed for stock. As a result, if the corporation does not succeed and cannot pay its debts or other financial obligations, creditors cannot usually seize or sell the corporate investor's home, car or other personal assets.

*Example:* Rackafrax Dry Cleaners, Inc., a California corporation, has several bad years in a row. When it files for bankruptcy it owes $50,000 to a number of suppliers and $8,000 as a result of a lawsuit for uninsured losses stemming from a fire. Stock in Rackafrax is owned by Harry Rack, Edith Frax and John Quincy Taft. Are the personal assets of any of these people liable to pay the money Rackafrax owes? Absent unusual circumstances, the answer is No.

**Note on Potential Personal Liability for Borrowed Money and Taxes Owed**   Often when a bank or other lender loans money to a small corporation, particularly a newly-formed corporation, it requires that the people who own the corporation independently pledge some of their personal assets as security for the debt. Be aware that if you do this you have waived the shield of limited liability as far as the assets you pledge as security are concerned.

Another common situation where limited liability may not protect corporate officers or directors is when the corporation has failed to pay income, payroll or other taxes. The IRS and the state Franchise Tax Board do not recognize the concept of limited liability in this instance, and attempt to recover unpaid taxes from "responsible" employees if they can't collect these taxes from the corporation.[3] In other words, make sure to withhold, deposit, report and pay corporate income and employment taxes on time. Detailed information on corporate taxes is provided in Chapter 6.

## 2. Tax Planning, Financial Flexibility and a Brief Summary of Corporate Tax Rules

In this section, we take a preliminary look at some of the tax aspects of incorporating which can provide a significant amount of financial flexibility to the owners of an incorporated business.

Taxation is a significant area where a corporation can give the owners of a small or medium-sized business flexibility in decision making and financial planning. As we've said, by forming a corporation, the owners immediately become eligible to split business income between themselves, personally, and the separate taxable entity, the corporation. For example, corporate income can be paid out to the owner-employees in the form of salaries, bonuses, fringe benefits, etc. These payouts are deductible by the corporation and, therefore, are not taxed at the corporate level. Such salaries and bonuses will only show up and be taxed on the individual's federal income tax return.

In conjunction with the payment of deductible salaries and other amounts to the owner-employees, a portion of corporate income can be left in the corporation to meet the future needs of the business, or paid out as salaries or other deductible amounts to the owner-employees in later years (this way, the owners can control the amount of individual income they realize from their business in each year).

For small corporations with modest-to-medium profits this can often result in substantial tax savings since initial corporate tax rates on profits left in the corporation are low (we discuss corporate tax rates and provide examples of corporate tax savings in Chapter 4B2). The ability to split up and shelter such business income is a unique attribute of the corporation—the Internal Revenue Code specifically allows most corporations to accumulate up to $250,000 of retained earnings in the corporation, no questions asked (amounts above this limit can be accumulated for the reasonable needs of the business).

Partnerships and sole proprietorships, on the other hand, must report all business income on their individual tax returns in the year in which it is earned. In a very good (high income and high tax) year, this can sometimes result in unincorporated individuals wondering if they might have come out ahead if they had not done quite so well.

**Note**  Certain personal service corporations (those whose principal function is the performance of services in the fields of health, law, engineering, architecture, accounting, actuarial science, performance arts or consulting, and whose stock is owned by the professional employees of the corporation) are subject to a flat corporate tax rate of 35%. In other words, any taxable income left in the corporation at the end of the corporate tax year is taxed at the maximum corporate income tax rate.[4] (See Chapter 4B1.)

Also, owner-employees of a corporation are eligible for certain deductible fringe benefits not available to (deductible by) noncorporate business owners, such as sick pay, group term-life insurance, accident and health insurance, reimbursement of medical expenses, disability insurance and other employee benefits. The reason for this favorable tax treatment is simple: as we've said, when you incorporate your business, you become an employee of your own corporation, eligible for employee benefits. These benefits are deductible by the corporation and, for the most part, are tax-free to the owner-employees (they do not have to show these benefits as income on their individual federal tax returns).[5] (See Chapter 4G for further information on corporate fringe benefits.)

What about the old bugaboo of double taxation? Isn't it true that corporate income is taxed twice—once at the corporate level and again a second time when it

is paid out to shareholders? In theory this is possible. However, in practice it seldom occurs when it comes to small corporations. The reason is simple. Employee-owners don't pay themselves dividends (which are taxed twice), but pay themselves salaries and bonuses (taxed to the individual, not the corporation). If this is not practical because the business owner has absolutely no role in corporate operations or planning, owners also have the option of electing federal S corporation tax status which, we will see in the next paragraph, also avoids double taxation.

An added tax flexibility allowed to many corporations is the ability to elect to have profits and losses pass through the corporation directly to the shareholders and reported on their individual federal tax returns (in effect, allowing the corporation to be taxed as if it was a partnership) by electing federal S corporation tax status. In some circumstances it is wise to do this. For example, an S corporation is a handy way of passing initial start-up losses through to the shareholders to be deducted on their individual federal tax returns while retaining the legal status and benefits of a corporation.

The S corporation election also makes sense if the owners of the business find that corporate taxable income (net corporate income after subtracting all deductions including business expenses, salaries, bonuses, depreciation, etc.) will be subject to more taxes at the corporate level than if taxed to the individuals personally. However, your corporation must be substantially profitable before electing S corporation status for this reason. Again, this is because federal taxes owed on lower and moderate levels of corporate income are less than the taxes that apply to the same levels of individual income (see Chapter 4B2).

**Exception**  If you form one of the special personal service corporations listed above, you will be taxed at the maximum corporate tax rate of 35% and may, therefore, wish to elect S corporation status to have any taxable income left in the corporation at the end of the tax year pass through to the individual shareholders to be taxed at their lower individual tax rates. (See Chapter 4B1.)

Again, in Chapter 4B2 we discuss individual versus corporate taxation and what is really involved for typical small corporations in more detail.

There are several other unique tax advantages of the corporate form, such as the ability, in many cases, to have the corporation keep its books and pay taxes based upon a tax year which is unrelated to the tax year of the owners of the business (i.e., to elect a noncalendar tax year for the corporation).[6] As a result, many corporations can choose to prepare tax returns and year-end financial statements at a time which is most convenient for them and which best reflects their own unique business cycle.

Although corporate pension and profit sharing plans are, for the most part, similar in terms of their advantages to noncorporate Keogh plans, corporate plans still provide the added advantage of allowing plan participants to borrow as much as $50,000 of the funds contributed to the plan without penalty. Also, corporate-defined benefit plans allow a significantly larger level of contributions to be made to the plan by participants than those permitted to Keogh participants. (See Chapter 4G2.)

Other specific tax provisions favor the corporate form, one example being the ability of a corporation to make tax deductible charitable contributions— other businesses cannot deduct such contributions as a business expense.

There is, however, one tax rule that may make it disadvantageous to incorporate under some circumstances. At the risk of totally confusing you with legal gobbledygook, this is called the repeal of the General Utilities doctrine and it affects who pays taxes on gains from business liquidation. Simply put, both the corporation and its shareholders may have to pay taxes when the corporation is sold or dissolved.

While this sounds bad (why incorporate if you're going to get taxed twice if you wind up a profitable

business?), there are a number of reasons why this does not normally produce this unhappy result for smaller corporations. Here are two: First, this corporate tax rule only applies towards appreciated assets held by the corporation. Many corporations (particularly those that provide services) do not hold significant assets which have appreciated during the life of the corporation (often the fair market value of assets will decrease rather than increase), and will not be subject to this corporate level tax even if they do liquidate. Second, if a corporation anticipates that its assets (such as real estate) will appreciate, it may elect federal S corporation tax treatment prior to any substantial appreciation and avoid this corporate tax, since appreciation occurring while the corporation maintains its S corporation tax status is generally not taxable under this rule.

Of course, these are just some of the tax provisions which apply to corporations. The relative importance of these special provisions will vary from one business to another.

In determining whether or not to incorporate your particular business for tax reasons, the only sound advice we can give you is to actually sit down (usually with your accountant or financial planner) and determine if the corporate form will really save you money, based upon a careful examination of your own unique situation, taking into account such factors as:

- the specific sources and amount of income and expenses associated with your particular business;
- the amount of money you will wish to continue to receive individually (as a corporate salary);
- the nature and extent of deductible fringe benefits you wish to provide for yourself;
- the amount of money you wish to keep in the corporation to meet the future needs of your business (or simply to shelter from individual taxation).

Moreover, as we've said, tax considerations are just one factor in arriving at your decision to incorporate. For example, depending on the type of business you are engaged in, the corporate advantage of limited liability (particularly in these days of overpriced or unsatisfactory liability insurance coverage) may be far more important to you. Also, the availability of special corporate fringe benefits to the owner-employees of the corporation, and the certainty and formality of the corporate form as a means of acquiring and disposing of ownership interests in the incorporated business through stock ownership, are often of equal, or greater, importance in arriving at the decision to incorporate.

## 3. Formality

A more subtle, but very real, reason many people choose to incorporate is the sense of business respectability that goes with being a corporation. While this benefit is obviously intangible, many proprietorships and partnerships feel (often justifiably) that their operations are seen by the business or financial community as too informal. Incorporating is one way for business people to put others on notice that theirs is an established business whose operations are carefully planned and routinely reviewed. In other words, although placing an "Inc." after your name will not directly increase sales, it forces you to pay serious attention to the structure and organization of your business, something that is likely to improve all aspects of your business including sales. Besides, in a world where everyone else proclaims the professionalism of their business, you too are entitled to a little self-validation.

## 4. Commercial Loans and Capital Investment

The corporate form often "lends" itself to a number of arrangements for the borrowing of funds for business operations. Lending institutions are familiar with the various types of debt instruments which have been developed through the years to provide corporations with funds and the risk-conscious corporate lender with special preferences. Examples include corporate bonds (secured promissory notes) and debentures (unsecured notes), which can confer voting or management rights on the lender or can be convertible by the lender into shares which carry special dividend, liquidation or other rights. Furthermore, although this book is not designed to show you how to make a public offering of stock, this is one valuable future option that can provide a successful corporation with needed capital.

## 5. Perpetual Existence

A corporation is, in some senses, immortal. Unlike a sole proprietorship or partnership which terminates upon the death or withdrawal of the owner or owners, a corporation has an independent legal existence which continues despite changeovers in management or ownership. Of course, like any business, a corporation can be terminated by the mutual consent of the owners for personal or economic reasons and, in some cases, involuntarily, as in certain bankruptcy proceedings. Nonetheless, the fact that a corporation does not depend for its existence on the life or continual ownership interests of particular individuals does influence creditors, employees and others to participate in the operations of the business. This is particularly true as the business grows.

## C. Disadvantages of Incorporating

We've touched upon the basic advantages of incorporating your business. Let's look at a few potential drawbacks of doing business as a corporation.

- One disadvantage of the corporate form involves complying with the formalities of the California Corporations Code and other state statutes and regulations. This includes the payment of an initial minimum franchise tax of $800 and a $100 filing fee to the California Secretary of State. This franchise tax amount must be paid as a minimum franchise tax each year. Note that this minimum annual tax payment is credited against your annual California corporate tax liability—the computed taxes paid by most profitable California corporations (based on a percentage of corporate taxable income) will equal or exceed this minimum payment level in most tax years.

- Corporate tax rates may not save you tax dollars. We've already looked at the basic tax issues earlier in this chapter. Make sure you sit down and calculate the net effect of incorporating on your total tax situation, both personal and business. Again, many people decide to incorporate for nontax reasons (e.g., to obtain limited liability). If the payment of corporate taxes on money left in the corporation results in an increased tax bill, you can decide to elect S corporation tax status to pass corporate income through to the shareholders to be taxed at their individual tax rates only.

- The basic model of the corporate entity under legal and tax rules (this includes the S corporation tax rules discussed in Chapter 4C) is that the profits, losses and liquidation proceeds of the corporation are allocated to shareholders in proportion to their capital investment in the enterprise (e.g., a 10% shareholder receives 10% of any dividends declared or 10% of any assets remaining after a dissolution of the corporation).[7] Limited partnerships, on the other hand, can afford limited partner investors with the protection of limited liability while allowing the profits and losses of the venture to be split up as agreed among the partners, disproportionately to capital contributions if desired. This flexibility does come with some built-in disadvantages however. First of all, the general partner (you must have at least one) will be personally liable for the debts and liabilities of the partnership. Second, as mentioned in Section A2 above, generally the losses of a limited partnership are considered passive losses under federal tax law and, as such, cannot be used to shelter (offset) the partner's share of active partnership income (e.g., salaries paid by the partnership or guaranteed payments or allocations of partnership income) or outside income of the partners (nonpartnership wages, salaries, bonuses, professional or personal service fees, etc.) to reduce the partner's individual tax liability.

- The corporate form can result in increased accounting and bookkeeping fees, particularly if you have not already set up a double entry bookkeeping system and a system to generate accurate financial statements. Such double entry accounting journals and a general ledger are usually considered to be a necessity if you plan to operate as a corporation. Frankly, because there are many excellent reasons to establish good financial controls anyway, this item should probably be treated as an advantage.

- Upon forming your own corporation, you immediately become a statutory employee and will be subject to state and federal employment tax withholding and reporting requirements as discussed in Chapter 6.

- Another disadvantage of incorporating has traditionally been the $1,000 (or often far more) that you could expect to pay an attorney. This book, together with a little effort on your part, effectively eliminates this drawback.

**Note**   You also may fear that the corporate form may prove too difficult to administer, subjecting you to a constant barrage of time-consuming, record-keeping details. This fear is largely groundless: Routine, ongoing corporate formalities are mostly limited to annual meetings documented with standard minute forms. Legal stationers as well as public law libraries, have standard minute forms on hand that you can use for this purpose.

Another perceived disadvantage of incorporating in California, in the view of some incorporators, is that California incorporation fees and ongoing formalities are more cumbersome than those found in other states. This issue, which is largely illusory, is addressed immediately below.

## D. Incorporating Out-of-State (Or the Myth of the "Trouble-Free, Tax-Free" Delaware Corporation)

No doubt you have heard about the possibility of incorporating in another state, most notably Delaware, where initial and ongoing fees are lower and regulations are less restrictive than in California.

Even though California's corporation laws create a more relaxed atmosphere for corporation operations than many other states, it is true that the laws of some other states, such as Delaware, do allow for an added degree of corporate flexibility (particularly in areas of concern mostly to large publicly-held corporations—such as fending off corporate raiders) and slightly lower fees. For most California-based businesses, however, out-of-state incorporation is not desirable.

It is true that you may legally incorporate in any state you please. However, if your corporation is considered to be transacting intrastate (within California) business, it must qualify to do so with the California Secretary of State. Generally, corporations entering into repeated and successive transactions in California must qualify.[8]

To qualify to do business in California, a corporation which is formed in another state (legally referred to as a "foreign" corporation) must file initial and annual statements with the California Secretary of State, must pay an annual corporate franchise tax based on the amount of net profits it earns in California (computed by payroll, property and sales factors, with an $800 minimum payment each year), and must also pay an extra $350 qualification fee. When you realize that the corporation must also pay fees and file papers in the state of incorporation, you see that for the small or medium-sized business, incorporating in another state means that both fees and paperwork are nearly doubled. Obviously, putting your business in this situation is silly.

Also, a foreign corporation which has more than half its shareholders located in California and which meets other tests (generally, if an average of more than half its property, payroll and sales are within California) is subject to many of the same provisions of the California Corporations Code which apply to corporations formed in California.[9]

If a foreign corporation transacts intrastate business and doesn't qualify by filing the appropriate forms or paying the above fees, it cannot use the courts of this state to assert a claim based upon its business in this state. However, it can be sued in any county in the state and is subject to a fine of $20 per day. Further, if the failure to qualify was not due to reasonable cause, the corporation is subject to an additional $2,000 yearly penalty. If an unqualified foreign corporation later decides to qualify in order to use the courts of California to assert a claim based upon a California business transaction, it must pay a $250 fine in addition to all the qualification fees, franchise, business and property taxes owed due to previous operations in California. Finally, California law provides for a $500 to $1,000 criminal misdemeanor penalty against corporations that fail to qualify with the Secretary of State.

The conclusion to this discussion is simple: Unless your corporation actually intends to transact all or most of its business outside of California or to really be based in another state, it is usually simpler, cheaper and far more sensible to incorporate in California. ■

## Endnotes

[1] For detailed information on living trusts and estate planning, see *Plan Your Estate* by Clifford (Nolo Press).

[2] Also see *Nolo's Partnership Maker*, a stand-alone software program that allows you for prepare a partnership agreement for use in any state using an IBM-PC compatible computer.

[3] Under California Revenue & Taxation Code Section 6829(a), the responsible officers of a corporation are personally liable for California sales taxes owed by the corporation if the corporation is dissolved and the officers willfully failed to pay the tax. Also note: Under federal bankruptcy statutes, personal liability for unpaid federal trust fund taxes (such as employment withholding taxes, sales taxes, etc.) cannot be discharged in bankruptcy. See *U.S. v. Sotelo*, 436 U.S. 268 (1978); *George v. State Board of Equalization*, 95 B.R. 718 (1989).

[4] Also note: Corporations engaged in the practice of these specific professions or activities are limited to an automatic accumulated earnings credit of $150,000 (instead of the standard $250,000 credit). (See Chapter 4H.)

[5] These special corporate fringe benefits are not available to shareholders who own 2% or more of the stock in S corporations. (See Chapter 4C.) Also note that unincorporated business owners are allowed to deduct a portion (25%) of the premiums paid for themselves and their spouses for health insurance. (See Chapter 4G3b.)

[6] As a general rule, federal S corporations and personal service corporations (defined here as those whose principal activity is the performance of personal services substantially performed by the employee-shareholders of the corporation) are required to choose a calendar tax year for the corporation. However, exceptions to this calendar year rule for these corporations do exist. For example, one automatic IRS criterion for allowing a noncalendar tax year is if the corporation derives 25% or more of its gross receipts during some other period in the year. There are other exceptions which allow these corporations to elect a noncalendar (fiscal) tax year. (See Chapter 4D for more information.)

[7] Of course, many of these standard corporate ground rules may be altered by implementing a complex, multi-tiered shareholder structure with different series and classes of stock. Further, although not a common practice (as explained in Chapter 2A3), California law does allow certain small corporations to elect statutory close corporation status, and waive normal corporate participation rules with dividends and liquidation proceeds split up disproportionately to shareholders. If you are interested in implementing any of these nonstandard organizational features, you will need to see a lawyer.

[8] If you are interested in more information in this area, see California Corporations Code Section 191.

[9] See Corporations Code Section 2115.

# CHAPTER 2

# A Closer Look at California Corporations

This chapter gives you detailed information on the legal, financial and practical considerations relevant to California corporations. Much of the information discussed here will be important to you in considering whether or not to incorporate. Some information relates to the day-to-day operations of the corporation. The rest is simply nice to know.

## A.  Kinds of California Corporations

California classifies corporations in several, sometimes overlapping, ways. The first classification is "domestic" versus "foreign." A domestic corporation is one which is formed under the laws of California by filing Articles of Incorporation with the California Secretary of State. A corporation which is formed in another state, even though it may be physically present and doing business in California, is a foreign corporation. We've already taken a look at the relative advantages and disadvantages of setting up a foreign corporation in Chapter 1D.

Corporations can also be classified as "profit" and "nonprofit." The California Corporations Code does not contain any precise definition of these terms, but does refer to regular profit corporations as "business corporations" to distinguish them from nonprofit corporations. We will refer to regular business corporations as profit corporations. A nonprofit corporation is one which is set up under the special provisions of the California Nonprofit Corporation Law.

Another corporate category is the "professional" corporation. This type of corporation is regulated by special statutes and, as its name implies, is a separate type of corporation formed for the purpose of engaging in the practice of certain professions.

Finally, the Corporations Code contains provisions for setting up a unique type of small profit corporation, the "close corporation." A close corporation is one with a limited number of shareholders which allows them to enter into a shareholders' agreement which waives or alters many of the provisions of the Corporations Code. Specifically, the shareholders of a close corporation may agree to divide dividends and liquidation proceeds in a manner which is disproportionate to their percentage of stock ownership, dispense with a board of directors and, in effect, operate their business as an "incorporated partnership." Setting up this hybrid and somewhat amorphous type of corporate entity is rarely an advantage and is often a hindrance to the orderly operation of the business of the corporation, both internally and externally. Reasons for this negative assessment include the fact that banks routinely require the board of directors to approve the corporation's credit line or a loan transaction, and that most shareholders wish to participate proportionately in corporate proceeds according to their percentage of stock ownership, etc. We discuss the California close corporation in more detail in Section A3 below.

Now let's briefly describe each of these types of corporations, as well as the privately-held California profit corporation—the type of corporation for which this book was written—in more detail.

## 1.  Nonprofit Corporations

A nonprofit corporation is a corporation formed by one or more persons, for the benefit of the public, the mutual benefit of its members or religious purposes. California public benefit nonprofit corporations are usually formed for tax-exempt purposes under Section 501(c)(3) of the Internal Revenue Code for religious, charitable, literary, scientific or educational purposes. For example, child care centers, shelters for the homeless, community healthcare clinics, museums, hospitals, churches, schools and performing arts groups normally incorporate as nonprofits.

Except with respect to mutual benefit nonprofit corporations, the California Corporations Code prohibits the distribution of profits to members of nonprofit corporations. Most nonprofit corporations dedicate all corporate assets to another nonprofit corporation upon dissolution to comply with the stricter provisions of state and federal tax laws and to obtain exemptions from payment of corporate income tax (the main reason for organizing a nonprofit corporation). For example, if you establish a nonprofit corporation to educate the public as to the need to preserve wetlands for birds, you might state that upon dissolution all remaining money goes to the Audubon Society.

Nonprofit corporations, like regular profit corporations, have directors who manage the business of the corporation. Instead of shares of stock, membership interests can be issued whose purchase price, if any, is levied against the members. The nonprofit corporation may also collect enrollment fees, dues or similar amounts from members. Like regular corporations, a nonprofit corporation may sue or be sued, pay salaries and provide fringe benefits, incur debts and obligations, acquire and hold property, and engage, generally, in any lawful activity not inconsistent with its purposes and its nonprofit status. It also provides its directors and members with limited liability for the

debts and liabilities of the corporation and continues perpetually unless steps are taken to terminate it. If you are interested in more information, see *The California Nonprofit Corporation Handbook,* by Mancuso (Nolo Press).

## 2. Professional Corporations

The California Moscone-Knox Professional Corporation Act requires certain, but by no means all, professionals to incorporate their practices by complying with special state incorporation formalities. In some cases this also involves obtaining a certificate of registration from the governmental agency which regulates the profession (e.g., the State Bar for lawyers). The Act provides that professional services may be rendered by a professional corporation only through individuals who are licensed to practice the particular profession in which the corporation is engaged. It also limits ownership of corporate shares to licensed individuals and makes the corporation subject to the rules, regulations, and disciplinary powers of the agency that regulates the particular profession. Special forms and procedures must be used to incorporate a professional corporation. This book does not show you how to form this special type of California corporation.

It is essential that you clearly understand that only a few professions, in the everyday meaning of the term, are required under state law to incorporate their practices as professional corporations. For example, engineers, computer scientists, real estate brokers, financial advisors, and most professions outside the areas of law, healthcare and accountancy, do not incorporate as professional corporations but as regular profit corporations (the type of corporation formed by using this book). If you are contemplating incorporating a professional practice and must incorporate as a professional corporation, see *The California Professional Corporation Handbook,* by Mancuso (Nolo Press).

The following is a list of professions which must incorporate as professional corporations (professions marked with an asterisk may incorporate either as a

regular business corporation or as a professional corporation):

Accountant
Acupuncturist
Architect*
Attorney
Audiologist
Chiropractor
Clinical Social Worker
Dentist
Doctor (medical doctors including surgeons)
Marriage, Family and Child Counselor
Nurse
Optometrist
Osteopath (physician or surgeon)
Pharmacist
Physical Therapist
Physician's Assistant
Podiatrist
Psychologist
Shorthand Reporter
Speech Pathologist
Veterinarian*

**Architects and Veterinarians Reality Note**   As you can see, architects and veterinarians have the option to incorporate as a professional corporation or as a regular profit corporation. Typically, to avoid extra formalities and operating restrictions associated with the professional corporation, architects and veterinarians often choose to incorporate as regular profit corporations. If you decide to use this book to form your architecture or veterinary corporation, check with your state Board to make sure these rules are current (that you have the option to form a regular profit corporation instead of a professional corporation).

**Tax Note for Certain Professionals**   As mentioned earlier and explained in Chapter 4B1, professionals engaged in the fields of health, law, engineering, architecture, accounting, actuarial science or consulting will be subject to the maximum 35% federal corporate tax rate if substantially all the stock of the corporation is owned by the employees who perform professional services for the corporation. This rate will be applied to any taxable income left in the corporation (not paid out as salary, fringe benefits, etc.) at the end of the corporation's tax year whether or not the individuals involved are organized as a California professional or regular profit corporation.

## 3. The Close Corporation

A California profit corporation with thirty-five or fewer shareholders may, by including special "close corporation" provisions in its Articles of Incorporation and on its stock certificates, elect to be organized as a California close corporation in order to take advantage of special provisions of the California Corporations Code.[1]

As mentioned earlier, the primary reason for electing close corporation status is to operate the corporation under the terms of a close corporation shareholders' agreement, which can provide for informal management of the corporation and allow the corporate entity to operate under partnership-type rules. For example, a shareholders' agreement can dispense with the need for annual director or shareholder meetings, the need for corporate officers, or even for the board of directors itself, allowing shareholders to manage and carry out the business of the corporation without having to put on their director or shareholder hats. As with a partnership, profits can be distributed without regard to capital contributions (stock ownership); thus a 10% shareholder could, for example, receive 25% of the profits (dividends). In effect, a close corporation can waive many of the statutory rules which apply to regular California profit corporations and establish its own operating procedures according to the terms of a close corporation shareholders' agreement.

*Example:* Kelley Greene, a successful junior tennis champion, forms her own California close corporation together with her financial backer, What a Racquet, Ltd., a California limited partnership shareholder consisting of a general partner and ten limited partner investors. In the close corporation shareholders' agreement, the limited partnership is given complete managerial control of the corporation, the limited partner investors are provided with a participation in 80% of the profits and liquidation proceeds of the corporation, while Kelley is assured an annual salary and a 20% share in corporate profits and liquidation proceeds.

Complex investment arrangements of this sort are the primary use of the close corporation. Most incorporators will not wish to organize their corporation as a close corporation. Indeed, less than 2% of all California profit corporations are formed in this manner.

There are a number of reasons for the lack of popularity of the close corporation. To begin with, most corporations do not need, or wish, to operate their corporation under informal or nonstandard close corporation shareholder agreement rules and procedures. In fact, many incorporators form a corporation

in order to rely on the traditional corporation and tax statutes which apply to regular profit corporations. Secondly, shares of stock in a close corporation contain built-in (automatic) restrictions on transferability, and most incorporators do not want their shares to contain these transfer restrictions. Third, there are a number of potential problems related to the use of a close corporation shareholders' agreement which make it inadvisable without further inquiry and outside consultation with an attorney and an accountant. So, please see a lawyer if you are interested in forming this special type of California corporation.

## 4. The Privately-Held California Profit Corporation

This is the type of corporation for which this book was written. More specifically, the forms and information in *How to Form Your Own California Corporation* will enable you to form a regular profit corporation which is eligible to issue its initial shares under the California limited offering exemption contained in the Corporate Securities Law of California. Essentially, this means that your corporation will offer and issue its shares of stock privately, without public solicitation or advertisement (the limited offering exemption is explained in detail in Chapter 3). The remainder of this book is devoted to implementing and explaining the rules and procedures which apply to organizing and operating this standard type of California profit corporation.

In the material in this book, you will occasionally encounter the term "closely-held corporation." The Internal Revenue Code contains a definition of this term which we will refer to when explaining special corporate tax rules.[2] However, when we use this term outside of its technical tax context, all we mean is that the corporation is formed and operated by a small number of people who will be active in the affairs of the corporation, and that it will not rely on the resources and capital of outside investors or public subscribers to its shares—in fact, the type of corporation most readers will wish to set up.

## B.  Corporate Powers

The California Corporations Code gives profit corporations carte blanche to engage in any lawful business activity. In legalese, lawful doesn't just mean non-criminal; it means not otherwise prohibited by law. Generally this means that a corporation can do anything that a natural person can do. The Code, by way of illustration, lists the following corporate powers:[3]

1.  To adopt, use, and alter a corporate seal.
2.  To adopt, amend, and repeal Bylaws.
3.  To qualify to do business in any other state, territory, dependency or foreign country.
4.  Subject to certain restrictions, to issue, purchase, redeem, receive, or otherwise acquire, own, hold, sell, lend, exchange, transfer, or otherwise dispose of, pledge, use, and otherwise deal in and with its own shares, bonds, debentures, and other securities.
5.  To make donations, regardless of specific corporate benefit, for the public welfare or for community fund, hospital, charitable, educational, scientific, or civic or similar purposes.
6.  To pay pensions and establish and carry out pension, profit-sharing, stock bonus, share pension, share option, savings, thrift, and other retirement, incentive and benefit plans, trusts and provisions for any or all of the directors, officers and employees of the corporation or any of its subsidiary or affiliated corporations and to indemnify and purchase and maintain insurance on behalf of any fiduciary of such plans, trusts, or provisions.
7.  Except with respect to certain restrictions as to loans to directors and officers which we discuss later, to assume obligations, enter into contracts, including contracts of guaranty or suretyship, incur liabilities, borrow and lend money or otherwise use its credit, and secure any of its obligations, contracts or liabilities by mortgage, pledge or other encumbrance of all or any part of its property, franchises and income.
8.  To participate with others in any partnership, joint venture or other association, transaction or arrangement of any kind, whether or not such participation involves the sharing or delegation of control with, or to, others.

## C.  Corporate People

While a corporation is a legal "person" capable of making contracts, paying taxes, etc., it needs real people to carry out its business. These corporate people are classified in the following ways:

- Incorporator
- Director
- Officer
- Shareholder

The courts and the California Corporations Code have given these corporate people varying powers and responsibilities. In the subsections below, we discuss these Code provisions and a few court-developed rules.

**Note**  Distinctions between these different roles often become blurred in a small corporation since, under California law, one person may simultaneously serve in more than one, or all, of these capacities. For example, if you form your own one-person California corporation, you will be your corporation's only incorporator, director, officer and shareholder.

## 1. Incorporators

Legally, an incorporator is a person who signs the Articles of Incorporation which are filed with the Secretary of State when the corporation is formed. In a practical sense, the incorporators are the key people who make the business happen. Typically, these are the entrepreneurs who make arrangements for obtaining money, property, people and whatever else the corporation will need to make a go of it. An incorporator (sometimes called a "corporate promoter" in legalese) is considered by law to be a fiduciary of the corporation. This means that he or she has a duty to make full disclosure to the corporation of any personal interest in, and potential benefit from, any of the business he or she transacts for the corporation.

*Example:* If the incorporator (promoter) arranges for the sale of property to the corporation in which he has an ownership interest, the fact of such ownership interest and any personal benefit he plans to realize from the sale must be disclosed.

The corporation is not bound by the incorporator's (promoter's) contracts with third persons prior to actual formation of the corporation unless they are later ratified by the board of directors or the corporation accepts the benefits of the contract (e.g., uses office space under a lease). An incorporator (promoter), on the other hand, may be personally liable on these pre-incorporation contracts unless she signs the contract in the name of the corporation only and clearly informs the third party that the corporation does not yet exist, may never come into existence and, even if it does, its board of directors may not ratify the contract.

So, a simple suggestion: If you want to arrange for office space, hire employees or borrow money before the formation of the corporation, make it clear that any commitments you make are for and in the name of a proposed corporation and are subject to ratification by the corporation when, and if, it comes into existence. The other party may, of course, refuse to do business with you under these conditions and tell you to come back after the corporation is formed. This is usually the best approach to pre-incorporation business anyway (namely, to postpone it until the corporation is formed).

## 2. Directors

Except for certain specific decisions which require shareholder approval, the directors are given the authority and responsibility for managing the corporation. The directors meet and make decisions collectively as the board of directors, with a majority of a quorum vote usually being necessary for board action. However, the Corporations Code does permit the board to delegate, by resolution, most of the management of the corporation to an executive committee consisting of two or more directors. This arrangement is often used when one or more directors are unable or unwilling to assume an active voice in corporate affairs, and the remaining directors wish to assume full control.

The passive directors should still keep an eye on what the other directors are up to since the courts, in extreme circumstances, have been known to hold passive directors liable for the mismanagement of active directors. The board of directors may also delegate management of the day-to-day operations of the corporation to a management company or other persons, provided that these people remain under the ultimate control of the board.

Directors, like promoters, are fiduciaries of the corporation and must act in its best interests and exercise care in making management decisions. What does this mean? The law doesn't help much. It says a director must act "in good faith, in a manner [which the] ... director believes to be in the best interests of the corporation and its shareholders and with such care, including reasonable inquiry, as an ordinarily

prudent person in a like position would use under similar conditions"[4] (ever wonder what law students find to talk about for three years?). In effect, the Code leaves it up to the courts to define what type of good-faith duty a director owes the corporation. Courts, in turn, usually decide cases on an individual basis. Broadly speaking, however, the courts say honest errors in business judgment are OK, while fraudulent or grossly negligent behavior isn't. The Code specifically allows a director to rely on the apparently accurate reports of attorneys, accountants and corporate officers in arriving at decisions, unless there is some indication of the need for independent inquiry by the director. We discuss special provisions of California law below which allow you to insulate your directors in many cases from personal liability for breach of their duty to the corporation or shareholders. (See "Special California Director Immunity and Indemnification Rules" below.)

The director has a duty of loyalty to the corporation and usually must give the corporation a "right of first refusal" as to business opportunities he becomes aware of in the capacity of corporate director. If the corporation fails to take advantage of the opportunity after full disclosure (purchase of inexpensive land, for example) or if the corporation clearly would not be interested in it, the director can go ahead for himself.

Directors normally serve without compensation since their work, as directors serving on the board, is usually done because they are intimately involved with the business and will gain financially if it does well by being able to pay themselves a better salary and/or eventually selling the business. Reasonable compensation for directors is allowed, however, if it is paid for the performance of real services to the corporation. A director may also receive advancement or reimbursement for reasonable out-of-pocket expenses (e.g., travel expenses) incurred in the performance of any of her corporate duties. Any compensation, advancement or reimbursement paid to a director should be authorized in advance of such payments.

The board of directors may properly vote on a matter in which one or more of the directors has a personal interest (the Code uses the term "material financial interest"), provided the following conditions are met:

1. The director's interest in the transaction is fully disclosed or known to the board;
2. The vote to pass the resolution is sufficient without counting the vote of the interested director; and
3. The contract or transaction is just and reasonable as to the corporation.

The Code contains additional rules and procedures which can be used to validate actions which benefit directors (see Corp. Code Section 310).

Subject to some exceptions, if the corporation lends money or property to, or guarantees the obligations of, directors, these transactions must be approved by the shareholders (by a majority vote of the shares not counting those held by benefited directors or by the unanimous vote of all shareholders).[5] Of course, full disclosure of the nature and extent of the benefit to the directors should be made to the shareholders prior to taking the shareholder votes.

If a director violates one of the above rules, in that he grossly mismanages or takes advantage of the corporation, receives unauthorized or unwarranted compensation, or participates in unauthorized or unfair transactions, he can be subject to personal financial liability for any loss to the corporation, shareholders and creditors. In addition to actual damages, the director can also be subject to monetary penalties awarded as part of a lawsuit (punitive damages), be temporarily or permanently ousted from directorship and, in certain cases, can be subject to criminal penalties.

It is interesting, and possibly a little comforting, to note that a corporation can purchase insurance to cover legal expenses, judgments, fines, settlements, and other amounts incurred in connection with a lawsuit brought against a director for breach of duty to the corporation, its creditors or shareholders, or simply because of her status as a director of the corporation.

Insurance coverage or not, however, the corporation must reimburse (indemnify) a director for legal expenses if she is sued and wins the suit. The statutory indemnification rules (contained in Section 317 of the Corporations Code) become a bit more complicated if the director is seeking indemnification for judgments, fines, or settlements, or if she loses the suit. In the very rare eventuality that you face this sort of situation, you should consult an attorney. (We discuss these statutory indemnification rules and special provisions of California law which allow your corporation to indemnify your directors and officers beyond the limits contained in Section 317 of the Corp. Code in a separate subsection—see "Special California Director Immunity and Indemnification Rules" below).

**Reality Note**  Of course, if you are forming your own closely-held corporation with, let's say, just you and another business associate acting as the corporation's only directors, shareholders and officers, much of the discussion in this and the subsequent sections regarding formal corporate director, officer and shareholder procedures will not apply to you. In such cases, formal director's meetings will probably be held infrequently (the tear-out Bylaws in this book provide for an annual meeting of the Board of Directors) and you will not have to worry about unfairly taking advantage of your own corporation or its shareholders since, obviously and by definition, you cannot defraud or take advantage of yourselves as shareholders. In other words, since there will be an identity of interest between you and your closely-held corporation, it's not so important that you deal with your corporation at arm's length. However, if even a few others invest in your corporation, all the rules and legal principles regarding fair dealing discussed above apply.

## a. Special California Director Immunity and Indemnification Rules

California corporations, like corporations in other "liberal" jurisdictions (such as Delaware), can add provisions to their Articles of Incorporation which, in many cases, eliminate the personal liability of their directors for monetary damages and allow the corporation to indemnify them (pay them back) for expenses, settlements, fines, judgments and other costs associated with lawsuits brought against the directors beyond the limits on indemnification contained in the California Corporations Code.

**Director Immunity**  Provisions of California law (Corp. Code. Secs. 204(a)(10) and (11), 204.5 and 317) allow California corporations to include language in their Articles limiting or eliminating the personal liability of directors, as directors, for monetary damages, in suits brought by or in the right of the corporation for breach of a director's duties to the corporation and its shareholders. The essential point to grasp here is that this language must be included in your Articles of Incorporation for your corporation to qualify for this higher level of director protection. The tear-out Articles of Incorporation included in this book contain this director immunity language.

**Important** These provisions do not insulate directors from liability which arises in a suit brought by a third party (e.g., for damages to an outsider caused by the act or omission of a director). They can be used, however, to protect directors from personal liability in shareholder derivative suits in many situations where the director is acting in good faith and according to law. A shareholder derivative suit arises when a shareholder sues the directors in the name of the corporation for damages caused to the corporation or to the shareholders.

*Example:* If your board of directors makes what turns out to be a poor management decision resulting in a monetary loss to the corporation (and a corresponding reduction in the value of the shareholders' stock), a shareholder (perhaps one who has been at odds with the directors for years) may decide to sue the directors personally in a shareholder's derivative action to have the corporation recover the amount of this loss from the directors. Of course, if the same shareholder is also injured in his individual capacity (he slips on the floor while walking through corporate headquarters), the shareholder could not bring this type of derivative action in the name of the corporation but, rather, would have to sue the directors (and the corporation) in a regular third-party lawsuit (the director immunity rules would not protect the directors in this type of lawsuit).

However, even in shareholder derivative suits there are some situations where the limitation or elimination of the personal liability of a director is not allowed.[6] These exceptions are discussed in the shaded box just below. Generally, they involve illegal or unethical director conduct and won't come into

play if your board of directors conducts business in a conscientious fashion.

**Indemnification** It is important here at the outset of this discussion of the special indemnification rules to underscore the distinction between the concept of "indemnification" and that of "director immunity" discussed above. Here's the basic difference: Although the director immunity rules may relieve a director of personal liability for a judgement in a particular case involving a director's breach of her duty of care, there are many other costs or payments which potentially arise in the course of defending or disposing of a lawsuit, such as settlement amounts, attorney fees, court costs and other litigation-related expenses, which are not covered by the director immunity rules. Generally, California's indemnification rules allow the corporation to pay a director (and officers, employees and other corporate agents) back for some or all of these additional types of lawsuit-related payments if certain requirements are met (see our brief earlier discussion of Corp. Code Section 317). With the high incidence of out-of-court settlements (regardless of the actual merits of the case) and the mammoth costs of preparing for and implementing the defense of even the most frivolous lawsuit (e.g., depositions, attorneys' fees, etc.), this director indemnification protection is essential.

Again, the basic background to California's indemnification rules is that Section 317 of the Corporations Code allows, and in some cases requires, corporations to indemnify (pay back) a director, officer, employee or other corporate agent (all of these corporate people are called "agents" under the statute) for expenses (court costs, attorneys' fees, etc.) incurred in defending a shareholder's derivative suit, and for expenses, judgments, fines and settlements incurred in third party actions—specific requirements must be met in all cases. There's a lot more to Section 317 but, for purposes of this discussion, we'll emphasize the following point: Prior to the enactment of the special rules discussed here, these indemnification provisions were.

## EXCEPTIONS TO SPECIAL DIRECTOR IMMUNITY AND INDEMNIFICATION RULES

You cannot protect your directors from personal liability (or provide additional indemnification for corporate agents) in the following circumstances:

1. Acts or omissions that involve intentional misconduct or a knowing and culpable violation of law;

2. Acts or omissions which the director believes to be contrary to the best interests of the corporation or its shareholders, or that involve the absence of good faith on the part of the director;

3. Any transaction from which the director derived an improper personal benefit;

4. Acts or omissions that show a reckless disregard for the director's duty to the corporation or its shareholders in circumstances in which the director was aware, or should have been aware, in the ordinary course of performing a director's duties, of a risk of serious injury to the corporation or its shareholders;

5. Acts or omissions that constitute an unexcused pattern of inattention that amounts to an abdication of the director's duty to the corporation or its shareholders;

6. Liability arising under Section 310 (for certain unauthorized transactions between the corporation and a director of a corporation in which the director has a material financial interest) and Section 316 (for certain unauthorized distributions, loans or guarantees made by directors);

7. Liability for acts occurring prior to the effective date of the immunity or indemnification provisions in the Articles (prior to the filing of your Articles); and

8. Liability for acts while acting as an officer of the corporation. The rules indicate that the limitation or elimination of the liability of an officer, while acting as an officer, is not permitted under these special rules, notwithstanding the fact that the officer is also a director or that the directors have ratified the officer's actions.

"exclusive"—meaning that corporations could not go beyond Section 317 and seek to indemnify directors and officers for circumstances and amounts not specifically allowed under Section 317.

With the enactment of these special rules, this exclusivity rule has been changed: now, a California corporation can include language in its Articles authorizing the indemnification of corporate agents in excess of the indemnification expressly permitted by Section 317.

Two key points to keep in mind when reviewing these special indemnification provisions:

1. The corporation can authorize and provide additional indemnification for directors and officers in situations where they have breached a duty to the corporation or its shareholders (shareholder derivative suit situations) and where they have incurred liability for acts or omissions affecting others (third-party liability situations); and

2. In situations where the director or officer has breached a duty to the corporation or the shareholders, additional indemnification is not allowed for the same types of prohibited acts and conduct discussed above in relation to director immunity (e.g., intentional or reckless action, where the agent derives an improper personal benefit, etc.— see the accompanying boxed discussion) nor can this type of indemnification be authorized in or for circumstances still expressly prohibited by Section 317.[7]

In the tear-out Articles of Incorporation provided in this book, we have included language from Section 317(g) which authorizes indemnification *to the fullest extent permissible under California law*. This is "magic" language, which allows the corporation to provide for additional indemnification for directors and officers both for breach of duty situations (shareholder suit situations) and third-party liability situations. Article VII of the tear-out Bylaws actually provides for the indemnification, and simply contains a general statement requiring indemnification of directors and officers in all cases not prohibited by the California Corporations Code. This generalized formulation should suffice for most smaller California corporations. If you wish to provide your own language for additional director and officer indemnification, see Sections 317 and 204(a)(11) of the Cal. Corp. Code and refer to the discussion and suggestions in Chapter 5, Step 4.

## 3. Officers

Officers (president, vice-president, secretary and chief financial officer) are in charge of supervising or actually carrying out the day-to-day business of the corporation. For example, in smaller corporations, the president will often actively run the business and the chief financial officer (treasurer) will actually sign checks, make deposits, prepare invoices and receipts, etc. In larger corporations, the officers will oversee various corporate departments or regular corporate personnel who will perform these day-to-day activities. The powers, duties and responsibilities of the officers are set by the Articles, the Bylaws or the board of directors.

Like directors, officers owe a fiduciary duty to the corporation and are subject to the same requirement of acting in good faith and in the best interests of the corporation. Although not specified by statute, this day-to-day authority of officers should not include authority to enter into certain major business transactions which are generally understood to remain within the sole province of the board of directors (e.g., the mortgage or resale of corporate property). Special authority should be delegated to the officers by the board for these, and other, major transactions.

Again, in smaller corporations the board of directors and the officers will often be the same people. However, the directors, as such, should still meet as a board to approve major corporate transactions to ensure that courts and the IRS will treat your business as a viable corporate entity (see Section I below for a further discussion of this issue).

Officers are considered agents of the corporation and can subject the corporation to liability for their negligent or intentional acts which cause damage to people or property, if such acts were performed within the course and scope of their employment. The corporation, moreover, is bound by the contracts and obligations entered into or incurred by the corporate officers if they had legal authority to transact the business. This authority can be actual authority (a bylaw provision or resolution by the board of directors), implied authority (a necessary but unspecified part of duties set out in the Bylaws or a board resolution), or apparent authority (where a third party reasonably believes that the officer has certain authority).

Apparent authority is a tricky concept. What does it mean? The California Corporations Code defines the far-reaching nature of apparent authority. Section 313 of the Code allows any third party to rely on the signature of the president, vice president, secretary or assistant secretary, chief financial officer or assistant treasurer on any written instrument, whether or not this officer had any actual or implied authority to sign the instrument on the part of the corporation, as long as the third party did not actually know that the corporate officer didn't have the authority to sign it.

**Note** Of course, any act performed by an officer without the legal authority discussed above binds the corporation if it accepts the benefits of the transaction or if the board of directors ratifies it after the fact.

Corporate officers are normally compensated for their services to the corporation, either as officers or simply as employees of the corporation. The compensation should be reasonable and given for services actually performed for the corporation.

*Example:* Jason Horner and Elmore Johnson form their own publishing company. Jason is the President and Elmore is the Treasurer of the corporation. Jason is paid a salary for acting as the Publisher (not for serving as President). Elmore is paid a regular annual salary as Treasurer (for the bookkeeping, bill paying and other ongoing work related to the financial operations of the corporation). The point here is that the title of the person being paid is not critical (officer title versus an employee title). What does matter is the nature and extent of the work for which the person is being compensated.

The rules that apply to approving loans and guarantees made to directors (see the previous section) also apply to officers. Officers, like directors, can be insured or indemnified against liabilities under the insurance and indemnification rules discussed in the preceding section (the special indemnification rules discussed earlier for directors also apply to officers).

## 4. Shareholders

Again, when reading this material, remember our earlier reality note: If you are forming a closely-held corporation and will not bring in any outside shareholders (by outside shareholders we mean outsiders who do not also manage and operate the corporation as directors and officers), you will not need to protect yourself or your own corporation against your own actions, and much of the following discussion will not apply to you. Also realize that the directors of closely-held corporations without passive investors are not likely to wish to pay themselves dividends, preferring instead to compensate themselves directly as employees by way of deductible salaries and bonuses (see Chapter 1B2).

Shareholders, unlike directors or officers, are not normally considered fiduciaries of the corporation with the responsibility of acting in the best interests of the corporation. They are required, however, to pay the corporation the full value of the shares they purchase. Moreover, in some cases involving larger corporations, the courts have treated majority shareholders as fiduciaries with a duty of full disclosure and fairness to the corporation and the minority shareholders when transferring their majority interests to outsiders. Remember, the general rule is that shareholders enjoy the protection of limited liability and are not normally personally liable to or for the corporation.

Shareholders vote for the board of directors and do, therefore, have an indirect, and strong, voice in the management of the corporation. In addition, the Corporations Code requires shareholder approval of certain corporate acts including, with some exceptions:

1. The amendment of the Articles of Incorporation after the issuance of stock;
2. The sale, option or lease of all, or substantially all, of the corporate assets other than in the usual and regular course of business, except for mortgages and the like given to secure corporate obligations;
3. A decision with respect to certain mergers, or other reorganizations, of the corporation.

As already mentioned, shareholder approval may be sought to approve loans, guarantees or indemnifications made by the corporation in favor of a director or officer. Shareholders also have the power to act independently of the board of directors in certain limited situations, the most important, aside from electing directors, being a unilateral shareholder decision to:

1. Amend the Bylaws of the corporation;
2. Remove any or all of the directors from the board;
3. Dissolve the corporation.

In the absence of provisions to the contrary contained in the Articles or Bylaws, shareholders are given one vote per share (i.e., if you own 100 shares, you cast 100 votes for or against a shareholder action), with a majority of a quorum vote usually necessary to decide an issue subject to shareholder approval. Shareholders whose names appear on the books of the corporation (as of a certain date which may be specified by the board of directors) are entitled to vote on the matter in question. If a record date is set, it must

be no more than 60, nor less than ten, days prior to the shareholder meeting.

Aside from the limited participation in corporate affairs discussed above, shareholders' rights primarily include the right to participate in the profits of the corporation through dividends (again, most small corporations rarely pay dividends) and the right to participate, after the creditors are paid, in the liquidation proceeds of a dissolved corporation.

A shareholder, like any other person, can sue the corporation for personal wrongs or damages suffered on account of corporate action. If, however, the shareholder is damaged in her capacity as a shareholder (wasting of corporate assets by the officers or directors which devalues stock), the law says that the real injury is to the corporation. An injured shareholder, in this case, must ask the board of directors to bring suit or to take the appropriate action. Of course, where the damage was caused by the mismanagement, negligence or fraud of the directors, the shareholder is, in effect, asking them to take action against themselves and, as you might guess, this doesn't always bring immediate results.

If the shareholder can't get the directors to bring suit, as in the situation described above, or if an attempt to get them to do this through intra-corporate channels would be futile, the shareholder can sue in his own name. This legal action is called a shareholder's derivative suit since, as the theory goes, the shareholder derives the right to sue from, and on behalf of, the corporation, which is considered to be the party sustaining the injury. (We've already touched on shareholder derivative suits in our earlier discussion of director immunity and indemnification rules above). The corporation, somewhat inconsistently, is required to be named as a defendant along with the officers and directors who are responsible for the alleged damage. The court, however, does treat the corporation as the co-plaintiff of the shareholder for whose benefit the suit is brought. If, after initiation of the suit by the shareholder, the directors decide to bring the action themselves against those who are responsible for the injury, the court will dismiss the shareholder's derivative suit and litigate the case in this second action.

## D. How Many People May Organize the Corporation?

Section 200 of the California Corporations Code states that a corporation may be formed by one or more natural persons executing and filing Articles of Incorporation with the California Secretary of State. The person (or persons) filing the corporation's Articles are legally referred to as the corporation's incorporator(s).

California does not impose age, residency or other requirements on any corporate person (incorporator, director, officer or shareholder). However, in order to avoid contractual problems, we assume your incorporator(s) (the person(s) who sign your Articles), directors and officers will be at least 18 years of age.

Under California law, the Bylaws of your corporation must provide for at least three directors if your corporation has three or more shareholders. However, a corporation with two shareholders is allowed to have only two directors. Further, a corporation with only one shareholder is allowed to have only one or two directors.

The Code further states that a corporation must have the following officers: a president, a secretary and a chief financial officer (or treasurer).

Summing this up, a corporation must have the following minimum number of titled positions:

- If one shareholder: one incorporator, one director, one president, one secretary and one treasurer;
- If two shareholders: one incorporator, two directors, one president, one secretary and one treasurer;

- If three or more shareholders: one incorporator, three directors, one president, one secretary and one treasurer.

Notice that these are the minimum number of titled positions. The Code allows one person to act as an incorporator, director, president, secretary and treasurer of the corporation. In other words, the same person may be an incorporator, a director and hold all of the officer positions. One person, however, cannot occupy more than one director position. This means that a corporation can be organized and operated by the following minimum number of people:

- If one shareholder: one person;
- If two shareholders: two people (two directors);
- If three or more shareholders: three people (at least three directors).

These are the minimum number of positions and people necessary to incorporate a business. However, it is important to note that a corporation may have as many incorporators, directors, officers and shareholders as are desirable or expedient to carry out its business. As a practical matter, it is quite likely that major corporate shareholders will wish to fill not only a director position, but will also wish to participate as officers in the day-to-day operations of the corporation. Subject to providing and filling the required positions, the details of these arrangements are up to you.

## E. Capitalization (Or How Much Money You Need to Form Your Corporation

A corporation needs people and money to get started. In the common sense definition of the term, the money or dollar value of assets used to set up a corporation is called "capital," and the process of raising the money or other assets is called "capitalizing" the corporation. There are no minimum capitalization requirements for corporations in California—theoretically, you could start a corporation with next to no money, property or other assets. There must be some consideration (e.g., money or property) given for shares, even if it's only a one-person corporation, but there are no statutory requirements as to how much is necessary.

While it often makes sense to start many types of businesses on a shoestring and to learn as you earn, the idea of starting a corporation without any money or assets is usually impractical. Profit corporations are in business to make money, and, depending on how capital intensive the type of business you contemplate is, you will usually need at least some assets to start with. In a legal and tax context, moreover, an under-capitalized corporation may be risky. Even though California doesn't require that a corporation have any minimum amount of assets, the courts and the IRS look at "thin" (undercapitalized) corporations with a leery eye, and in the past have occasionally subjected the shareholders of such corporations to personal liability for corporate debts and taxes (see Section I

below). To give yourself the best chance of making a success of your corporation and to protect yourself from such individual liability, you should pay into the corporation enough money and other assets to commence operations and cover at least foreseeable short-range taxes, expenses and potential liabilities that might occur in the particular business in which you plan to engage.[8]

There are several ways to get the assets necessary to capitalize a corporation. Perhaps the most common is to transfer the assets of an existing unincorporated business to the new corporation in return for shares of stock. In most other situations, a corporation is capitalized with money or property contributed to the corporation in return for its initial shares of stock, or with money which is loaned to the corporation in return for a promissory note.

It should be realized that the term "capitalization" refers loosely to the assets that a corporation starts out with and, as we've said, there should be enough to guarantee a good start. In bookkeeping terms, however, capitalization has a specific meaning and refers to the way the organizational assets are carried on the

corporate books—either as equity or debt. Equity capital is, generally, the amount of money or dollar value of property transferred to the corporation in return for shares of stock. Debt is, quite logically, money borrowed by the corporation in return for promissory notes or other debt instruments which should specify a maturity date, repayment schedule and a given (reasonable) rate of interest.

It is often true that the nature of the assets capitalized will, in and of itself, determine whether these assets will be carried on the books as equity or debt. In many cases, however, particularly in closely-held corporations, the incorporators can choose whether their contribution to the corporation will be handled as an equity or debt transaction. For example, they can loan money to the corporation, contribute it in return for shares of stock, or, as is customary, elect a combination of both techniques.[9] Because there are significant practical, legal and tax differences between equity and debt capital, it is often important to seek the advice of an experienced accountant or other financial advisor before opting for a particular capitalization method. However, we'll take a brief look at these differences here to give you a general idea of some of the considerations relevant to your decision.

In practical terms, a contribution of equity capital to a corporation in return for shares of stock is a risk investment. The shareholder will receive a return on this investment if, and only if, the corporation makes a profit and is able to distribute dividends to shareholders or, upon its dissolution, has assets left after payment of the corporate creditors to distribute to the shareholders. When equity contributions are made to a new corporation that has not operated previously in any form, this is indeed a high risk investment. Although still risky in terms of a start-up venture, a debt transaction is more certain, safer and generally more short-term, with the lender relying on the terms of a promissory note as to the date or dates of repayment and the rate of return (interest).

As we've already mentioned, a loan to a new business from an outside institution such as a bank will often require an added degree of safety, with the bank demanding that the personal assets of the incorporators (directors) be pledged as security for the loan. A standard note, however, unlike a stock certificate, doesn't carry with it the attractive possibility of providing the lender with a percentage of the profits or the liquidation assets of a successful enterprise.

The situation is altered somewhat for a closely-held corporation in that the shareholders of the corporation are not normally passively investing in an enterprise but are rather simply incorporating their own business, which will pay them a salary in return for their efforts and provide them with favorable corporate tax advantages. Nonetheless, if the incorporators lend money to the corporation, they too will be able to look to the specific terms of a promissory note in seeking a guaranteed rate of return on their investment, rather than relying solely on the profits of the corporation to pay them money by way of salary.

For tax purposes, an equity contribution may result in the recognition of taxable income by the shareholders: Dividends paid to shareholders are taxed to them as income at their own individual income tax rates. In addition, payment of dividends to shareholders is a distribution of profits, and the corporation is not allowed a business expense deduction for these payments. Debt capital, on the other hand, provides certain tax advantages to the corporation and to the noteholder. Interest payments, like dividends, are taxed to the recipient as income, but the repayment of principal is simply a return of capital giving rise to no individual tax liability. The corporation, moreover, is allowed to deduct interest payments as a business expense on its tax return.

### Warning—Debt to Equity Ratios Should Be Reasonable

The courts and the IRS have often been suspicious of corporations with a high ratio of debt to equity, feeling that creditors were inadequately protected, and that the corporation was a sham designed to insulate incorporators from personal liability and to grant them undeserved tax benefits (see the Section I below for more on this). For instance, if a disproportionate amount of money is "loaned" to the corporation by the incorporators of a closely-held corporation rather than paid in for stock, and the repayment terms are unduly permissive or generous, it might be held that the contribution was, in essence, an equity transaction contrived as debt to obtain favorable tax treatment. In this situation, the interest payments are subject to being treated as dividends, with the corporation unable to deduct these payments as a business expense and the lender-shareholder having to report repayment of the principal of the loan as income rather than a return of capital.

Another practical reason for watching your debt to equity ratio is that banks are unlikely to loan money to your corporation if this ratio is particularly lopsided (too much debt/not enough equity).

A guideline (that is subject to loads of exceptions depending on specific circumstances) is that a 3 to 1 debt to equity ratio (e.g., $30,000 of debt, $10,000 of equity) is considered to be relatively safe, while higher debt to equity ratios are considered to be progressively more risky, particularly those which exceed 10 to 1.

The courts have listed a number of criteria which they will consider when attempting to determine if a purported debt arrangement should be treated as a real debt obligation or whether it should be reclassified to the less favorable status of an equity contribution. Briefly stated, the courts have indicated that the debt instrument should be drawn up as a regular promissory note with a fixed maturity date and a specified rate of interest, and the corporation should have the right to enforce the terms of the note. The corporation should not arbitrarily grant the person making the loan any special preferences over other lenders or allow this person to postpone payments on the note. If the corporation is "thinly" capitalized (has a high ratio of debt to equity), can obtain loan funds

from outside lenders or uses the loan proceeds to acquire capital assets, these factors will make disallowance of the loan more likely.

### Loans and the California Securities Law

The basic point we want to make here is that notes issued by a corporation to lenders (shareholders, investors, etc.) are considered securities and must be qualified by the Commissioner of Corporations—usually by a somewhat complicated and costly procedure requiring the assistance of an attorney—unless the notes are exempt under a special rule from qualification. As you'll see in Chapter 3, we assume all the initial securities issued by your corporation to your shareholders (this includes both stock and shareholder loans) will be exempt from qualification under the California limited offering exemption. Many small corporations do not substantially capitalize their corporation with loans, or if they do, their loan transactions will be exempt from qualification under the California limited offering discussed in the next chapter. Nonetheless, because of the technicalities involved with this area of law, and since our focus in Chapter 3 must, as a practical matter, be limited primarily to the issuance of shares only, we think it would be wise to obtain the opinion of a lawyer regarding compliance with state and federal securities laws if you substantially capitalize your corporation with loan proceeds.

## F.  Sale of Stock

Corporate stock may be sold for:
- money
- labor done
- services actually rendered to or for the benefit of the corporation in its formation or reorganization

- debts cancelled and
- tangible or intangible property actually received by the corporation.

If shares are sold for other than money, the board of directors must state, by resolution, the fair value to the corporation in monetary terms (that is, they must state a dollar amount which represents the fair market value) of the services, property or other form of payment given for the shares.

Shares cannot be sold in return for promissory notes of the purchaser (shareholder) unless secured by collateral other than the shares themselves, nor can they be sold in return for the performance of future services (unless as part of an employee or director stock purchase or option plan).

*Example:* Thomas and Richard, after a bit of brainstorming, decide to form a Beverly Hills hang gliding tour service, called "Two Sheets in the Wind, Inc." Unfortunately, they know only one person who would be willing to actually strap himself in as their tour guide, a fellow flying enthusiast, Harold. Harold sees the unique possibilities associated with this enterprise and insists on owning shares in the corporation rather than being a mere employee. Since all parties concede that not just any Tom, Dick or Harry would be willing to assume this position, it is decided that Harold will receive one-third of the corporation's shares in return for entering into an employment contract with the corporation. Although this arrangement may seem extremely fair under the circumstances, the California Corporations Code, as we've said, does not allow shares to be issued in return for future services, and Harold will have to contribute something else of value for his shares. Harold suggests that the corporation issue its shares to him in return for a long-term note (he'll pay for them after he's survived a few tours). Again, since shares cannot normally be issued in return for promissory notes, this idea is discarded, and Harold decides to pay (or borrow) enough cash to purchase his shares outright.

# G.  Payment of Dividends

The Corporations Code restricts the rights of corporations to declare dividends. Before dividends can be paid to shareholders, certain legal and financial tests must be met. For the most part, the law applies generally accepted accounting procedures to determine the validity of dividend payments.

For example, a dividend cannot be paid unless:

1.  The amount of retained earnings of the corporation, immediately prior to the payment of the dividend, equals or exceeds the amount of the proposed dividend; or
2.  Immediately after the dividend:
    a.  the sum of corporate assets (not including goodwill and certain other assets) would at least equal $1\frac{1}{4}$ times the liabilities of the corporation (not including certain deferred items); and
    b.  subject to certain exceptions, the current assets of the corporation would be at least equal to its current liabilities or, in some cases, at least equal to $1\frac{1}{4}$ times its current liabilities.

In addition, no dividend can be paid if the corporation is, or as a result of the payment of a dividend would be, likely to be unable to meet its liabilities, not otherwise provided for, as they become due. Certain other tests apply for payment of a dividend to certain classes of stock if the corporation has more than a one-class stock structure.

The rules for determining the validity of payments of dividends (referred to, and included in, the term "distribution to shareholders" by the Code) are contained in California Corporations Code Section 500 and following. As you can see, these tests apply technical accounting standards, and you should consult an accountant or a lawyer before declaring and paying a dividend. If a dividend is paid and does not meet the appropriate tests, the directors of the corporation may be held personally liable to the creditors and shareholders of the corporation for the amount of the illegal dividend.

## H. Dissolution of a Corporation

We're sure the dissolution of your corporation is, literally and figuratively, the last thing on your mind at this point. Nevertheless, it might be comforting to know that you can wind up the affairs and business of your corporation with a minimum of legal formality. Here is a quick look at the basic rules which apply when voluntarily dissolving a California corporation:[10]

Any California corporation may, on its own motion and out of court, elect to voluntarily wind up and dissolve for any reason by the vote of at least 50% of the voting power of the shareholders.

In addition, the board of directors may elect to dissolve the corporation, without shareholder approval, if any of the following conditions apply:

- The corporation has not issued any shares.
- An order for relief has been entered under Chapter 7 of the Federal Bankruptcy Law for the corporation.
- The corporation has disposed of all its assets and hasn't conducted any business for the past five years.

Voluntary dissolution, upon the request of the corporation, three or more creditors, or other interested parties, may be subject to court supervision.

In any voluntary (or involuntary) dissolution, the corporation must cease transacting business except to the extent necessary to wind up its affairs and, if desired, to preserve the goodwill or going-concern value of the corporation pending a sale of its assets. All shareholders and creditors on the books of the corporation must be notified of the dissolution. All debts and liabilities, to the extent of corporate assets, must be paid or provided for, with any remaining assets distributed to shareholders in proportion to their

stockholdings and any special stock preferences. A certificate of dissolution must be filed with the Secretary of State, and the Franchise Tax Board must issue a tax clearance to the Secretary of State indicating that all corporate franchise taxes have been paid.

Corporate dissolutions subject to Superior Court supervision must include the publication of a notice to creditors at least once a week for three successive weeks in the county in which the court is located. Creditors not filing claims within a specified period (ranging from three to six months after publication) are barred from participating in any distribution of the general assets of the corporation.

### Voluntary Dissolution—How to Do It

The dissolution of a small corporation is, as we've said, usually a relatively simple procedure (unless it is subject to court supervision). Two forms must be prepared and filed with the California Secretary of State: First, a Certificate of Election to Wind Up and Dissolve,[11] and second (after the creditors have been paid in full or as far as the assets of the corporation permit, and after any remaining assets have been distributed to the shareholders), a Certificate of Dissolution. The Certificate of Dissolution or a separate statement attached to it must indicate the corporation or an individual agrees to assume any taxes owed or that may be assessed against the corporation. The Secretary of State will wait to get a tax clearance for the corporation from the Franchise Tax Board before filing the Certificate and dissolving the corporation. These formalities are simple and there is no fee for filing these forms. For further information on the voluntary dissolution of a California corporation, together with sample forms and instructions, obtain the *Corporations Check List* from the California Secretary of State's office (there is a small fee for this booklet—call the Secretary's office at 916-445-0620 for current ordering and price information).

## I.  Piercing the Corporate Veil

### (Or, If You Want to Be Treated Like a Corporation, It's Best to Act Like One)

After you've set up a corporation, you must act like one if you want to be sure to qualify for the legal protections and tax advantages the corporate form offers. Filing your Articles of Incorporation with the Secretary of State brings the corporation into existence and transforms it into a legal entity. You should be aware, however, that this is not enough to ensure that a court or the IRS will treat you as a corporation.

Courts occasionally do scrutinize the organization and operations of corporations, particularly closely-held corporations where the shareholders also manage, supervise and work for the corporation as directors, officers and employees. If a corporation is inadequately capitalized, doesn't issue stock, diverts funds for the personal use of the shareholders, doesn't keep adequate corporate records (e.g., minutes of annual or special meetings) or, generally, doesn't pay much attention to the theory and practice of corporate life, a court may disregard the corporate entity and hold the shareholders liable for the debts of the corporation. Using the same criteria, the IRS has been known to treat corporate profits as the individual income of the shareholders. In legalese this is called "piercing the corporate veil."

**Please Note**    Piercing the corporate veil is the exception, not the rule. If you follow the basic precautions mentioned below, you should never face this problem.

To avoid problems, your corporation should be adequately capitalized; issue its stock; keep accurate records of who owns its shares; keep corporate funds separate from the personal funds of the shareholders, officers and directors; and keep accurate records of all votes and decisions which occur at formal meetings of the board of directors and the shareholders. These formal meetings should be held at least annually and whenever you wish to document a change in the legal or tax affairs of your corporation (such as an amendment of your Bylaws, board approval of an important tax election, etc.) or an important business transaction (purchase of corporate real estate, authorization of a bank loan, etc.).

**Reality Note**    Of course, many corporations, regardless of their size, hold frequent meetings of directors, shareholders, staff, department heads, committees, etc. Here, we are talking about more formal legal or tax-related meetings documented by formal minutes. For one-person or other small corporations, these formal meetings will often be held on paper, not in person, to document corporate actions or formalities which have already been agreed to ahead of time by all the parties.

## J.   Summing Up—More Questions

The preceding sections of this chapter on general corporate law and practices may have raised a few questions that will require additional information for you to competently answer. Sorry. We could not (and at this stage you probably wouldn't want us to) squeeze a complete corporate law course into this chapter. Hopefully, we have given you an appreciation of some of the complexities of corporate law as well as an awareness that corporations are closely regulated by statute, subject to scrutiny by courts, and that there are certain problem areas which may require the advice of a tax or legal expert.

This doesn't mean you can't organize and operate a corporation on your own (we obviously believe you can) or that you should suffer mental anguish wondering whether your debt-equity ratio is the right size, whether you're forming a "thin" or a "fat" corporation, etc. The great majority of small, sensibly run corporations will not face any of these problems. It does mean that you should use your own business judgment as to when and why to pay a financial or legal advisor to answer specific questions related to your individual problems. The fact that you can competently do many things yourself does not mean that you will never need to see an accountant or a lawyer. ■

## Endnotes

[1]Technically, California close corporations are referred to as "statutory close corporations" since they are set up and operated under special California statutes. We will usually refer to this type of corporation simply as a "close corporation."

[2]Under Internal Revenue Code Sections 469(j)(1), 465(a)(1)(B) and 542(a)(2), a closely-held corporation is one where more than 50% of the value of the corporation's stock is owned by five or fewer individuals during the last half of the corporation's tax year.

[3]See Corporations Code Section 207.

[4]Corporations Code Section 309(a).

[5]See Corporations Code Section 316.

[6]See Corporations Code Section 204(10).

[7]For example, Section 317(c)(1-3) prohibits indemnification in certain circumstances where the director is found liable to the corporation for a breach of his duty to the corporation and its shareholders, for amounts paid in settling a case without court approval and for expenses incurred in defending an action which is settled without court approval.

[8]Nolo Press publishes an excellent book, How to Write a Business Plan, by McKeever, which contains step-by-step instructions to design your own business plan and loan package, which will be extremely useful if you wish to borrow money.

[9]Be careful if you are incorporating an existing business and plan to transfer the assets of the business to your new corporation partly for shares and partly in return for a promissory note—this sort of transaction is likely to be treated as a taxable exchange under IRC Section 351 (see Chapter 4F1b and check with your accountant).

[10]The rules in this section concern what is legally referred to as a "voluntary dissolution" of the corporation (where a majority of your shareholders mutually agree to dissolve the corporation). The California Corporations Code also contains involuntary dissolution procedures where a court is petitioned (by dissatisfied or deadlocked shareholders, directors or the Attorney General) to force the dissolution of a corporation. If you're interested in these special rules, see the California Corporations Code, starting with Section 12620.

[11]Under Corporations Code Section 1901(c), an election form is not required to be filed if the election to dissolve was approved by all outstanding shares, and this fact is noted on the Certificate of Dissolution.

CHAPTER 3

# Small Corporations and the Securities Laws

This chapter will provide specific information on an important incorporation issue: offering and selling your shares in compliance with California and federal securities laws. To use this book, you must be eligible for the California limited offering exemption when issuing your initial shares.

**Forms Note** In Step 6 of Chapter 5, you will prepare tear-out shareholder representation letters containing required and recommended information under the limited offering exemption. In Step 7 of Chapter 5, you will prepare the tear-out Notice of Transaction form, which must be filed with the California Department of Corporations when issuing shares under the limited offering exemption.

Since all stock transactions are also subject to the federal securities laws, we also provide information in Section C of this chapter on making sure you are exempt from registering your stock offering and issuance under the federal Securities Act and its associated regulations.

On first impression, some of the information in this chapter may seem complicated. If so, don't despair—it will make sense when you actually go through the steps in Chapter 5 and prepare the documentation necessary to issue your initial shares under the limited offering exemption. So for now, relax, read this information carefully and, if it still seems muddy, read it again when you go through Steps 6 and 7 of Chapter 5.

**Note** If for any reason, after reading this chapter, you conclude that you are not eligible to form a California corporation using the limited offering exemption, or if you have any questions, see a lawyer.

## A. Securities Laws and Exemptions

One of the most important steps in forming your corporation is the issuance of your initial shares of stock. You have the responsibility of making sure that your shares are offered and sold in strict compliance with the securities laws of California and the federal Securities Act. Federal securities law is primarily directed toward ensuring that corporations make full disclosure of all relevant facts to all prospective purchasers of shares. California law goes a step beyond this and looks to see that the stock issuance transaction is fair, just and equitable to all offerees and purchasers of stock (i.e., your shareholders). The California system is therefore referred to as a "merit" system (as opposed to the federal "disclosure" system), and is considered by many securities specialists to be the most rigorous in the nation.

You should realize that the securities laws of another state may also apply to your stock issuance transaction if you offer to sell your shares outside of California, or even if your offer to sell shares is directed to people in another state. Although the securities laws of a number of states provide exemptions similar to California's limited offering exemption for shares privately offered and sold to a limited number of people within the state, we cannot go into the details and exceptions here. We simply urge you to consult a lawyer to make sure you comply with the securities laws of any other state in which you plan to offer or sell your shares or where you plan to have shareholders. Remember, technical violations of the securities laws (even though no one is defrauded or unfairly treated) can often come back to haunt you later on—this is particularly true if you decide to have distant (out-of-state) investors in your corporation.

In California, your stock issuance must be "qualified" (approved) by the Commissioner of Corporations, usually by means of obtaining a permit for the issuance of shares, unless an exemption from qualification is available under the California Securities Law.

At the federal level, you must register your stock issuance with the SEC unless a federal exemption is available. Qualifying or registering a stock issuance requires the preparation and submission of complex legal and financial statements, takes time, and can be expensive due to accountant, attorney and filing fees.[1]

Fortunately, stock issuance exemptions exist in California and at the federal level which should allow most small, closely-held corporations to privately offer and sell their initial shares of stock without having to obtain a permit from the Department of Corporations or register with the SEC. Specifically, most small closely-held corporations should be able to qualify for the California limited offering exemption. As you'll see, one-person corporations, small family corporations and pre-existing businesses that are incorporating their current operations should find it particularly easy to meet the requirements of this exemption.

## B. The California Limited Offering Stock Issuance Exemption

As noted above, the California Corporations Code contains an exemption for the offer and sale of securities, called the limited offering exemption.[2] Although this exemption is available for various types of securities and securities transactions, we limit our focus here to how this exemption relates to the issuance of your initial shares.

The limited offering exemption is available, generally, if you will be issuing shares privately to your shareholders without advertisements or public solicitation for your shares and if other general requirements related to your stock issuance are met. We discuss these general rules in the section immediately below.

Additionally, you must meet special shareholder requirements and rules (in other words, you must look at each shareholder's qualifications, not just at your stock issuance in general). We discuss these special rules in Subsections 2 and 3 below. Finally, in Subsection 4, we give you a series of down-to-earth examples to put this rather technical information in a more practical context.

As an introductory comment, we want to make one very basic observation. Most small closely-held corporations should not have any trouble meeting the general requirements listed in the following subsection since they are reflective of the way most small corporations actually sell their shares. For example, the rules prohibit the publication of any advertisement for your shares and require that each purchaser buy shares for investment and not for resale. Most small corporations will be able to meet these and the other general requirements of the limited offering exemption easily.

**Caution for Future Stock Issuances**   The limited offering exemption contains technical rules relating to future stock issuances which we do not cover here. If you issue shares again after your initial stock issuance, you will need to be sure that you are not jeopardizing the exemption for your initial stock issuance and that this future stock offering meets the requirements of the securities laws.

## 1. General Rules of the Limited Offering Exemption

In this subsection we discuss the general requirements of the limited offering exemption. Again, most small corporations which plan a limited, private offering and sale of their initial shares should not have a problem meeting these basic requirements.

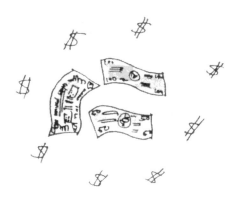

## THE CALIFORNIA SMALL OFFERING EXEMPTION

If your proposed stock issuance does not qualify under the California limited offering exemption discussed in this chapter, you may be able to rely on another California stock issuance exemption—the small offering exemption. In practice, this exemption may serve as a useful alternative if you will be issuing stock to all your shareholders for cash only (the other situations covered by the small offering exemption are, generally, also covered by the limited offering exemption, although in broader terms).

Under the small offering exemption, a lawyer is required to sign an Opinion of Counsel statement on a Notice form (which is filed with the Department of Corporations), stating that in the lawyer's opinion, the stock offering and issuance meets the requirements of the small offering exemption. Other formal requirements of this exemption require that a special transfer restriction legend be printed prominently on the face of each stock certificate, and that each shareholder be given a copy of a specific section of California law when receiving her stock certificate.

Because the small offering exemption is truly limited in scope, and because you must, in all cases, have a lawyer sign an opinion statement when relying on it, this book does not contain the small offering exemption notice form and we do not discuss its various requirements. However, if you experience any difficulty in understanding or meeting the (sometimes subjective) requirements of the limited offering exemption discussed here, we urge you to discuss this alternative with a lawyer.

FORMS NOTE   The forms contained in the Appendix of this book, such as the Articles of Incorporation, Bylaws, and most of the resolutions in the Minutes of your first meeting, will work fine if you utilize the small offering exemption instead of the limited offering exemption. However, it's important to realize that this book doesn't take you through the steps of a stock issuance under the small offering exemption since, in order to use it, you are required to see a lawyer anyway to have the required Opinion of Counsel statement signed, order special stock certificates, etc.

### a. The Investment Representation Rule

All purchasers[3] of shares issued under the limited offering exemption are required to represent that they are purchasing their shares for their own account and not with a view to resale in connection with any distribution of the shares. Shareholders in small closely-held corporations should not have any problem in making this representation. A more common example of shares which are purchased with an

intent towards resale are those which are publicly traded and listed with a national securities exchange. This investment representation must be made in writing.

**Forms Note** This investment representation is included in the tear-out shareholder representation letter contained in the Appendix.

### b. The No-Advertising Rule

This rule states that your offer or sale of shares must not be accompanied by the publication of any advertisement. The California Corporations Code defines "advertisement" to mean any written or printed communication or any communication by means of recorded telephone messages or spoken on radio, television, or similar communication media, published in connection with the offer or sale of a security (e.g., stock). "Publish" means publicly to issue or circulate by newspaper, mail, radio or television, or otherwise to disseminate to the public. Although these terms cover a lot of ground, the rules specifically indicate that this prohibition is to be interpreted to facilitate the circulation of disclosure materials to offerees, so long as these materials are not disseminated to the public.

If the disclosure of material about your stock issuance is limited to persons reasonably believed to be interested in purchasing the shares or to persons whom the corporation reasonably believes may meet the qualifications required of purchasers under this exemption, you should be within the rules as long as neither the corporation nor an agent acting on its behalf offers or sells the securities by any form of general solicitation or general advertising. In other words, use common sense in communicating the fact that you are setting up a corporation and will be issuing your initial shares. Obviously, you should keep these types of discussions with potential investors on a private level and not disclose the availability of your shares in any public way.

For example, you won't want to advertise your new corporation in the Business Opportunities section of the classifieds or use mailing lists as a means of targeting potential shareholders. Perhaps less obviously, you shouldn't hold a seminar or a meeting to which the public is invited where you plan to make even a soft pitch for your shares.

To sum up this section: We expect that most incorporators of small, closely-held corporations will naturally limit any overtures to invest in the corporation to close friends, relatives or business associates who are considered suitable purchasers under this exemption (purchasers who fit within one of the specific limited offering categories as explained in Subsection 3 below), in the context of a one-to-one conversation. If you do this, you should not have a problem complying with this no-advertising rule.

### c. The Consideration for Shares Rule

The limited offering exemption does not contain any specific requirements as to what type of consideration (e.g., money or property) may be received for shares. However, as we have discussed in Chapter 2F, other California laws state that you may only issue shares for certain types of consideration, such as money paid, tangible or intangible property received by the corporation, labor done or services rendered the corporation, or the cancellation of debts (the cancellation of debts owed by the corporation to the person receiving the shares). Shares cannot be issued under California law in return for future services or promissory notes (unless the notes are adequately secured by collateral other than the shares themselves). This means, for example, that you shouldn't issue shares to a key employee in return for her entering into an employment contract with the corporation—this is really issuing shares in return for the performance of future services. Similarly, you can't normally issue shares in return for the promissory note of a shareholder who promises to pay for the shares over time or at some later date. For further details on how to issue shares in return for different types of consideration, see Chapter 5, Step 5, Section A.

### d. The Notice of Transaction Rule

When relying on the limited offering exemption for the issuance of shares in a corporation (as we assume you are), your corporation must file a notice of transaction form with the Department of Corporations within 15 calendar days after the first sale of a security in the transaction in this state.

**Forms Note**   You will prepare this tear-out Notice form as part of Step 7 of Chapter 5. As you'll see, we show you how to prepare and file this notice just before the actual issuance (sale) of your shares to stay on the safe side of this deadline date.

### e. The Disclosure of All Material Facts Rule

Although the limited offering exemption does not contain any specific requirements relating to the disclosure of specific facts to shareholders, Section 25401 of the Corporations Code states: "It is unlawful for any person to offer or sell a security in this state or buy or offer to buy a security in this state by means of any written or oral communication which includes an untrue statement of a material fact or omits to state a material fact necessary in order to make the statements made, in light of the circumstances under which they were made, not misleading."

The Code also contains provisions for liability if this section is violated. Since you will undoubtedly be making at least oral communications in issuing your shares, make sure you are completely honest in your dealings with potential shareholders and that you disclose all material facts concerning your incorporation and share issuance to them.

## 2. Special Shareholder Suitability Rules

As we've said, special rules of the limited offering exemption require you to look at each of your shareholders to make sure he qualifies to be issued shares under the limited offering exemption. Specifically, each purchaser must fit within one of six suitability categories (we've broken the three main statutory categories into six more narrowly defined categories to make them more comprehensible). As you'll see, the basic purpose of these suitability categories is to ensure that each of your shareholders is able to protect herself when purchasing shares in your corporation.[4]

Before dealing with this specific material, a note of optimism: Most incorporators will not need to get bogged down in the more technical categories discussed below. In the usual case, all your shareholders will fit nicely into Category 1 (inside shareholders such as directors or officers) and Category 6 (spouses or relatives of another suitable shareholder). Since each shareholder only need fit within one suitability category, in these common instances you can simply review these two categories then skip ahead to the next section of this chapter. Simple.

## CATEGORY 1.  INSIDE SHAREHOLDERS

In this category, we discuss the most common types of suitable shareholders under the limited offering exemption: Those with a close relationship to the corporation, who we refer to as "inside shareholders."[5] Many small corporations will find that most, if not all, of their shareholders will fall into one of the inside shareholder definitions discussed here and will not need to be concerned with any of the other shareholder suitability categories discussed in the other sections below.

Here's a list of the different types of shareholders who fit within this inside shareholder category:

### a.  Directors or Officers of the Corporation

Since many small corporations will only issue shares to directors or officers, all of their shareholders will be suitable shareholders and their stock issuance will, therefore, easily meet the requirements of the limited offering exemption.

### b.  Executive Officers of the Corporation

We can't give you a precise definition here—all the law says is that "persons who occupy a position with the corporation with duties and authority substantially similar to those of an executive officer" are suitable shareholders under the limited offering exemption. However, the background material to this exemption seems to indicate that this rule relates to people who function more or less as directors or officers but who have different titles. If you find that you will be issuing some of your initial shares to a managerial or supervisory employee who isn't also a director or officer of the corporation, and you cannot qualify this shareholder under any other shareholder suitability category, then this inside shareholder suitability rule may come in handy.

### c.  Promoters of the Corporation

In this context, the word "promoter" means any person who, acting alone or in conjunction with one or more persons, takes the initiative in founding and organizing the business or enterprise of the corporation. Readers of this book who form their own corporation should be considered the promoters of their corporation. You should, however, not normally need to have to rely on this promoter status since your promoters will usually serve as the directors or officers of your corporation and therefore already be qualified as inside shareholders as discussed above. We mention this rule in case some person instrumental in organizing your corporation does not meet another shareholder suitability test of the limited offering exemption.

To sum up this category: If you find that all of your shareholders qualify as inside shareholders since they will be directors or officers (or, less commonly, because they can be considered executive officers or promoters) of your corporation, you don't have to bother with the more complex shareholder suitability requirements discussed in Categories 2 through 6 of this section.

## CATEGORY 2.  SHAREHOLDERS WITH AN EXISTING RELATIONSHIP TO DIRECTORS OR OFFICERS

Shareholders with a pre-existing personal or business relationship with the corporation or any of its officers, directors or controlling persons are also considered suitable shareholders under the California limited offering exemption.[6] The rules (the regulations contained in the California Code of Regulations as footnoted earlier) give a general (and not very helpful) description of this kind of relationship as follows:

"any relationship consisting of personal or business contacts of a nature and duration such as would enable a reasonably prudent purchaser to be aware of the character, business acumen and general business and financial circumstances of the person with whom such relationship exists."

As you can see, this is general language and will require a subjective determination of the suitability of a shareholder under this category. The rules state that the relationship of employer-employee, or of a shareholder of the corporation, will not necessarily meet this test (e.g., if you issue shares to someone who is already an employee of the business, you can't automatically assume that this person meets this relationship requirement).

For simplicity, we assume that a shareholder will need to have an existing personal or business relationship with a director or officer of your corporation to qualify under this category.

*Example:* You and three other business friends plan to incorporate your existing software development business, "Bits and Pieces, Inc." (The three of you will be directors of the corporation and will therefore qualify as suitable shareholders under the limited offering exemption as Inside Shareholders under Category 1 above). For the past five years, you have worked closely with Jessica, a professional outside programmer, in developing and marketing various programs, and you plan to bring her in as an initial shareholder in your corporation. Since Jessica has been closely associated personally and financially with you and the other principals of your corporation over a continuous and extended period of time, you conclude that she has the required relationship with you and the other directors which enables her to meet the pre-existing relationship test of this category.

**Additional Special Rule Note** If any of your shareholders qualify as suitable under this Category 2, please see Subsection 3, below, which contains information on a special 35-shareholder rule which may apply to you. As we explain further below, this special rule limits you to no more than 35 shareholders from certain limited offering exemption categories.

## CATEGORY 3.   SOPHISTICATED SHAREHOLDERS

Shareholders who, by reason of their business or financial experience can "reasonably be assumed to have the capacity to protect [their] interests in connection with the [stock issuance] transaction" are also considered suitable shareholders under the limited offering exemption. We refer to these suitable shareholders as "sophisticated" shareholders.

*Example:* You and your spouse are forming your own California corporation. Over a mixed doubles tennis match with your friends, Althea and Walter, each ask if they can invest as shareholders in your new venture. Althea is a CPA and Walt is an investment advisor and active trader of his own large portfolio of stocks. You conclude that both meet the sophisticated investor test stated above and will qualify as suitable shareholders under this category.

**Additional Special Rule Note** If any of your shareholders qualify as suitable under this Category 3, please see Subsection 3, below, which contains information on a special 35-shareholder rule which may apply to you. As we explain further below, this special rule limits you to no more than 35 shareholders from certain limited offering exemption categories.

## CATEGORY 4. MAJOR SHAREHOLDERS

Certain types of "major shareholders" (this is our term, used for convenience to help characterize this category) qualify as suitable shareholders under the limited offering exemption. These major shareholders must make a specified investment in the corporation or be able to meet either a net worth or income test (and must meet additional requirements as explained below). Here is a list of the three types of major shareholders suitable under this category (these three basic rules are contained in Sections 260.102.13(e) and (g) of Title 10 Cal. Code Regs.):

- A shareholder who purchases $150,000 or more of the corporation's shares;
- A shareholder whose net worth,[7] or joint net worth with a spouse, at the time of the stock purchase exceeds $1,000,000; or
- A shareholder whose income, or joint income (see footnote 6) with a spouse, exceeded $200,000 in each of the two most recent years, and who reasonably anticipates an income in excess of $200,000 in the current year.

In addition to these basic requirements, a major shareholder must meet (or the corporation must reasonably believe the shareholder meets) one of the following requirements (contained in Section 260.12.13(e) of Title 10 Cal. Code Regs.):

1. The shareholder's investment does not exceed 10% of her net worth or joint net worth with her spouse;
2. The individual, or her professional advisor, has the capacity to protect her own interests in connection with the stock transaction; or
3. The individual is able to bear the economic risk of her investment in the transaction.

You've no doubt noticed that these additional tests are either couched in vague, subjective terms or relate to additional financial tests. We won't dwell on these terms here. In the unusual event that you do need to use one of these major shareholder tests, it will usually be to qualify an outside shareholder (one who is passively investing in your corporation). Since these shareholders are outsiders and since, under these rules, they should have sufficient resources and business sophistication, we think your best bet is to ask them to check with their lawyer to make sure they meet the technical requirements of this category. Another way is to simply have them designate a professional advisor who will protect their interests in connection with their purchase of shares in your corporation (as explained in Category 5 just below).

## CATEGORY 5. RELIANCE ON PROFESSIONAL ADVISORS

Shareholders who, by reason of the business or financial experience of their professional advisor, can "reasonably be assumed to have the capacity to protect [their] interests in connection with the [stock issuance] transaction" are suitable shareholders under the limited offering exemption. This language is the same as that used for suitable shareholders in Category 3 above. The difference here is that the shareholder is relying on the business and financial experience of a professional advisor, not on his own individual experience.

A professional advisor is defined as "a person who, as a regular part of such person's business, is customarily relied upon by others for investment recommendations or decisions, and who is customarily compensated for such services, either specifically or by way of compensation for related professional services, and attorneys and certified accountants."[8] Besides lawyers and CPAs, the following professionals and institutions are also listed as examples of professional advisors:

Persons licensed or registered as broker-dealers, agents, investment advisers, banks and savings and loan associations.

Professional advisors must be unaffiliated with, and must not be compensated by, the corporation. If a shareholder relies upon a professional advisor to qualify under this category as a suitable shareholder, she must designate the advisor in writing. We discuss professional advisors further in Chapter 5, Step 6 of the book. For now, please note that Step 6 of Chapter 5 shows you how to designate a professional advisor for one or more of your shareholders when preparing the tear-out shareholder representation letter contained in the Appendix.

**Please Note**   This professional advisor category can be very helpful in qualifying any shareholder who does not neatly fit within any of the other categories. For example, if you wish to issue shares to an outside investor and are not sure if he meets the requirements of another category (e.g., if the only other possible Category is #3, and you don't feel comfortable in classifying the shareholder as a sophisticated investor under the language of that category), then simply have the shareholder designate a professional advisor (as further explained in Chapter 5, Step 6) in order to meet the more certain requirements of this category.

**Additional Special Rule Note**   If any of your shareholders qualify as suitable under this Category 5, please see Subsection 3, below, which contains information on a special 35-shareholder rule which may apply to you. As we explain further below, this special rule limits you to no more than 35 shareholders from certain limited offering exemption categories.

### CATEGORY 6.   RELATIVES OF OTHER SUITABLE SHAREHOLDERS

Spouses, relatives or relatives of the spouses (in-laws) of another shareholder who have the same principal residence as this other shareholder are automatically considered suitable as shareholders under the limited offering exemption.

This means that once you have determined that a particular shareholder is suitable under any of the above limited offering exemption suitability categories (Categories 1-5), then the spouse, relatives and in-laws of this shareholder who share the same principal residence with this shareholder qualify as suitable shareholders.

Note that the rules indicate that the term "relative" means a person who is related by blood, marriage or adoption. To give you one example of how this category works, if, as is common, you are only issuing shares to the directors and officers of your corporation and to their spouses (we assume that the spouses share the same principal residence), then all of these shareholders will be automatically qualify as suitable shareholders under the limited offering exemption: The directors and officers qualify as inside shareholders under Category 1; the relatives qualify under this Category 6. As we've said, most small closely-held corporations will only need to rely on Categories 1 and 6 in qualifying their shareholders as suitable under the limited offering exemption.

### 3.  Special 35-Shareholder Rule for Categories 2, 3 and 5

The limited offering exemption contains a special rule which prohibits you from having more than 35 shareholders[9] who fall within Categories 2 (Existing Relationship), 3 (Sophisticated Shareholders) or 5 (Reliance on Professional Advice). This rule is very unlikely to apply to you for the following reasons:

1. It's unusual for privately-held corporations to issue initial shares to more than 35 shareholders from all categories;
2. Even if you do plan to issue initial shares to more than 35 shareholders, the odds are over-

whelmingly against you having more than 35 shareholders in just these three special categories (Categories 2, 3 or 5). Remember, most shareholders of closely-held corporations will be directors or officers (Category 1) or their spouses or live-in relatives and in-laws (Category 6).

For these reasons, and since, as a practical matter, you are forming a much larger and more broadly-based corporation than we envision in this book if you plan to have more than 35 shareholders who fit within just these three special categories, we suggest you see a lawyer if this rule poses a problem for you. We're sure most readers can move on to Section 4 at this point without having to worry about this special rule.

## 4. Examples of How to Use the Limited Offering Exemption

Now that we've thrown a basket full of legal technicalities at you, let's look at the limited offering exemption in a more down-to-earth, real life context.

We assume that you will not have any trouble complying with the special rule of this exemption relating to the number of Category 2, 3 and 5 shareholders (35 or less in these categories as discussed in the preceding section) and the other rules set out in Subsections 1a-e above, such as the prohibition on advertising, the purchase of shares for investment purposes and not for resale, etc. Consequently, your main responsibility will be to make sure that your shareholders are eligible as suitable shareholders under one of the six categories discussed in Section 2 above. For many, if not most, incorporators of small corporations, doing this will not be difficult.

To get a better idea of how qualifying under one or more of the six categories works in practice, let's look at some specific situations.

*Example 1:* Assume Bob wants to form his own corporation and be the sole director and shareholder and fill all of the required officer positions himself. He will qualify as a suitable shareholder under the limited offering since, as a director and officer, he fits within the Inside Shareholder Category 1.

*Example 2:* Now let's assume that Bob wants to make his wife, Blanche, a shareholder, together with his mother-in-law, Beatrice, who has been living with them for the last fifteen years. No problem here also since Blanche and Beatrice qualify as Relatives of a Suitable Shareholder under Category 6: Blanche is Bob's wife; Beatrice is related to Bob's wife; and they both share the same principal residence as Bob.

*Example 3:* Changing this hypothetical situation around a little, let's now assume that Bob would like to incorporate his pre-existing partnership, Bob & Ray's delicatessen. Ray is Bob's brother and has decided to stay with the deli only as a part-time employee, allowing his half-interest in the business (worth $75,000) to be transferred to the corporation in return for half of the initial shares, with Bob managing the corporation as its only director.

Ray does not qualify as an Inside Shareholder under Category 1 since he will not be a director, officer, founder or promoter of the corporation. He does not qualify as a Major Shareholder under Category 4, since he cannot meet any of the three alternate tests of this category: he will not be purchasing $150,000 of the corporation; he does not have a net worth of $1 million dollars; and he has not, and does not expect to, earn $200,000 annually (you'll have to take our word for it). Further, although Ray is related to Bob (Bob is a suitable purchaser), he does not qualify as a Relative of a Suitable Shareholder (Category 6) since Bob and Ray don't share the same principal residence.

Consequently, we'll have to look at the other categories to qualify Ray as a suitable shareholder under the limited offering exemption. The logical choice here is Category 2 (shareholders who have a sufficient pre-existing personal or business relationship with the corporation, its directors, officers or controlling persons). Ray should be able to fit in this category in view of the fact that Bob and Ray have been doing business together for the past ten years. This should give Ray the type of pre-existing personal and business relationship with a corporate director (Bob) sufficient to allow him to "be aware of the character, business acumen and general business and financial circumstances" of that person. Of course, if Blanche and Beatrice still wanted to be let in as shareholders (let's say for cash), there would be no problem since they would qualify as suitable shareholders under the reasoning set out in Example 2, just above.

*Example 4:* Now, let's go one step further in this fantasy and say that Bob, in one of his infrequent yet customary calls to his stockbroker Bernie to check on the status of his small investment in pork belly futures, casually mentions that he is forming a corporation. Since the hogs have been good to Bernie too, he has a little extra money and thinks it would be a neat idea to purchase a few shares in a business that will get the hogs to market (and, hopefully, bring in a little bacon on the side). Bernie should be able to qualify as a Sophisticated Shareholder under Category 3, since he could be reasonably assumed to have the capacity to protect his own interests in connection with the purchase of his shares by reason of his own business and financial experience.

*Example 5:* Now let's assume that Bob, Blanche, Beatrice, Bernie and Ray succumb to pressure from Beatrice's younger brother Biff, who lives in the next town, and decide to let Biff in on this golden opportunity. Biff is a successful guitarist but lets his business manager take care of most of the details of the business side of his career. Biff doesn't stay in constant contact with the family, preferring to limit his visits to major holidays and occasional family get-togethers. Moreover, he rarely discusses family finances or business with his relatives and has never had anything to do with the deli. Biff will not qualify under the tests of Categories 1, 2, 3, 4, or 6. He is not an insider under Category 1; does not have a sufficient pre-existing personal or business relationship under Category 2; is

not a Sophisticated Shareholder under Category 3 (he does not have sufficient business or financial experience to be reasonably assumed to have the capacity to protect his own interests in the stock issuance transaction); cannot meet any of the tests for Major Shareholders contained in Category 4; and does not satisfy the relationship test of Category 6 (although he is related to the spouse of a suitable shareholder—he is the brother of Blanche, Bob's wife—he does not share Bob's principal residence).

Therefore, Biff's only way of being considered a suitable shareholder is under Category 5 if he designates a professional advisor such as a CPA or attorney who can protect his interests for him. We discuss the rules relating to professional advisors further in book Chapter 5, Step 6.

*Example 6:* As a final scenario, let's assume that Bob, Blanche, Beatrice, Bernie, Biff and Ray all decide, in separate moments of sober reflection, that the idea of an incorporated delicatessen is silly, and the incorporation is called off. However, as an alternative, Bob decides to go ahead with an idea that he's had for some time: manufacturing and marketing an extremely efficient and novel sausage stuffing machine of his own invention. Some of his friends and neighbors who are regular customers of the deli have seen his machine in operation and, favorably impressed, have expressed an interest in investing in Bob's creation. Bob, who knows these people only casually, decides to see if any of them are interested in becoming shareholders in a corporation set up to exploit his invention.

Assuming that none qualify as Major Shareholders under Category 4 (a logical assumption in most cases), each of these people must qualify under Categories 2 or 3 (none are insiders such as directors or officers or related to another suitable purchaser). Of course, if a particular shareholder qualifies under Category 2 or 3, then his or her spouse or other "live-in" relative would automatically qualify as a relative of suitable shareholder (Category 6). Looking at these latter categories, since these people don't know Bob or his business except as customers of the deli, none of them will qualify as having a pre-existing personal or business relationship with him and therefore each doesn't qualify under Category 2. What about Category 3? To qualify under this category, each prospective share-holder must have the requisite financial or business experience discussed above. As a practical matter, it is unlikely that all of these people will be able to meet this test and some, if not most, will have to designate and seek the advice of a professional advisor under Category 5 if the shares are to be issued under the limited offering exemption.

The alternative to the limited offering exemption in this type of situation is, as we've said, to have the corporation's initial stock offering and issuance qualified by obtaining a permit from the Department of Corporations.[10] Since Bob is dealing with so many outsiders, it may be best, and more direct, to hire a lawyer to obtain a permit for his stock issuance rather than to have to qualify each one of these people as suitable purchasers.

The point of these last two examples is that you should be careful about considering relatives, friends, neighbors, business associates and particularly casual acquaintances, customers or clients of your business, etc., as meeting the suitability standards of this ex-emption. They may not have a close enough personal or business relationship with one of the corporation's directors or officers or may not have sufficient per-sonal business or financial experience to enable them to make an informed investment decision and protect their own interests. The best and only suggestion we can give you when making distinctions of this type is to use common sense, be a bit conservative, and, if you have any doubts about the suitability of a pro-spective purchaser, make sure that their interests are protected by a qualified professional advisor (Cat-egory 5).

## C.  Federal Securities Act

The Federal Securities Act also applies to the offering of shares by a corporation. You must register your initial offering of stock with the federal Securities and Exchange Commission (SEC) unless you fall under a specific exemption from registration. There are several exemptions available and most small closely-held California corporations eligible for the California limited offering exemption should qualify under at least one, and therefore not need to register their initial stock issuance with the SEC.

Traditionally, most small, closely-held corpora-tions wishing to privately issue their initial shares to a limited number of people have been able to rely on the federal "private offering" exemption. As discussed below, we assume that readers using this book (who will be eligible for the California limited offering) will also qualify for this federal exemption since, as you'll see, the basic requirements of the two exemptions are similar. As always, you have the responsibility of making sure that our assumptions are accurate with respect to your particular incorporation. Before com-paring the California limited offering with the federal private offering exemption, let's look at the general requirements of this federal exemption.

The federal private offering exemption is a one-line exemption contained in Section 4(2) of the Securities Act for "transactions by an issuer [corporation] not involving any public offering." The courts have dis-cussed the basic elements which should be present when relying on this exemption:[11]

- the offerees and purchasers are able to fend for themselves due to their previous financial or busi-ness experience, relationship to the issuer (the corporation, its directors, officers), and/or signifi-cant personal net worth;

- the transaction is truly a nonpublic offering involv-ing no general advertising or solicitation;

- the shares are purchased by the shareholders for their own account and not for resale;

• the offerees (persons to whom shares are offered) and purchasers are limited in number;

• the offerees and purchasers have access to or are given information relevant to the stock transaction in order to evaluate the pros and cons of the investment (the same type of information supplied on an SEC registration statement).

In order to better understand the factors which should, and should not be, present when relying on this exemption, the SEC has issued Release No. 33-4552. This release contains several statements and examples regarding the private offering exemption—please see the accompanying shaded box for a summary of this release.

Of course, the guidelines contained in this release and the language of the court decisions are very general but, as you can see, they are similar to the general requirements of the California limited offering exemption. In order to make things a little clearer, the SEC has issued Rule 506 (this rule is part of a series of provisions referred to as "Regulation D") which pro-

vides a "safe harbor"[12] set of rules and procedures under Section 4(2) of the federal Securities Act and which, if followed, help ensure that the offer and sale of securities will really be a private offering. We don't show you how to formally offer and issue your shares under this rule by filing a Notice of Sales form with the Securities and Exchange Commission. However, we think that a discussion of the basic requirements of this rule will give you further insight into the nature of a private offering under the federal statute and a greater appreciation of the similarities between a private offering under the federal rules and a limited offering under California rules. In addition, as we discuss later in this section, we suggest that you informally comply with several Rule 506 requirements in order to add an extra measure of certainty to your conclusion that your share issuance is exempt as a private offering under Section 4(2) of the federal Securities Act (you'll see that the Notice form and the legend on the stock certificates contained in the Appendix help you do this).

Here are some of the requirements of Rule 506:

• There can be no more than 35 purchasers of shares. However, certain purchasers of shares are not counted, including certain "accredited investors" and the spouses, relatives and relatives of spouses of another purchaser if they share the same principal residence as the other purchaser. Accredited investors include directors and executive officers of the corporation and individuals with a net worth of more than $1 million dollars or with two years prior individual income in excess of $200,000 (or joint income with a spouse in excess of $300,000). With some differences in definitions, these categories of uncounted purchasers under the federal rule are similar to, but narrower than, Categories 1, 4 and 6 under the California limited offering exemption.

## SEC RELEASE 33-4552

Here is a summary and restatement of some the factors contained in this release issued to help explain the scope of the federal private offering exemption:

- Whether a transaction is one not involving any public offering is essentially a question of fact and requires a consideration of all surrounding circumstances, including such factors as the relationship between the offerees and the issuer (corporation), the nature, scope, size, type and manner of the offering.

- The number of persons to whom shares are offered is not determinative of whether this exemption is available. The real consideration is whether these people have sufficient association with and knowledge of the issuer so as to make the exemption available.

- Negotiations or conversations with, or general solicitations of, an unrestricted and unrelated group of prospective purchasers for the purpose of ascertaining who would be willing to accept an offer of securities makes the transaction a public offering and renders the exemption unavailable, even though only a few knowledgeable purchasers ultimately buy the shares.

- Limitation of the offering of shares to certain employees designated as key employees may not be sufficient to qualify for this exemption. However, an offering made to executive personnel who, because of their position, have access to the same kind of information that the Act would make available in the form of a registration statement (financial statements, etc.) may qualify for the exemption.

- The sale of stock to promoters who take the initiative in founding or organizing the business would come within this exemption.

- If the amount of the stock offering is large, it may be considered a public offering not eligible for the exemption.

- An important factor is whether the securities offered have come to rest in the hands of the initial informed group or whether the purchasers are merely conduits for a wider distribution. If the purchasers do, in fact, acquire the securities with a view to public distribution, the corporation assumes the risk of possible violation of the registration requirements of the Act and the imposition of civil penalties.

- The nature of the purchaser's past investment and trading practices or the character and scope of his or her business may be inconsistent with the assumption that the purchaser is buying the shares solely for investment purposes and not for resale. In particular, purchases by individuals engaged in the business of buying and selling securities require careful scrutiny for the purpose of determining whether they may be acting as mere conduits for a wider distribution of shares.

- The issuer may help control the resale of the securities and thereby make reliance on this exemption a little safer. For example, the corporation may secure a representation from the initial purchasers that they are acquiring the securities only for investment and place a legend to this effect on the stock certificates.

- What may appear to be a separate offering to a properly limited group will not be so considered if it is one of a related series of offerings (if, for example, you offer and sell shares after your initial stock offering, this future issuance, if similar in structure, purpose and scope, may be considered part of your initial stock issuance and may jeopardize your initial exemption).

- Whether or not an exemption is available for your stock offering, you cannot engage in any fraudulent activity (and should disclose all material facts to all potential shareholders) to avoid the possible imposition of penalties under other sections of the Act.

- The shares cannot be offered or sold by any form of general solicitation or advertising. The rules restricting the manner of offering and selling the shares are similar to those which apply under the limited offering exemption (see Section B1b, above).

- The corporation must reasonably believe that each purchaser who is not an accredited investor (either alone or together with his "purchaser representative") has such knowledge and experience in financial matters that he is capable of evaluating the merits and risks of the prospective investment. Note that this requirement resembles the "sophisticated investor" test under the limited offering exemption Category 3. Finally, as briefly stated above, this rule allows a purchaser to rely on the experience of his "purchaser representative." This concept is similar to that of reliance on the financial or business experience of a "professional advisor" under the limited offering exemption Category 5. As with the limited offering exemption, this purchaser representative must be designated by the purchaser in writing.

- The corporation must furnish specific types of information (financial statements, written disclosure of resale restrictions, etc.) to nonaccredited investors a reasonable time prior to sale of the shares (to be safe, the regulation suggests that this information be disclosed to accredited investors as well).

- The corporation must also give each purchaser the opportunity to ask questions and receive answers concerning the terms and conditions of the offering and to obtain any additional information which the corporation possesses, or can acquire without unreasonable effort or expense, that is necessary to verify the accuracy of information already furnished to the purchaser. The rule also indicates that the anti-fraud provisions always apply to any offer or sale of securities, and that the corporation must, generally, provide all material information to ensure that purchasers are not misled.

- The corporation must make a reasonable inquiry to determine if the purchaser is acquiring the securities for herself (not for other persons). Actions the corporation should take include: (1) making a written disclosure to each purchaser, prior to the sale, that the securities have not been registered under the Act and cannot be resold unless they are registered or are exempt from registration; and (2) placing a legend on the share certificates which indicates that the securities have not been registered and which refers to these restrictions on the transferability and sale of the shares.

- A Notice of Sales of Securities form (Form D) must be filed with the SEC.

It is not coincidental that Rule 506 resembles so closely the California limited offering exemption. Both were passed at approximately the same time, and were drafted and amended so as to achieve uniformity between federal and state security law exemptions. Perhaps the most significant procedural differences between the California limited offering exemption and Rule 506 is that the latter involves the furnishing of specific information to certain purchasers of shares, including the disclosure of transfer restrictions on these shares to purchasers and the placement of a legend to that effect on the share certificates.

As mentioned above, the assumption we've followed in this book, and one which is customarily made by lawyers, is that you should be able to meet most of the general guidelines to the federal private offering exemption under Section 4(2) of the federal Securities Act when issuing your initial shares under the California limited offering exemption, and you should also be able to simultaneously meet most of the "safe harbor" provisions of Rule 506 just discussed.

**Forms Note**   To help conform your limited offering stock issuance to some of the additional required and suggested procedures of Rule 506, we have:

(1) included a statement of the restrictions on transfer of shares in the shareholder representation letters prepared in Step 6 of Chapter 5; and (2) placed a nonregistration legend on the share certificates contained in the Appendix of this book (the stock certificates contained in the corporate kits offered at the back of this book also contain a nonregistration legend).

**A Short Disclaimer**   Remember, although we provide what we think is a practical and traditional method of issuing your shares under the general guidelines of the federal private offering exemption promulgated under Section 4(2) of the federal Securities Act and under some of the provisions of Rule 506, we can't anticipate the particular facts and circumstances surrounding your incorporation, and can't, of course, guarantee that the federal private offering exemption will apply to you. As always, technical provisions of law (particularly of the securities laws) can be analyzed ad infinitum, and entire volumes, indeed libraries, have been devoted to the task. What we can do is provide you with (hopefully) helpful information, and repeat the reminder that you have the responsibility of making sure that you comply with the securities laws.

Finally, one other point bears repeating: Whether or not you have to register or provide notification to the SEC of your stock offering, the anti-fraud and civil liability provisions of the Securities Act always apply, so DISCLOSE, DISCLOSE, DISCLOSE! ■

# Endnotes

[1]California has added a simplified securities permit procedure under Cal. Corp. Code Section 25113(b)(2) that allows a corporation to raise up to $1 million in a small public offering and requires the filing of a relatively simple question-and-answer form (Form C-7, based upon a national model form, Form U-7, commonly referred to as a Small Corporate Offering or SCOR form). A fee of $2,500 is charged, plus up to $1,000 more based upon the Department's actual costs of processing the form. Use of Form U-7 is being recognized in a number of other states, and may soon be the best way to obtain moderate amounts of equity capital from investors under state securities registration laws. There were some initial problems with California's version of this procedure which are being worked out. If you are interested in raising capital through a small stock promotion, you may wish to check out this simplified permit procedure with a lawyer. Note: The minimum stock price under this procedure is $5, proceeds from the sale of shares must be used in the business, and the corporation must have only one class of shares of voting common stock outstanding after the SCOR issuance.

Federal Securities Laws: Generally, the use of a state SCOR form is coordinated with the filing of a federal Form D, under Rule 504, with the SEC. We touch upon federal Regulation D in Section C below, but we do not discuss the specific requirements of the federal Rule 504 exemption contained in Regulation D.

[2]The statute which contains this limited offering exemption is Section 25102(f) of the California Corporations Code. The regulations which have been promulgated in order to clarify the meaning of the statute are contained in Title 10 of the California Code of Regulations, Sections 260.102.12 through 260.102.14.

[3]A technical point: The limited offering exemption statute and the rules often refer to a "purchaser." Since this term simply means the purchasers of your shares, we use the terms "purchaser" and "shareholder" interchangeably.

[4]In our discussion of suitable shareholders, we are only looking at types of shareholders that are most relevant to small corporations issuing shares to individual shareholders, and we have excluded rules relating to "affiliates" and other types of shareholders which are unlikely to apply to you.

[5]For the legally minded: These shareholders (sometimes referred to as "uncounted shareholders" by lawyers) are "automatically" suitable under the limited offering exemption—by this we mean that they do not have to meet one of the subjective suitability standards discussed in Categories 2 and 3 of this section. This automatic suitability of uncounted purchasers has been confirmed in two Opinions of the Commissioner of Corporations (Opinions 83/2C and 83/3C) and now is formalized in Rule 260.102.12(d)(2) of Title 10 of the California Code of Regulations. For clarity, we have split up the major automatically suitable (uncounted) shareholder categories and treat additional types of automatically suitable shareholders (shareholders who meet specific investment, net worth or income requirements and relatives, spouses, and in-laws of suitable shareholders) in separate Categories 4 and 6.

[6]A "controlling person" is defined to include a person who, in conjunction with transactions within one year of the formation of the corporation, is a promoter of the corporation, and a promoter, as we've said, means any person who, acting alone or in conjunction with one or more other persons, takes the initiative in founding and organizing the business or enterprise of the corporation.

[7]The regulations indicate that the terms "net worth" and "income" shall be interpreted in a manner consistent with Rule 230.501(a), subsections (6) and (7) under SEC Regulation D (see Section C of this chapter for a brief discussion of this federal securities law regulation). Also note: It is likely that the joint income requirement mentioned here may be raised to $300,000 to conform to changes made to the parallel SEC stock exemption rule under federal Regulation D. Also, California may soon decide to eliminate purchasers of $150,000 worth of shares from this major shareholder category to conform to the latest federal rules.

[8]Section 260.102.12(g) of Title 10 Cal. Code Regs.

[9]Again, we only look at rules which relate to individual shareholders—if you plan to have corporate, partnership, institutional or other types of organizational shareholders, you should check with a lawyer concerning counting rules for these special types of shareholders.

[10]As we've noted earlier, the California small offering exemption may be helpful in a small number of cases when the limited offering exemption is unavailable—it may be available

here if all shareholders buy their shares for cash. Remember, the law requires you to have a lawyer sign an opinion statement that the small offering exemption is available for your stock issuance.

[11]A leading case on this exemption is SEC v. Ralston Purina Co., 346 U.S. 119 (1953).

[12]A "safe harbor" is a set of rules which have been enacted to define a safe procedure to follow to comply with general requirements of another rule or statute. In effect, a "safe-harbor" means "this is one way to comply with the law—you don't have to follow this procedure but, if you do, you will be safe."

# Corporate Taxation

Corporations, like individuals, are subject to state and federal taxes. In this chapter we will discuss some of the tax consequences of starting and operating a corporation, and also talk about some special tax elections many small corporations will want to make. This information is meant to introduce you to the most important areas of corporate taxation and to provide the necessary background for you to study them in greater depth with a tax advisor, if you feel this is necessary.[1]

# A. California Taxes

## 1. California Corporate Franchise Tax

A California profit corporation is subject to an annual corporate franchise tax. This is an annual fee which is paid to the state for the privilege of doing business as a corporation. The tax is computed each year on the basis of your corporation's previous year's net income derived from business activity in California (and, sometimes, outside California). The California franchise tax rate is 9.3% of the corporation's taxable income, with a minimum yearly payment of $800 regardless of the amount of annual income or profits. A newly-formed corporation pays the minimum $800 amount at the time of incorporation—this payment is simply for the privilege of operating as a corporation in California.

**Important Tax Note** As explained in Chapter 6C1, you will be required to begin estimating and prepaying your first year's California corporate franchise taxes soon after you incorporate. This means that you will be required to make a second $800 payment to the Franchise Tax Board by the end of your first tax quarter. Be prepared for this second tax payment.

## 2. California Personal Income Tax

Corporate profits are reported on the personal income tax returns of individual shareholders (and taxed to them at their personal income tax rates) when and if these profits are distributed to them as dividends or salaries. Dividends are taxed twice: at the corporate level and at the individual level (dividend payments cannot be deducted by the corporation). As a practical matter, however, most small corporations rarely pay dividends (and, therefore, are not subject to double taxation on corporate profits). Why? Because one of the primary reasons to incorporate is to have the flexibility to either retain earnings in your corporation at corporate tax rates or to pay out profits to the employee-shareholders in the form of salaries, fringe benefits, etc., which are deductible by the corporation. Either way, only one tax is paid (corporate or individual) and double taxation is avoided. In addition, a California corporation may wish to elect state and federal S corporation tax status: These tax elections allow the corporation to bypass regular corporate level taxes on corporate taxable income (although the state still assesses a small-percentage corporate-level tax as explained below), with the taxable income of the corporation passed through to the shareholders to be taxed only once on their individual tax returns. We explain how these special S corporation tax elections work in subsequent sections of this chapter.

## 3. California S Corporation Tax Election

California corporations that are qualified for, and have elected, federal S corporation tax status are eligible for S corporation tax treatment in California.[2] This state tax election parallels the federal S corporation tax election and allows the corporation to avoid the full California corporate franchise tax rate (9.3%) on state corporate net taxable income, passing the corporation's taxable California income through to the individual state tax returns of the corporation's shareholders. We explain the advantages and disadvantages of the S corporation tax election in detail in Section C below. For now let's note a few special requirements of the California S corporation tax election:

- As opposed to federal S corporation tax status where the S corporation does not normally pay any federal corporate income taxes, California S corporations must still pay the California Franchise Tax Board a 2.5% tax on net California corporate income and must pay the minimum corporate franchise tax each year.
- If your California S corporation has out-of-state shareholders, each must file a consent with the California Franchise Tax Board agreeing to be subject to California taxes on his or her pro rata share of the corporation's income that is attributable to California sources.
- The Franchise Tax Board automatically presumes that corporations that have elected federal S corporation tax treatment have also elected S corporation status in California unless they specifically elect not to be treated as an S corporation in California (by filing FTB form 3560).

You may wonder: Why should a California S corporation pay a 2.5% corporate level tax when corporate income will pass through and be taxed at the individual California tax rates as well? Or, to ask the question more directly: Isn't this double taxation? Yes, this is indeed double taxation if your corporation shows a profit. But, as we explain in Section C, below, one common reason to elect S corporation tax status is to pass initial corporate losses directly onto the individual tax returns of the shareholders, where they can

be used to offset other active shareholder income (wages, salaries, professional income, etc.). Since a corporation which loses money will not have to pay any tax because of this 2.5% rate (2.5% x 0 = 0), this added tax is not a problem in this context (remember, however, that even a losing California S corporation will have to pay California's annual minimum franchise tax each year). Of course, if your corporation is profitable and you elect California S corporation tax status, then you do indeed pay a price of 2.5% of your corporation's California net taxable income each year for making this election.

Is California S corporation tax status worth the price, particularly if your corporation is making a profit? There's no easy answer here—you'll have to add up the total cumulative tax impact of this state tax election to your corporation and to you personally as a shareholder to see if this state tax election saves you tax dollars. Depending upon the outcome of your calculations, you may wish to elect California S corporation tax status, or decide that it makes better sense just to elect federal S corporation tax status without making this parallel state S corporation election (remember, this is a voluntary state tax election—you can elect federal S corporation tax status and choose not to make the California S corporation tax election).

## B. Federal Taxes

### 1. Federal Corporate Income Tax

Federal corporate income taxes and tax rates are as follows:

| Taxable Income | Tax |
| --- | --- |
| $0-$50,000 | 15% of taxable income |
| $50,001-$75,000 | $7,500 + 25% of income over $50,000 |
| $75,001-$100,000 | $13,750 + 34% of taxable income over $100,000 |
| $100,001-$335,000 | $22,250 + 39% of taxable income over $100,000 |
| $335,001-$10,000,000 | $113,900 + 34% of taxable income over $335,000 |
| $10,000,001-$15,000,000 | $3,400,000 + 35% of taxable income over $10,000,000 |
| $15,000,001-$18,333,333 | $5,100,000 + 38% of taxable income over $15,000,000 |
| over $18,333,333 | $6,416,667 + 35% of taxable income over $18,333,333 |

Essentially, the first $50,000 of taxable corporate income is taxed at 15%, the next $25,000 at 25%, and the remainder of taxable income over $75,000 at 34%. To make larger corporations pay back the benefits of the lower graduated tax rates of 15% and 25%, corporate taxable incomes between $100,000 and $335,000 are subject to an additional 5% tax—this 39% "bubble" leaves the corporation paying a flat 34% tax rate on all corporate income below $10 million. For highly profitable corporations, an additional 35% tax bracket is applied to taxable incomes over $10,000,000, with an additional 38% bubble set up to make corporation's with incomes over $18,333,333 pay taxes at a flat 35% tax rate (to eliminate the advantage of the lower graduated tax brackets below 35%).

As discussed further below, most smaller corporations will not have taxable incomes over $100,000 and will therefore be able to take advantage of the lower corporate tax brackets of 15%, 25% and 34%.

**Maximum Corporate Tax Rate on Certain Personal Service Corporations** Under special provisions of the Internal Revenue Code, the taxable income of certain personal service corporations is taxed at a flat corporate tax rate of 35% (the lower 15%, 25% and 34% federal corporate tax brackets do not apply to these

corporations). Specifically, this flat maximum federal corporate tax rate is applied to corporations: (1) where substantially all the stock of the corporation is held by the employees performing professional services for the corporation and (2) where substantially all the activities of the corporation involve the performance of one of the following professions or activities:

• health
• law
• engineering
• architecture
• accounting
• actuarial science
• performing arts
• consulting

A few comments on this special federal flat corporate tax:

First, remember that the practice of the professions of health, law and accounting are required to be incorporated as California professional corporations, not as regular California profit corporations (architects have a choice—see Chapter 2A2 for further information). Similarly, performing arts groups typically incorporate as California nonprofit corporations—see Chapter 2A1.

Second, even if this flat tax provision applies to you (because you are using this book to form a regular profit corporation engaged in engineering, actuarial science, architecture or consulting and all of your corporation's stock will be owned by the professionals), this doesn't mean that you will be paying 35% of your income to the IRS each year—this tax only applies to any taxable income left in the corporation at the end of the corporate tax year. If, like many professionals, you have no need to accumulate money in your corporation and prefer to pass corporate profits to yourself each year in the form of a deductible salary, fringe benefits, a substantial contribution to your pension plan, etc., then this tax provision will have little, if any, impact on your corporation's tax liability. Further, if you do end your corporate tax year with income left in the corporation and wish to avoid the imposition of this tax, electing federal S corporation tax status will pass corporate profits to you automatically each year and avoid corporate level taxes altogether (however, this election will limit your ability to pay yourself deductible fringe benefits—see Section C, below).

Third, this flat tax provision contains some general terminology which may require you (or your tax advisor) to explore current and future Treasury regulations. For example: When is all the stock of one of these personal service corporations substantially owned by the professional employees? If 25% of the stock of a consultancy corporation is owned by non-employees—or by employees who simply work administratively for the corporation, not as consultants—is the corporation subject to this flat tax? What if 75% of the activities of the corporation involve consulting and 25% are derived from other sources? Are substantially all the activities of the corporation derived from consulting and, therefore, subject to this flat tax provision? For that matter, what is "consulting" for purposes of the imposition of this special federal tax rate? If you may be subject to this flat tax, see the box below and consult your tax advisor for further guidance.

Fourth, this special tax provision applies to the same professions and activities to which the lower federal corporate accumulated earnings credit of $150,000 applies (see Section G below for a further explanation of this credit).

## 2. Federal Individual Income Tax

The federal government taxes corporate profits when distributed to shareholders as dividends or salaries. The shareholders must pay federal individual income tax on the amounts received. As we've mentioned earlier, however, since the payment of dividends results in double taxation, owners of small corporations normally use one of several methods to get money out of the corporation without being subject to double taxation. When the owner works for the corporation, the simplest tax strategy is to pay out corporate profits in the form of deductible salaries, bonuses and employee fringe benefits, rather than as dividends. As long as salaries are not unreasonable and the benefits are paid in accordance with IRS guidelines (see Section G, below), the IRS should have no objection. Of course, money paid in salaries and bonuses is a deductible business expense of the corporation and is thus not taxed to the corporation, only to the individual.

In effect then, incorporating a business you actively participate in allows you to split your income between two tax entities, the corporation and yourself, as an employee-shareholder, in order to obtain the most favorable (smallest) tax rate on this income. You can pay salaries to yourself and other employees that will be taxed at individual federal tax rates while retaining earnings in the corporation that will be taxed at the lower federal corporate tax rates of 15% or 25%.[3] (Again, certain personal service corporations pay federal corporate taxes at a flat 35% rate as explained in the previous subsection).

## CORPORATIONS SUBJECT TO FLAT 35% TAX RATE

Treasury Regulation Section 1.448-1T(e)(4) contains definitions and examples of the types of "qualified personal service corporations" engaged in health, consulting and the performing arts fields which are subject to a flat corporate tax rate of 35%. Here are a few examples:

HEALTH SERVICES   This means the providing of services by physicians, nurses, dentists and other similar heathcare professionals. This category does not include the performance of services unrelated to the health of the person who receives services. For example, the operation of health clubs or spas that provide physical exercise or conditioning is not included in this category.

CONSULTING SERVICES   This means giving advice and counsel and does not include sales, brokerage or economically similar services. The manner in which the corporation (or other person) is compensated for services (e.g., whether the compensation is contingent on sales or some other factor) will help determine whether the services are considered consulting or sales.

The regulation includes examples of services which will or will not be considered consulting services. One example is a taxpayer (corporation) that determines a client's data processing needs after studying the client's business and focusing on the types of data and information relevant to the business and the needs of the client's employees to access this information. The taxpayer does not provide the client with computer hardware or additional computer programming services—just recommendations regarding the design and implementation of data processing systems to be purchased elsewhere. The taxpayer is considered to be engaged in consulting services (and will be subject to a flat corporate tax rate of 35%).

This regulation contains definitions and clarifications of other terms used in Section 448(d)(2) to determine if a corporation is subject to a 35% flat tax rate (and is subject to other provisions of the IRC). You or your accountant should consult this regulation for further information.

This feature of income splitting is unique to the corporate way of life—partnerships and sole proprietorships are not tax entities separate from their owners. All income realized by these unincorporated businesses is automatically counted as part of the individual income of the business owners each year, and is taxed at their individual federal income tax rates. In other words, even if profits are needed to expand the business and don't end up in the unincorporated business owner's pocket, federal individual income taxes must be paid.

If you anticipate, or find, that corporate taxable income (net corporate income after subtracting all deductions including business expenses, salaries, bonuses, depreciation, etc.) will be subject to more taxes at the corporate level than if taxed to you and the other shareholders personally, your corporation may be able to elect federal S corporation tax status—as explained in Section C, below, this federal tax election passes corporate income through to your shareholders where it is reported and taxed on their individual federal tax returns only.

### A Comparison of Individual and Corporate Tax Rates and Payments for Owners of Smaller Corporations

Incorporating and paying taxes as a corporate entity generally results in paying less tax on business income than you would pay as an individual or as a partner if your corporation has a taxable income of approximately $150,000 or less.[4] The table below compares individual and corporate tax rates and tax payments for various levels of taxable income.

There are two basic reasons why corporate tax payments are less than individual payments on lower levels of taxable business income:

1. Federal corporate tax rates on taxable incomes of $75,000 or less are 15% on the first $50,000, and 25% on the next 25,000, as opposed to the 15%, 28% and 31% federal individual rates that apply to these income levels,[5]

2. More importantly, while federal individual rates jump to 28% at modest levels of taxable income, the lower 15% and 25% corporate rates stay in effect over wide ranges of taxable income (for example, the 15% corporate rate is in effect up to and including $50,000 of taxable income; the 28% individual rates kick in well below this amount for noncorporate taxpayers—see the table below).

The result is that a fairly high level of taxable income must be reached before it makes sense for your corporation to choose to be taxed at individual rates (by electing federal S corporation tax status) rather than the standard corporate rates. Again, remember, since salaries, employee fringes and other expenses of doing business are deducted by the corporation first, it is not common for smaller businesses to report more than $150,000 of taxable income.[6]

In fact, the majority of small corporations will show a taxable income of less than $50,000, and will, therefore, pay taxes at a flat 15% minimum corporate tax rate. After the corporation pays deductible salaries and corporate fringe benefits to the owner-employees of the corporation (and to other corporate personnel) and deducts other corporate business expenses, gross receipts, even in the millions of dollars range, are commonly reduced to a small taxable income amount and are taxed at the lower corporate tax rates.

Here is an example of how, with proper planning, a smaller incorporated business is able to split income between the corporation and its owners, retain money in the corporation for necessary expenditures, and lower the corporation's tax liability to an amount that is actually less than what would have to be paid by the principals of the same business if it was not incorporated:

## INDIVIDUAL VS. CORPORATE TAX RATES & TOTAL TAXES OWED

| Taxable Income Over | Individual Rate (Single)[1] | | Individual Rate (Married Filing Jointly)[1] | | Corporate Rate[2] | |
|---|---|---|---|---|---|---|
| $ 0 | 15% | | 15% | | 15% | |
| $ 22,100 | 28% | $3,315 | 15% | $3,315 | 15% | $3,315 |
| $ 36,900 | 28% | $7,459 | 28% | $5,535 | 15% | $5,535 |
| $ 50,000 | 28% | $11,127 | 28% | $9,203 | 25% | $7,500 |
| $ 53,500 | 31% | $12,107 | 28% | $10,183 | 25% | $8,375 |
| $ 75,000 | 31% | $18,772 | 28% | $16,203 | 34% | $13,750 |
| $ 89,150 | 31% | $23,158 | 31% | $20,165 | 34% | $18,561 |
| $ 100,000 | 31% | $26,522 | 31% | $23,528 | 39% | $22,250 |
| $ 115,000 | 36% | $31,172 | 31% | $28,178 | 39% | $28,100 |
| $ 140,000 | 36% | $40,172 | 36% | $35,928 | 39% | $37,850 |
| $ 150,000 | 36% | $43,772 | 36% | $39,528 | 39% | $41,750 |
| $ 250,000 | 39.6% | $79,772 | 39.6% | $75,528 | 39% | $80,750 |

HOW TO USE THIS TABLE    Each time a tax rate changes, we start a new row and calculate the total amount of taxes paid by the taxpayer up to that point. We have also included columns for taxable incomes above $100,000 to show tax rates and taxes owed on higher levels of earnings.

For example, to compare tax rates and taxes owed on $100,000 of taxable income, find the $100,000 row. The three columns in this row show that individual taxpayers pay a tax rate of 31%, and corporations a rate of 39%, on taxable incomes *above* this threshold amount. The first column shows that a single taxpayer will owe a total of $26,522 in taxes up to this point (on $100,000 of taxable income) and a married couple filing jointly will owe $23,528. A corporate taxpayer will owe $22,250 in taxes on this amount of taxable income.

By looking at the rows to the right, you can see that although corporations pay taxes at a higher *rate* once taxable income exceeds $75,000, they do not pay as much in taxes as single taxpayers until taxable income exceeds $150,000. Corporate taxes are also less than those paid by married couples filing jointly on taxable incomes roughly below $115,000.

[1]Because of the phaseout of personal exemptions and limitations on itemized deductions for individuals with higher incomes, upper-income taxpayers are subject to a top effective tax rates in excess of 39.6%.

[2]Once a corporation earns a taxable income over $335,000, its marginal (top) tax rate is reduced to 34%. In other words, the 39% "bump" that occurs in the corporate tax rate schedule is meant to eliminate the savings of the lower tax rates and leave the corporation paying a flat 34% on all taxable income if it earns more than $335,000. Also note that an additional marginal tax rate of 35% has been added for taxable incomes in excess of $10 million, with an additional 38% "bump" in the $15 to $18.3 million range (to make the corporate pay a flat 35% tax rate if it earns over $18.3 million in taxable income).

*Example:* Sally and Randolph run their own incorporated lumber supply company (S & R Wood). With the boom in home renovations, their sales increase to a $1.2 million yearly pace. After the close of the third quarter, S & R's accountant reports that they are on course to make $110,000 net profit (net taxable corporate income) for the year. Sally and Randolph are pleased and call a meeting. They decide to reward themselves and other key employees with moderate raises in pay, provide a small year-end bonus to other workers, and purchase some needed equipment, including another cross-cut saw to increase their productivity. As a result, their net taxable corporate income is reduced to $40,000—an amount they feel is prudent to retain in the corporation for future expansion or in case next year's operations are less profitable. Taxes are therefore paid at the lowest 15% corporate rate.

Incidentally, if Sally and Randy wanted to get a larger personal return they could have increased their salaries (which are a tax deductible corporate expense). They see no reason to declare a stock dividend, as a big corporation would, since doing so would subject them to a double tax of 15% at the corporate level plus an individual tax at their marginal tax rate (the top rate that is applied to any additional income they must report individually).

If S & R Wood had not incorporated but instead operated as a partnership, the entire net profits of the business ($110,000 minus the bonuses to workers and expenditures for equipment) would pass through to Sally and Randy. The result would be that the $40,000 (which was retained in the business in the corporation example above) would be taxed at their higher individual tax rates.

But now suppose that the owners of smaller corporations anticipate corporate taxable income substantial enough that they would benefit by being taxed at lower individual rates. Fine. They have the opportunity to do so by electing S corporation tax status. By doing this, these owners can take advantage of the legal, financial and other advantages of the corporation (such as limited liability, ease of obtaining investment capital, etc.) while having corporate earnings and profits taxed at individual rates. This federal tax election, which is available, generally, to corporations with 35 or fewer shareholders, passes corporate income, losses, deductions, credits, etc., directly through to the owners of the corporation. In essence, the S corporation achieves the tax status of a partnership while enjoying the legal and other benefits of the corporate form.

## C.  Federal S Corporation Tax Status

A corporation which has 35 or fewer shareholders and which meets other basic requirements may elect to fall under special federal tax provisions contained in Subchapter S of the Internal Revenue Code.[7] Corporations which make this election are known as S corporations. Generally, a corporation which elects to become an S corporation has its profits and losses passed through the corporation to its shareholders. This means, with exceptions, that profits and losses are not taxed to, or deducted by, the corporation, but by the individual shareholders in proportion to their stockholdings. The corporation side-steps taxation on its profits and its shareholders (like partners) get the tax benefit of the losses, credits, deductions, etc., of the corporation. Profits of the S corporation pass through to shareholders on a per-share, per-day basis, whether or not such profits are actually distributed to them.[8] Consequently, S corporation tax status can be a very flexible planning tool, providing corporations with the ability to live in two different worlds, enjoying a corporate legal life (including limited liability status for its owners) and partnership tax status.

This pass-through of corporate income and losses to the shareholders can be advantageous to some newly-formed or existing corporations. Here's a few typical situations where electing S corporation tax status can save tax dollars:[9]

1. In start-up businesses that expect initial losses before the business begins to show a profit, S corporation tax status can pass these initial losses to the individual tax returns of the shareholders who actively participate in the business. This allows them to offset income from other sources with the losses of the corporation (see the sidebar below entitled "What Constitutes Material Participation?" for further information).

*Example:* Will and Bruno decide to form a part-time air charter business and incorporate it. They'll continue to work during the week at their salaried jobs until their new business gets off the ground. They know that the first few years of corporate life will generate substantial losses (modest profits from weekend flying charters accompanied by large expenditures for the purchase of a plane, required charter insurance, etc.). Rather than take these losses at the corporate level and carry them forward into future profitable years of the corporation, they decide they would be better off electing S corporation tax status and deducting these losses immediately against their individual full-time salary income on their individual tax returns.

2. If corporate taxable income is substantial, S corporation tax status can be a handy way of taking advantage of the lower individual rates (if corporate taxable income is high, these profits can be passed through and taxed at the shareholders' lower individual rates.

Example: Tomas and Gerald form their own video production company. They anticipate first year gross receipts of $2 million and, after deducting all salaries, business expenses, depreciation, etc., a corporate taxable income of $350,000. Since corporate taxable incomes above $335,000 are taxed at a flat rate of 34% (the highest 35% corporate rate only applies to companies with taxable incomes in excess of $10 million), they decide to elect S corporation tax status

to have this income pass through to them and be taxed at their lower individual tax rates.

3. As discussed in Chapter 1B2, regular corporations with appreciated assets are subject to a corporate level tax when the corporation dissolves. S corporations are generally not subject to this tax.[10] For some corporations, this can be a decisive factor in electing S corporation tax status.

*Example:* Sam and his sister Terry decide to form a corporation to hold title to real property. During the anticipated ten-year life of their corporation, they expect the property to appreciate considerably. In order to avoid a corporate level tax on this appreciation when the corporation is dissolved and the property sold, they decide to elect S corporation status prior to the purchase of any property by their corporation.

The point of these examples is simple. In some businesses, at least some of the time, it is better for business owners to be taxed as if the business was a partnership. With some technical exceptions (see the partnership differences sidebar below), electing S corporation status allows you to do this. If later, for the reasons discussed in Section B above (for example, to split business income between your corporation and yourself) or for any other reason, you no longer wish to be an S corporation, you can revoke or terminate this tax status.

Here now are some potential disadvantages of S corporation tax status:

• The amount of losses that may be passed through to the business owners (shareholders), and the ability to allocate these losses in different proportions to different individuals, are restricted by various technical provisions of the Internal Revenue Code and Treasury Regulations. Generally, you can only deduct losses in an S corporation up to the "basis" (tax value) of your stock plus amounts loaned by you to your corporation.[11] If these losses cannot be deducted by you in a given year, they can be carried forward to and deducted in future tax years if you then qualify to deduct the losses.[12]

## WHAT CONSTITUTES MATERIAL PARTICIPATION?

In order for an S corporation shareholder to deduct corporate losses against active income, such as salary or wages, on his individual tax return, the shareholder must materially participate in the business of the S corporation. As mentioned in Chapter 1A2, this material participation rule also applies to limited partners.

Here are some of the ways in which an S corporation shareholder, limited partner or other person can satisfy the IRS that he materially participates in a business activity during a taxable year:

- The person participates in the business for more than 500 hours during the year;

- The person participates in the business for more than 100 hours during the year, and that participation is not less than any other individual's participation in the business;

- The person participates in the business for more than 100 hours during the year and participates in other activities for more than 100 hours each, for a total of more than 500 hours during the year;

- The person's participation in the business for the year constitutes substantially all the participation in the business of all individuals for that year;

- The person materially participated in the business for any five of the last ten taxable years;

- The business involves the performance of personal services in the fields of health, law, engineering, architecture, accounting, actuarial science, performing arts or consulting, and the person materially participated in the business for any three preceding taxable years; or

- The person can show, based upon all facts and circumstances, that she participates in the business on a regular, continuous and substantial basis during the year.

NOTE   For more information, see, Temp. Reg. Sections 1.469-1T, -2T, -3T, -5T and -11T, and related regulations issued under Section 469 of the Internal Revenue Code.

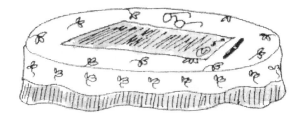

The important point is this: If you plan to elect S corporation status to pass corporate losses through to you on your individual tax return, make sure you will have sufficient basis in your stock plus enough qualified indebtedness to allow you to deduct these losses at the individual level. An experienced corporate tax advisor should be intimately familiar with this issue and able to help you make sure you can deduct S corporation losses on future individual tax returns.

- Unlike regular corporations, S corporations must generally choose a calendar-year as their corporate tax year. Exceptions exist under IRS Revenue Procedures which allow S corporations to elect a non-calendar tax year in certain circumstances, including: (1) if the S corporation can show a valid business purpose for the non-calendar year; or (2) if the non-calendar year results in a deferral of income for three months or less and other requirements are met. Please see Section D below for additional information on choosing a corporate tax year.
- S corporations cannot adopt an employee stock ownership plan (although they are permitted to adopt a stock bonus plan).
- S corporations, like partnerships, cannot provide tax deductible fringe benefits to owners (i.e., shareholder-employees owning more than 2% of the S corporation's stock) such as:
  1. Qualified accident and health plans;[13]
  2. Medical expense reimbursement plans;
  3. $50,000 of group term life insurance;
  4. $5,000 death benefit;
  5. Free meals and lodgings furnished for the convenience of the corporation (e.g., furnished on company premises).

## 1. Qualifying for S Corporation Tax Status

In order for a corporation to qualify for S corporation tax status, it must be a "small business corporation" under Subchapter S of the Internal Revenue Code. To so qualify, the corporation must meet the following requirements:[14]

1. It must be a domestic (U.S.) corporation;
2. None of the shareholders may be non-resident aliens;
3. There must be only one class of stock (all shares have equal rights, e.g., dividend, liquidation rights). However, differences as to voting rights are permitted.[15]
4. All shareholders must be individuals or estates or certain trusts;
5. There must be no more than 35 shareholders. Shares which are jointly owned by a husband and wife are considered to be owned by one person;
6. The corporation cannot be a member of a group of affiliated corporations. If your corporation plans to own stock in, or have its stock owned by, another corporation, it might be an affiliate and thus not qualify for S corporation tax treatment.

In the past, some incorporators avoided electing S corporation status since doing so would place restrictions on contributions to their corporate pension and profit-sharing plans. However, these additional restrictions to S corporation retirement plans have, for the most part, been eliminated with S corporations and regular corporations (referred to as "C" corporations in the Internal Revenue Code) now being placed on a relatively equal footing with respect to most corporate plan provisions. (However, S corporation plans are still prohibited from lending money to a participant owning more than 5% of the corporation's stock—see Section G2 below for general information on regular corporate pension and profit sharing plans.)

**PARTNERSHIP DIFFERENCES**

Partnership tax status is still more flexible than S corporation tax status in some areas. For example:

1. Partnerships can admit any person or entity as a partner. S corporation shareholders must be individuals, estates or certain types of trusts.

2. Partnerships can divide profits and losses among partners as they see fit. S corporations generally must allocate dividends, liquidation proceeds and corporate losses in proportion to stockholdings. To do otherwise invites an IRS attack on the grounds that the S corporation had created an impermissible second class of stock.

3. Under technical tax provisions, partners may be able to personally deduct more business losses on their tax returns in a given year than corporate shareholders. (In calculating the amount of partnership losses that may be deducted individually, a partner gets to count her pro-rata share of all money borrowed by the partnership. An S corporation shareholder can only count money borrowed by the corporation directly from the individual shareholder.)

## 2. Electing Federal S Corporation Tax Status

If a corporation wishes to become an S corporation and meets the foregoing requirements, it must make an election by filing Form 2553 with the IRS indicating the consent of all shareholders. The election must be made on or before the 15th day of the third month of the corporation's tax year for which the S status is to be effective, or any time during the preceding tax year. For newly-formed corporations that wish to start off as an S corporation, this means making the election before the 15th day of the third month after the date the corporation's first tax year begins.

For purposes of the S corporation election, the corporation's first tax year begins when it issues stock to shareholders, acquires assets or begins doing business, whichever occurs first. Generally, your first tax year will begin on the date you file your Articles of Incorporation. Since your S corporation election will be invalid if made at the wrong time, please check with your tax advisor to ensure that you fully understand these election rules and make your election on time (see Chapter 6B1).

The S corporation election must be consented to by all persons who are shareholders at the time it is made, as well as by all persons who were shareholders during the taxable year before the election is made. Their consents should be indicated on the election form when it is mailed to the IRS. If the shares are held jointly (e.g., in joint tenancy) or are the community property of spouses (or if any income from the stock is the community property of spouses), each co-owner and each spouse must sign the consent form.

## 3. Revocation or Termination of Federal S Corporation Tax Status

Once your corporation elects to become an S corporation, it continues to be treated as one through later tax years until the status is revoked or terminated. A revocation is made by filing shareholder consents to the revocation. The consent of shareholders who collectively own at least a majority of the stock in the corporation is required to effect a revocation.

S corporation status will be terminated, however, at any time, if the corporation fails to continue to meet all the small business corporation requirements discussed above (e.g., if the corporation issues a second class of shares, issues stock to a 36th shareholder, etc.). Such a termination will be effective as of the date on which the terminating event occurs (not retroactively to the beginning of the tax year).

A termination will also occur in certain situations where the corporation has a specified level of passive investment income. This type of income generally includes royalties, rents, dividends, interest, annuities and gains from the sale or exchange of stock or securities. Many S corporations will not have to be concerned with this type of termination since it also requires that the corporation have "accumulated earnings and profits" from operating previously as a regular C (a non-S) corporation.

Once S status has been revoked or terminated, the corporation may not re-elect S corporation tax status until five years after the termination or revocation. Note that certain inadvertent terminations will be ignored, provided, among other things, that the corporation takes specified corrective action.

# D. Corporate Accounting Periods and Tax Years

The accounting period of the corporation is the period for which the corporation keeps its books and will correspond to the corporation's tax year. Generally, a corporation's accounting period (and its tax year) may be the calendar year from January 1 to December 31 or it may be a fiscal year, consisting of a twelve-month period ending on the last day of any month other than December (for example, from July 1 to June 30). In special situations, a corporation may wish to choose a "52-53 week" year. This is a period which ends on a particular day closest to the end of a month (e.g., "the last Friday of March" or "the Friday nearest to the end of March"). Most corporations will choose either a calendar year or a fiscal year as their accounting period (however, see the "Special Calendar Year Rules for S and Personal Service Corporations" below).

For some corporations, a calendar tax year will prove easiest, since it will be the same year as that used by the individual shareholders. Others, because of the particular business cycle of the corporation or simply because December is a hectic month, may wish to choose a different month to wind up their yearly affairs. Moreover, having the corporation's tax year end after that of the individual shareholders (after December 31), may allow special initial and ongoing tax advantages such as the deferral of income to the employee-shareholders of a small corporation.

You should also realize that choosing a fiscal rather than a calendar year is often in your accountant's interest, since she is usually busy preparing and filing individual tax returns after the end of the calendar year. In fact, some accounting firms provide discounts if you choose a fiscal year which ends after the individual tax season (January to April). So if your accountant suggests a fiscal tax year for your corporation, you might suggest a fiscal year discount on your accounting bill.

**Special Calendar Year Rules for S and Personal Service Corporations** If you plan to elect federal S corporation tax status (see Section C above) or if your corporation meets the definition of a "personal service corporation" (defined below), generally, you must choose a calendar year for your corporate tax year (and your accounting period) unless the IRS approves the use of a fiscal year (see the discussion of exceptions to these calendar tax year rules below).

Under provisions of the Internal Revenue Code, a personal service corporation (for purposes of choosing a corporate tax year) is defined as "a corporation the principal activity of which is the performance of personal services ... [if] such services are substantially performed by employee-owners." Also, "an employee-owner is any employee of the corporation who owns, on any day during the taxable year, any of the outstanding stock of the personal service corporation."[16] Note that federal S corporations will not be considered personal service corporations (however, as we have indicated, they too are required, generally, to adopt a calendar year as their tax year).

As a result of these special rules, your corporation will be subject to this calendar-year rule if: (1) you elect federal S corporation tax status, or (2) you are incorporating a service-only business or profession (for example, lawyers, architects, business consultants, financial planners, etc.). Of course, many of these incorporated professions must organize themselves as a special California professional corporation and will not be using this book to form their corporation (see Chapter 2A2 for a discussion of professional corporations).

You may need to consult Treasury Regulations and other clarifications to determine if your service-based corporation is subject to this calendar year rule for personal service corporations.[17] The main points to keep in mind are the following: If your corporation plans to derive income primarily from the performance of personal services, and if the owner-employees only, or primarily, will perform these services, then your corporation may be required to adopt a calendar year as the tax year of your corporation. Your tax advisor can help you determine if this special personal service corporation rule applies to you.

**Exceptions to Special Calendar Year Rules for S and Personal Service Corporations** Despite the above special calendar year rules, IRS procedures provide exceptions which allow certain S corporations and personal service corporations to adopt a non-calendar (fiscal) tax year. Please see the box below ("S and Personal Service Corporation Fiscal Tax Year Rules") for a summary of these rules.

**Note** This discussion of special fiscal year rules for S corporations and personal service corporations is intended only to introduce you to some highly technical and rapidly changing tax material. If you wish to elect a non-calendar tax year for your S or personal service corporation, make sure to discuss these and other applicable rules and regulations with your tax advisor and, above all else, be sure to file the required tax year election forms with the IRS on time.

# E. Section 1244 Ordinary Loss Treatment for Stock Losses

Under Section 1244 of the Internal Revenue Code, many corporations can provide shareholders with the benefit of treating losses from the sale, exchange or worthlessness of their stock as "ordinary" rather than "capital" losses on their individual federal tax returns, up to a maximum of $50,000 ($100,000 for a husband and wife filing a joint return) in each tax year. This is a definite advantage since, generally, ordinary losses are fully deductible against individual income, whereas capital losses are only partially deductible (normally the latter can only be used to offset up to $3,000 of individual income in a given tax year). Stock issued by a corporation that qualifies for this federal ordinary loss treatment is known as Section 1244 stock.

To qualify for Section 1244 stock treatment, the following requirements must be met:

• The shares must be issued for money or property (other than corporate securities) and more than 50% of the corporation's gross receipts during the five tax years preceding the year in which the loss occurred must have been derived from sources other than royalties, dividends, interest, rents, annuities or gains from sales or exchanges in securities or stock. If the corporation has not been in existence for the five tax years preceding the year in which the loss occurred, the five-year period is replaced by the number of tax years the corporation has been in existence prior to the loss.

• The corporation must be a small business corporation as defined in Section 1244 of the Internal Revenue Code. A corporation is a small business corporation under this definition if the total amount of money or the value of property received by the corporation for stock, as a contribution to capital and as paid-in surplus, does not exceed $1 million.

• At the time of loss, the shareholder must submit a timely statement to the IRS electing to take an ordinary loss pursuant to Section 1244.

**Note** Ordinary loss treatment for the stock loss is only available to the original owner of the stock.

Corporations formed by using this book should automatically meet most of these requirements. However, if you issue shares in return for cancellation of indebtedness, problems may arise in some situations (e.g., if the notes were secured). Also, if you anticipate problems in being classified as a small business corporation (as defined above), or significant income from passive sources such as dividends or interest, or if you plan to have partnership shareholders, you should check with your tax consultant to make sure you can rely on ordinary loss treatment should a loss occur.

You do not have to file a special election form with the IRS or adopt a formal Section 1244 stock plan to be eligible for this special tax treatment—you simply must meet the requirements indicated above.

## ANOTHER TAX BREAK FOR SMALL BUSINESS STOCK

The 1993 Federal Deficit Reduction Act created another tax break for small business corporation stock. Specifically, persons who own shares in qualified corporations can qualify for a special tax rate of one-half of the capital gains tax rate, or a special rate of 14%, when they report gains from the sale or other disposition of their shares.

To qualify for this tax break, a number of requirements must be met. They include the following:

- The stock must be acquired when newly issued by the corporation and after the date of enactment of the federal tax legislation (August 10, 1993).

- The shares must be held for at least five years. However, a person who is given shares or inherits them during the five-year period can add on the amount of time the shares were held by the donor or deceased shareholder.

- The stock must have been purchased with money or property other than shares in the corporation,ß or been paid to an employee as compensation.

- The corporation must have gross assets of $50 million or less on the date of stock issuance.

- The corporation must be engaged in the operation of an active business. The practice of an incorporated profession such as a medical, accounting or engineering practice, and other types of businesses such as investing, farming and mining, are specifically excluded and do not qualify under this tax provision.

This special tax rate for small business stock gains may be an important one for your shareholders. Check with your accountant for the complete rules on this recent tax break.

**Forms Note** The tear-out Minutes, prepared as part of Chapter 5, Step 5, contain a Section 1244 resolution which is used as formal documentation of your intent that future stock losses of your shareholders be eligible for Section 1244 tax treatment. We expect most incorporators will wish to include this resolution in their Minutes. If your corporation does not meet the Section 1244 requirements at the time of a stock loss, the loss will simply be treated as the usual capital loss associated with regular shares of stock. Of course, if Section 1244 treatment of future stock losses is a critical factor in your incorporation, you will want to check with your tax advisor to be sure you will be eligible for this special stock loss treatment should a loss occur.

## F.   Tax-Free Exchange Treatment of Your Incorporation

Many incorporators will wish to issue stock in return for the transfer of property to the corporation. If you plan to do this, you should realize that taxes may have to be paid by one or more of the transferors of the property unless special requirements contained in Section 351 of the Internal Revenue Code are met. If all of your shareholders will simply pay cash for their shares, you may ignore this section since an all-cash transaction of this sort is simply a purchase of shares, not a potentially taxable transfer of property to your corporation.

First, let's back up a little. As you know, anytime you sell an asset to someone (in the case of an incorporation, you are "selling" property to the corporation in return for stock), you are normally liable for the payment of taxes on the profit you make from the transaction. In tax terms, the profit is the difference between the selling price and your "adjusted basis" in the property. Without covering all the technicalities, the basic rule for business property is that your adjusted basis in the property will be the original cost of the property minus depreciation plus capital improvements.

Here's a (simplified) example: Assume that your business purchased a building at a cost of $180,000. It has taken $90,000 depreciation on the property and made $20,000 in capital improvements to the property since the property was purchased. The adjusted basis of the property is $110,000 (cost of $180,000-$90,000 depreciation + $20,000 improvements). If the property is sold for $210,000, the taxable gain (profit) is $100,000 ($210,000-$110,000 adjusted basis). Note that we are ignoring, for purposes of this example, the cost, sales price and basis of the land on which the building is located (land is not depreciable).

Naturally, most incorporators will not wish to pay taxes on the sale of property to their corporation in return for shares of stock. This is particularly true if property which has increased in value (appreciated property) is being transferred to the corporation.

*Example:* If a building which originally cost $60,000 and has been depreciated down to an adjusted basis of $30,000 is being transferred to the corporation for $100,000 (the current appreciated value of the building), the gain on the transfer would be $70,000 ($100,000-$30,000 adjusted basis).

Fortunately, many small corporations will be able to transfer property to their corporation in return for stock in a tax-free exchange without recognizing any gain or loss on the transfer. Specifically, under Section 351 of the Internal Revenue Code, the transfer of property in return for shares of stock will generally be treated as a tax-free exchange if, immediately after the transfer, the transferors (shareholders) meet certain "control" tests. The tests that must be met are:

## S AND PERSONAL SERVICE CORPORATION FISCAL TAX YEAR RULES

A new corporation that plans to elect S corporation tax status can apply for a fiscal year on its S corporation election form (IRS Form 2553). Personal service corporations request a non-calendar tax year by filing IRS form 1128 with the IRS within certain time limits.

25-Percent Test: IRS Revenue Procedure 87-32 allows S corporations and personal service corporations to elect a fiscal year for their corporation if they can show that the fiscal year requested represents the natural business year of the corporation. To make this showing, these corporations must meet the "25% test." Generally, this test is met if 25% or more of the corporation's gross receipts from services or sales have been recognized during the last two months of the requested fiscal year for the past consecutive three years (e.g., if an S corporation wishes a fiscal year ending on June 30th, then 25% or more of its receipts from services must have derived during the months of May and June during each of the previous three years). If the corporation has not been in existence for three years, then, generally, the IRS will look at the gross receipts of the pre-existing unincorporated business.

Business Purpose: Even if you cannot meet the 25% test explained above, you may be able to establish another business purpose for your non-calendar tax year (e.g., if the fiscal year requested corresponds to the natural annual business cycle of the corporation)—Revenue Procedure 87-57 contains eight factual examples of valid and invalid business purposes when requesting a fiscal year for an S corporation.

Three-Month Deferral of Income: Under Section 444 of the Internal Revenue Code, S corporations and personal service corporations may be allowed to adopt a non-calendar tax year if the tax year results in a deferral on income of three months or less. Specifically, if a fiscal year ending September 30th is requested, this tax year will be allowed for the corporation (if other requirements are also met) since this results in a three-month deferral of income when compared to the otherwise required calendar year ending December 31st. Please realize that use of this three-month deferral rule comes with a price tag: S corporations using this procedure have to make a "required payment" to the IRS each year; personal service corporations utilizing this election are limited in the amount of corporate deductions which can be taken for payments made to the employee-shareholders unless certain minimum distributions are made to these shareholders before the end of the calendar year and carrybacks of net operating losses of the personal service corporation are restricted. For further information on Section 444 elections, see Treasury Regulation Section 1.444-1T. For the manner and timing of making a Section 444 election, see Treas. Reg. Section 1.444-3T. For further guidance in making a Section 444 election, see IRS Notice 88-10 (1/15/88) and Notice 88-49 (4/4/88).

1. The transferors, as a group, must own at least 80% of the total combined voting power of all classes of issued stock entitled to vote; and

2. They must also own at least 80% of all other issued classes of stock of the corporation.

Most initial stock issuance transactions of small closely-held corporations using this book should meet these control tests and be eligible for this tax-free exchange treatment since this is your first stock issuance involving one class of common voting shares and you don't need to establish control over previously issued stock or other classes of stock. Also note that cash and intangible types of property such as the goodwill of a business or patents are considered property for purposes of Section 351.

*Example:* Harvey, Frank and Frances decide to form a corporation. The corporation will issue 500 shares of stock at a price of $100 per share. Harvey will receive 100 shares for a $10,000 cash payment; Frank and Frances will receive 200 shares apiece for their equal interests in the assets of their partnership valued at $40,000. The transaction qualifies for Section 351 tax-free exchange treatment since at least 80% (in this case, 100%) of all shares will be owned by the transferors of money and property after the transfer (Harvey is not personally affected by this tax-free exchange treatment since he is simply purchasing shares for cash; however, Frank and Frances do not want to recognize a taxable gain on the transfer of their partnership assets.) Moreover, even without considering Harvey's permissible transfer of money to the corporation for his shares, Frank and Frances themselves will control the required 80% of the corporation's shares after the transfer of their property (400 out of 500 shares).

Of course, nothing (or next to nothing) is really free under tax statutes and regulations. A tax-free exchange simply defers the payment of taxes until your shares are sold (e.g., when you sell your shares to someone else or your corporation, itself, is sold or liquidated). Technically (and, of course, with some exceptions), the adjusted basis of the property transferred to the corporation is carried over to your shares (the adjusted basis of the shareholder's property becomes the basis of the shareholder's newly-purchased shares).

*Example:* You transfer property with a fair market value of $20,000 and an adjusted basis of $10,000 to the corporation in a Section 351 tax-free exchange for shares worth $20,000. Your shares will then have a basis of $10,000. If you sell the shares for $30,000, your taxable gain will be $20,000 ($30,000 selling price minus their basis of $10,000). Note also, the corporation's basis in the property received in a tax-free exchange will also generally be the same as the adjusted basis of the transferred property (in this example, the corporation's basis in the property will be $10,000).

Even in a tax-free transaction, the shareholders will be taxed to the extent of any money or property they receive in addition to stock. For example, if you transfer a truck in a tax-free exchange worth $50,000 to the corporation in return for $40,000 worth of shares and a $10,000 cash payment by the corporation, you will have to report the $10,000 as taxable income.

## 1. Potential Complexities Under IRC Section 351

There are, of course, added complexities which may arise in attempting to qualify an exchange of property for stock in your corporation as a Section 351 tax-free exchange. Let's look at a few of the more common situations which may trigger special rules:

### a. Where shares are issued in return for the performance of services

Although California law allows stock to be issued for past services performed for the corporation (see Chapter 2G), services are not considered "property" for purposes of Section 351 (remember, stock must be issued in return for property to qualify for this tax-free exchange treatment). Consequently, you cannot normally count shares issued to shareholders for services in calculating the 80% control requirement. Moreover, even if you are able to meet the control test (not counting the stock issued for services), any shareholder who receives stock for services will have to report the value of her shares as taxable income.

*Example:* Upon its incorporation, your corporation plans to issue $50,000 worth of shares to you and the co-founder of your corporation, Fred. You will transfer property worth $30,000 for $30,000 in shares, while Fred will receive $10,000 in shares in return for services already performed for the corporation valued at $10,000. The transfer will be taxable to both you and Fred since the basic control test of Section 351 will not have been met: You are the only person who will transfer property in return for stock and you do not meet the control requirement of Section 351 since you will only own 75% of the shares of the corporation.

If the facts in this example are changed so that you receive 80% of the stock in exchange for property (you transfer $40,000 worth of property; Fred still receives $10,000 in shares for his services), the transfer will be tax-free under Section 351, but Fred will have to report the $10,000 in shares as taxable income.

### b. Where the corporation issues notes in return for the transfer of appreciated property to the corporation

Only stock may be received for property in a tax-free Section 351 exchange, not long- or short-term notes. For example, if you transfer appreciated assets (such as the assets of a business) to the corporation in return for shares of stock plus a promissory note from the corporation, you will need to report and pay taxes on the gain (technical rules are applied to determine the amount of gain that must be reported). See your accountant if you plan to incorporate an existing business and wish to receive a note in addition to shares back from your corporation.

### c. Where the corporation assumes (agrees to pay) liabilities associated with the transferred property

This technicality typically arises when an existing business is being incorporated (i.e., where the owners of a prior business transfer the assets and liabilities of the prior business to the corporation in return for shares of stock). Under this exception to Section 351 tax-free exchange treatment, the prior business owners will be subject to the payment of taxes if the liabilities assumed by the corporation exceed the basis of the business assets transferred to the corporation.

For example, if you transfer business assets with a basis of $40,000 to your corporation along with $60,000 worth of liabilities, the difference of $20,000 is, as a general rule, taxable to you.

As a conclusion to this discussion, we will simply note that this federal tax statute and its associated regulations contain many rules and exceptions to rules. As a result, if you will be transferring property to your corporation in return for shares of stock (and, possibly, notes to be repaid by the corporation), you will need to check with an accountant to ensure favorable tax results under IRC Section 351.

**Record Keeping Note** Federal income tax regulations require the corporation and each shareholder to file statements with their income tax returns listing specific information concerning the Section 351 tax-free exchange.[18] Permanent records containing the information listed in these statements must also be kept by the corporation and the shareholders.

# G. Tax Treatment of Employee Compensation and Benefits

## 1. Salaries

A corporation may deduct amounts paid to employees as salaries for corporate income tax purposes. To be deductible, salaries must be reasonable and must be paid for services actually performed by the employees. Substantial salary increases or large discretionary lump-sum bonuses paid to shareholder-employees of closely-held corporations may be scrutinized by the IRS, since they can be, and sometimes are, used as a means of paying disguised dividends to the shareholders (i.e., as a return of capital to the shareholder rather than as a bona-fide payment for services rendered by the employee).

If the IRS determines that a salary was not related to bona-fide services actually performed by a shareholder-employee or was paid in an unreasonable amount, it will treat the excess amount as a dividend. This will not have an adverse effect on the shareholder-employee's tax liability because the payment must be included on his individual tax return either way. However, it will prevent the corporation from deducting the disallowed payment as a business expense.

Therefore, try to avoid the payment of large discretionary bonuses and keep any increase in salaries tied to increased corporate productivity related to the employee's performance or the going rate of pay for employees in similar businesses.

**Reality Note** In the majority of small corporations, the owner-employees will rarely be in a position to pay themselves unreasonably large salaries (small business owners are notoriously under-compensated, particularly in contrast to their highly-paid, publicly-held corporation counterparts).

However, if you do decide to pay yourself a large salary, it may be wise to draw up an employment contract between yourself and your corporation. You may also wish to adopt a board resolution detailing your abilities, qualifications and responsibilities, showing why you are entitled to the wages the corporation is paying you. In these situations, paying out dividends occasionally (if possible) is also useful, since it helps demonstrate to the IRS that you are acting in good faith in not paying as salary what should be going out as dividends.

## 2. Pension and Profit-Sharing Plans

Corporations may deduct payments made on behalf of employees to qualified pension or profit-sharing plans. Contributions and accumulated earnings under such plans are not taxed until they are distributed to the employee. This is advantageous because employees generally will be in a lower tax bracket at retirement age, and the funds, while they are held in trust, can be invested and allowed to accumulate with no tax being paid prior to the distribution.

Corporate and noncorporate pension plans for business owners (i.e., Keoghs) are, for the most part, the same with respect to contributions and benefits for participants, integration with social security benefits, and most other plan provisions. There are also strict rules which apply specifically to "top-heavy" plans, whether corporate or noncorporate—those set up primarily to benefit key employees (this is the type of plan you will most likely have if you decide to have one at all).

However, corporate plans still contain a few advantages over noncorporate plans such as allowing loans of $50,000 to be made from the corporate plan to participants. Also, whereas corporate defined contribution plans (which guarantee a specified yearly contribution to the plan on behalf of the participant) and noncorporate Keoghs limit annual contributions for participants to a maximum of 25% of earnings (subject to a yearly maximum limit), corporate defined benefit plans (which guarantee a specified benefit upon retirement) may allow contributions that provide annual benefits of up to 100% of a participant's compensation[19] (the cost of administering defined benefit plans is higher however). Further, with respect to noncorporate individual plan arrangements (IRAs) where contributions for an individual are generally limited to $2,000, full or partial deductions for contributions to these plans are only permitted to individuals who are not covered by a company retirement plan or, if they are so covered, to individuals whose adjusted gross income does not exceed certain maximum limits (e.g., $35,000 for an individual; $50,000 for a married couple filing jointly).

**California Tax Note**    California retirement plan provisions are generally in keeping with the federal rules.

For further information on corporate plans and comparable or contrasting provisions for noncorporate plans, see the following IRS publications:

334:    *Tax Guide for Small Business*
560:    *Self-Employed Retirement Plans*
575:    *Pension and Annuity Income*
590:    *Individual Retirement Arrangements*
1048:    *Filing Requirements for Employee Benefit Plans*

The above rules and dollar limits are subject to constant change. Please consult the above publications, your accountant, tax advisor, plan trustee or financial planner for information on the latest federal and state corporate pension and profit-sharing plan rules.

## 3.  Medical Benefits

### a.  Medical Expense Reimbursement

Amounts paid by a corporation as part of a medical expense reimbursement plan to repay the medical expenses of employees, their spouses and dependents, are deductible by the corporation and are not included in the employee's income for tax purposes.

### b.  Accident and Health Insurance

A corporation may deduct premiums paid by the corporation for accident and health insurance coverage for employees, their spouses and dependents. The premiums paid by the corporation are not included in the employee's income for tax purposes. Similarly, insurance proceeds and benefits are not normally taxable. Coverage need not be part of a group plan, such as Blue Cross. The employee may pick her own policy, pay for it, and obtain reimbursement from the corporation.

**Sole Proprietorship and Partnership Tax Note**    Unincorporated business owners (and S corporation shareholder-employees) are allowed to deduct a portion (25%) of the premiums paid for themselves and their spouses for health insurance. These deductions do not, however, reduce the individual's liability for self-employment (Social Security) taxes, are not available if the individual is eligible to participate in an employer-sponsored plan, and are subject to non-discrimination and other coverage rules (e.g., employees of the unincorporated business must also be provided coverage).[20]

## 4. Life Insurance

A corporation can also deduct premiums paid on behalf of employees for group-term life insurance. This tax break is available only if the plan does not discriminate in favor of key employees. An employee covered by a qualified group-term insurance plan does not have to count premiums paid by the corporation for up to $50,000 worth of insurance coverage as taxable income. Death proceeds under such insurance are also generally not included in the employee's income for tax purposes if you set up the right kind of plan.

## 5. Disability Insurance

Premiums paid by a corporation for disability insurance coverage for its employees are deductible by the corporation. Any disability benefits, however, are

included in the employee's gross income, subject to a few exceptions involving permanent and total disabilities. If the premiums are paid by the employee, however, all benefits are nontaxable.

## H. Corporate Accumulated Earnings Credit

In this section, we discuss a benefit of doing business as a corporation: the federal accumulated earnings credit.

As we've discussed earlier in this book, the decision to incorporate is often based upon the desire of business owners to split business income between themselves and their corporation. The Internal Revenue Code helps corporations do this by allowing them an automatic accumulated earnings credit of $250,000.[21] What this means is that the IRS will allow you to retain this amount of earnings in your corporation without challenging you for not paying it out to the shareholders as dividends or salaries, or in other ways which would make it subject to taxation on their individual tax returns. Of course, the corporation must pay tax on these accumulated amounts at the corporate tax rate but these taxes are often lower than

individual taxes on the same levels of individual income (particularly on lower or more moderate levels of taxable business income—see Section B2 above).[22] Note that federal S corporations do not receive (or need) the benefit of this credit since the undistributed earnings of the corporation pass through to the shareholders of S corporations each year (see Section C above). This accumulated earnings credit is, as we've said, one of the advantages of doing business as a corporation—sole proprietors and partnerships do not enjoy this type of tax flexibility.

Most small corporations will not need (or be able) to accumulate earnings anywhere near this $250,000 credit since salaries, bills and other business expenses will reduce earnings below this amount. If, however, you do need to accumulate income in the corporation above this limit, you may do so, as long as these excess accumulations are held for the reasonably anticipated needs of the business (not just to shelter income).

**Important**    If the IRS determines that corporate earnings have been unreasonably accumulated above the automatic credit amount, it will assess a whopping 39.6% penalty on the excess accumulations—you will want to stay well clear of this hefty tax penalty.

# I.  Personal Holding Company Penalty

In this section we briefly discuss provisions of the federal tax law[23] which some closely-held personal service corporations will need to be aware of: the personal holding company penalty tax. If your corporation does not plan to derive income from passive sources (such as rents, royalties, dividends) or will not derive income from the performance of personal services, you may wish to skip this section.

This tax is a 39.6% corporate surtax, in addition to regular corporate taxes, on the income of certain types of corporations which receive a significant portion of their adjusted gross income from "passive" sources or from services performed under contract. With a few simple precautions, this tax should not pose a problem for these corporations—the only real danger is inadvertently becoming subject to this tax due to a lack of knowledge of these provisions.

Without discussing all of the technical definitions and exceptions of this federal tax law, the personal holding company tax may apply to a corporation if five or fewer of its shareholders own 50% or more of the corporation's stock, and if 60% or more of the corporation's gross income (minus several technical adjustments) for the tax year is from certain types of passive sources, such as dividends, interest, rents or royalties[24] or is derived from personal service contracts. Although many small corporations will have five or fewer shareholders who own at least half of the corporation's shares, most corporations using this book will derive most of their income from engaging in active business pursuits rather than these types of passive sources. Consequently, the concern here will usually be whether your corporation provides contracted services, and, if so, whether this income is subject to being classified as personal service contract income.

Under Section 543(a)(7) of the Internal Revenue Code, personal service contract income means, generally, "amounts received under a contract under which the corporation is to furnish personal services, if some person other than the corporation has the right to designate (by name or description) the individual who is to perform the services, or if the individual who is to perform the services is designated (by name or description) in the contract." In addition, the individual who is to perform the services, or who may be so designated, must be at least a 25% shareholder.

What does all of this mean? Simply stated, if your corporation is planning to provide services under the terms of a contract, you will want to make sure that the corporation has the right to designate the individual who will perform the contracted services (not the person or business for whom the services will be performed) and that the name of the individual who is to perform the services does not appear in the contract. By doing this you should be able to stay clear of this personal holding company penalty.

**Note When Incorporating a Pre-existing Business**
If you are incorporating a personal service business, such as your own computer repair and service corporation, you will not want to assign your individual personal service contracts to your new corporation without checking first with your tax advisor—this could trigger a penalty.

It should be of some comfort to note that the Internal Revenue Code anticipates that corporations will be subject to this penalty tax, usually due to an oversight or poor planning, and, consequently, allows them to avoid the imposition of this tax, in many cases, by the payout of what is known as a "deficiency dividend." Even under this procedure, however, the corporation is subject to interest and other penalty payments. Nonetheless, if you are incorporating a service business, or if your corporation plans to receive a substantial portion of its income from the types of passive sources which we've mentioned above, please check with your tax specialist to make sure you will not inadvertently run afoul of this penalty tax provision.

## J. Tax and Financial Considerations When Incorporating a Prior Business

In this section, we discuss a few key legal and tax issues involving the incorporation of an existing business—for a broader discussion of the basic considerations relevant to your decision to incorporate, please see Chapter 1. If you are simply incorporating a new business, you may wish to skip this section.

### 1. When Is the Best Time to Incorporate the Prior Business?

You will want to incorporate your prior business at a time which results in the most favorable tax treatment (mostly, this means the time which results in your paying the least amount of taxes).

*Example:* If you anticipate a loss this year and a healthy profit next year, you may wish to remain unincorporated now and take a personal loss on your individual tax return. Next year you can incorporate and split your business income between yourself and your corporation to reduce your overall tax liability.

### 2. Special Financial and Tax Considerations

Typically, when incorporating a pre-existing business, all the assets and liabilities of the prior business will be transferred to the new corporation which will then carry on the pre-existing business. Further, as explained in Section F above, most incorporators will want the transfer of the assets of the prior business to the corporation in return for shares of stock to qualify for tax-free exchange treatment under Section 351 of the Internal Revenue Code. In special circumstances, however, some incorporators may not wish to transfer all assets or liabilities of the prior business to the corporation, or, for special reasons, may not wish this transfer to qualify for Section 351 tax-free exchange treatment. We discuss these special circumstances in this subsection.

### a. Do you wish to retain (not transfer) some of the assets of the prior business?

In some instances, the prior business owners may not wish to transfer some of the assets of the prior business to their new corporation. For example:

- Sufficient cash should be retained to pay liabilities not assumed by the corporation (such as payroll and other taxes).
- You may wish to retain ownership in some of the assets of the prior business. For example, you may wish to continue to own a building in your name and lease it to your corporation. In this way, you can continue to deduct depreciation, mortgage interest payments and other expenses associated with the property on your individual tax return. (The corporation, moreover, can deduct rent payments made under the lease.)

### b. Do you wish to have the corporation assume some, but not all, of the liabilities of the prior business?

As with the assets of your unincorporated business, you may not wish to transfer (have your corporation assume) all of the liabilities of the prior business. Two considerations relevant to this decision are listed below:

- The assumption of the liabilities of the prior business may, in special situations, result in the recognition of taxable gain by the prior business owners under an exception to the tax-free exchange rule of Section 351 discussed in Section F1c above.
- Payment of liabilities and expenses by the prior business owners, rather than by the corporation, will allow the owners to deduct these expenses on their individual tax returns (to reduce their individual taxable incomes).

### c. Is a Section 351 tax-free exchange desirable?

Although not typical, a small number of incorporators may wish to have the transfer of assets of the prior business to the corporation be a taxable exchange. Since the general rule under Section 351 (discussed in Section F above) is that the exchange of property for stock by individuals who will be in control of the corporation after the exchange is a tax-free transfer, oddly enough, you may need to do a little advance tax planning to accomplish this taxable result. Reasons why a few incorporators may wish to be taxed on the transfer of the assets of their prior business to the corporation include the following:

- Some incorporators may wish to recognize taxable gain on the transfer of business assets to increase the corporation's "basis" in these assets.

*Example:* Let's assume that you will transfer assets with a fair market value of $50,000 to your corporation. Your basis in these assets is $30,000. If you transfer these assets to the corporation for $50,000 worth of stock in a taxable exchange, you will recognize a taxable gain of $20,000. However, the corporation's basis in these assets will be your basis before the sale ($30,000) plus the amount of gain recognized by the transferor (your individual gain of $20,000). Consequently, the corporation's basis in these assets will be increased to $50,000. This allows the corporation to take additional depreciation in these assets over time and will lower the gain the corporation will recognize upon a sale of these assets (if the corporation sells the assets for $60,000, the gain will be $10,000—the difference between the corporation's basis and the selling price).

If the assets in the above example had been transferred to the corporation in a tax-free exchange, the corporation's basis would be the same as your pre-transfer basis in the property ($30,000), and the gain recognized by the corporation from the sale of these assets would be the higher figure of $30,000 (the difference between the corporation's $30,000 basis and the $60,000 selling price). Of course, whether the advantages of obtaining a higher corporate basis in assets is worth the gain that you, the transferor, will be required to recognize in a taxable exchange, must be determined by the individual facts of your incorporation (for example, will you be able to offset this individual gain with losses or deductions on your individual tax return?, etc.). As we've said, normally, you will want to transfer assets to your corporation in a tax-free exchange to avoid the recognition of gain on the transfer.

- Some incorporators may wish to recognize a loss on the transfer of assets to their corporation. If you transfer assets to your corporation under Section 351, you cannot recognize either a gain or a loss on the transfer. If the value of the assets has decreased below your basis in the property, you may wish to take a loss on the transfer.

  *Example:* If your basis in a building is $75,000, and, because of market conditions, the current value of the building is now only $60,000, you will need to transfer the building to the corporation in a taxable exchange (and meet other technical requirements) to recognize this loss of $15,000. Again, this is not a typical situation but it may be relevant to some incorporators.

## 3. Liability for the Debts of the Prior Business

In addition to the above considerations involving the assumption of liabilities of the prior business by your new corporation, legal rules exist concerning the liability of the prior business owners and the corporation for the debts of the prior business.

**Note** These rules will have little significance for most newly-formed corporations which will wish, as a matter of course and as a matter of simple good-faith business dealings, to continue to carry on the business and continue to pay all the debts and liabilities associated with the business, whether incurred before or after incorporation. However, to underscore the fact that you cannot incorporate as a means of avoiding the liabilities of the prior business, and by way of briefly mentioning other specific considerations related to this issue, we include the following points:

- As a general rule, a new corporation is not liable for the debts or liabilities of the prior business unless it assumes them (as we've said, most new corporations will wish to assume these debts). However, whether or not the corporation assumes these liabilities, the prior owners will remain personally liable for any unpaid debts and liabilities of the prior business.

- Even if the corporation assumes the liabilities of the prior business, if the transfer of the business is in some way fraudulent or done with the intent to frustrate or deceive creditors, the creditors of the prior business may be able to seize the transferred business assets. Similarly, if the corporation does not, in fact, pay the assumed liabilities of the prior business, the transferred assets may be seized by creditors of the prior business.

- If transferred assets are subject to recorded liens (e.g., a mortgage on real property), these liens will survive the transfer and the assets will continue to be subject to these liens.

- The former business owners may be liable for debts incurred after incorporation if credit is extended to the corporation by a creditor who believes that he or she is still dealing with the prior business (i.e., a creditor who has not been notified of the incorporation). See Chapter 6A4 for the steps to take to notify creditors of the prior business of your incorporation.

- The corporation may be liable for delinquent sales, employment or other taxes owed by the prior business. ■

## Endnotes

[1]We have tried to include major changes which affect the tax areas discussed in this and other chapters. To check on any recent changes, check with your accountant or obtain the IRS and California tax publications mentioned throughout this book, particularly those listed in the "For More Information" box at the beginning of Chapter 6.

[2]If you have formed more than one corporation and have to file a combined state tax report for your corporations, you may not be eligible for California S corporation tax status.

[3]As you'll see in Section H of this chapter, the IRS allows most corporations to accumulate up to $250,000 of earnings in the corporation for this type of income splitting, no questions asked. Amounts above this amount may be accumulated to meet the reasonable business needs of the corporation.

[4]We are generalizing here. The table shows that corporate taxes catch up to individual taxes between $115,000 and $150,000, depending on whether the individual's tax filing status is as a single person or as a spouse filing a joint return. Married persons filing separate returns pay more taxes for the same levels of individual income than single taxpayers. Tax payments by heads of household fall somewhere between the taxes owed by single taxpayers and those owed by spouses filing joint returns.

[5]Individuals with incomes that exceed specified thresholds pay taxes at a top individual income tax rates of 36% or 39.6%. However, because of the reductions of deductions and the phasing out of personal exemptions that apply to higher levels of individual income, high-income individuals may end up paying an effective top tax rate even higher than 39.6%.

[6]One survey concluded that only 10% of all U.S. corporations report taxable incomes over $75,000—this 10% group pays 90% of all corporate taxes.

[7]This discussion is intended to treat the general aspects of S corporation tax status—for more detailed information regarding special rules, see IRS Publication 589, Tax Information on S Corporations.

[8]IRS rulings indicate that S corporation shareholders may have to estimate and pay individual federal income tax during the year on their pro rata share of the undistributed taxable income of the S corporation—previously S corporation shareholders included this income on their individual federal tax return at the end of the year. Please check with your tax advisor for current developments on this issue.

[9]Another potential advantage of S corporation status is that, traditionally, corporate profits that have been passed through to shareholders have not been subject to self-employment (Social Security) taxes. There has been some IRS resistance, however, where an active sole shareholder attempts to avoid all employment taxes by having all profits pass to the shareholder as undistributed S corporation earnings without the payment of any amounts as wages. Check with your accountant if you are interested in this tax issue.

[10]S corporations are subject to a "built-in gains" tax for any appreciation which occurred prior to the S corporation election (if these assets are disposed of within ten years after the effective date of the S corporation tax election). Please consult your tax advisor for information on these technical provisions.

[11]Generally, you start out with a basis in your shares equal to the price you paid for them (or the value of the property contributed for your shares).

[12]Also note: In order to use S corporation losses to offset the active individual income of a shareholder, the shareholders must materially participate in the business of the S corporation. See the sidebar in the text for a summary of several of the material participation regulations promulgated by the Treasury Department.

[13]Note, however, that S corporation shareholders are entitled to the same tax break for medical plans as sole proprietors and partners—see Sole Proprietorship and Partnership Tax Note in Section G3b of this chapter.

[14]See IRC Section 1361(b) and following for the statutory technicalities of, and exceptions under, the Subchapter S definition of "small business corporations."

[15]For further information on the second-class-of-stock rules for S corporations, see Treasury Regulation Section 1.1361-1.

[16]See Treasury Regulation 1.441-4T for further information on how this calendar year rule is applied to personal service corporations.

[17]Treasury Regulation Section 1.441-4T defines the nature and extent of personal service activities which will trigger the application of this calendar year rule for personal service corporations. For example, the regulation states that: (1) the fields of health, law, engineering, architecture, accounting, actuarial science, performing arts and consulting are personal services subject to this rule; (2) performing arts services do not include the personal services of managers and promoters; and (3) consulting does not include the performance of services such as sales or brokerage activities since compensation for these services is contingent on the consummation of the transaction that these services are intended to effect. Again, see your tax advisor for current developments and clarifications.

[18]See Treasury Regulation Section 1.351-3.

[19]Federal tax law now limits the annual amount of compensation that can be taken into account for retirement plan purposes (as well as Keogh plans) to $150,000. This amount is expected to be increased slightly in future years due to cost of living adjustments.

[20]This tax break is temporary and is expected to change when new, comprehensive federal health care legislation is approved by Congress.

[21]Section 535(c)(2)(B) of the Internal Revenue Code limits the amount of this credit to $150,000 for corporations whose principal function is the performance of services in the fields of health, law, engineering, architecture, accounting, actuarial science, performance arts, or consulting. This lesser credit should still be sufficient for most corporations. Note: Many of these professional service corporations must incorporate as California professional corporations (see Chapter 2A2).

[22]Note, however, that the personal service corporations listed in the previous footnote which are only allowed the $150,000 must pay a flat tax of 35% on retained corporate taxable income—see Section B1 of this chapter for further information on this special flat-tax provision.

[23]Internal Revenue Code Sections 541 through 547.

[24]Note for software developers and distributors: We know that many readers of this book will be deriving corporate income from the licensing of software. The Internal Revenue Code contains an important exemption here for software royalties which may be apply to you. Specifically, "active business computer software royalties," defined as those which are "received by the corporation during the taxable year in connection with the licensing of computer software," are not treated as personal holding company income if certain specific technical tests are met—see IRC Section 543(d) and check with your tax advisor for more information.

# CHAPTER 5

# Steps to Form Your Corporation

**T**his chapter will show you, on a step-by-step basis, how to form your California corporation by preparing and filing Articles of Incorporation, preparing Bylaws, preparing Minutes of and holding your first meeting of the board of directors, selling and issuing your initial shares of stock, and taking care of other essential organizational formalities. You'll see that these steps are really not complicated and involve, for the most part, simply filling in a small number of blanks on the tear-out forms contained in the Appendix at the end of this book. Take your time and relax; you'll be surprised at how easy it all is.

Although we provide you with standard tear-out forms and show you how to fill them in, we realize that some incorporators may have special needs dictated by the particular facts and circumstances of their incorporation. Since we can't customize these forms to fit the special needs of all businesses, some incorporators will need to check their papers with a lawyer and/or an accountant (see Chapter 7).

One more point on consulting a professional: A consultation with a lawyer and accountant to review the forms and other organizational aspects of your incorporation in light of your own special circumstances is far different from having them do it all for you. Their job in this context will be to answer your specific, informed questions and, if you feel it necessary, to review your papers at an hourly fee agreed upon in advance, not to do the routine paperwork or re-assess all your decisions.

**SPECIAL UPGRADE OFFER FOR COMPUTER USERS**

Nolo Press offers a special records binder with disk edition of this book. This special edition includes a disk containing computer files for each of the tear-out incorporation forms in the Appendix of this book. These files have been prepared in the most popular wordprocessing formats, as well as text-only versions that can be read by all word processors. This special edition also contain tear-out and computer disk files to prepare minutes of ongoing director and shareholder meetings or to take action by written consent of directors or shareholders without a meeting. Separate stock register and transfer pages are also provided to help you keep track of share ownership in your corporation. Nolo Press offers a special upgrade offer to purchasers of this book—for the details, see the order pages at the front of this book.

ANOTHER WAY TO INCORPORATE USING YOUR COMPUTER    If you want more than forms on disk, you may be interested in purchasing Nolo's *California Incorporator* software. This stand-alone program guides your through each step in the incorporation process and prompts you to supply the information necessary to have the program fill in the blanks on the incorporation forms for you. See the sidebar below for further information.

**CALIFORNIA INCORPORATOR COMPUTER PROGRAM**

*California Incorporator* is an interactive computer program which will assemble and print your incorporation forms for you, including Articles of Incorporation, Bylaws, Minutes of First Meeting, Shareholder Representation Letters, and Notice of Stock Transaction. The program works like this: You are led through an orderly sequence of steps starting with choosing a corporate name and ending with preparing the documentation for your initial stock issuance. In each step, you answer specific questions following instructions on the screen. Your answers are used by the program to fill in the blanks, and assemble and print the incorporation document(s) associated with each step. You can leave the program at any time and return later to pick up where you left off (or to go to any other step in the program to review and change information, re-print forms, etc.).

Although *Incorporator* will produce and print all incorporation documents on its own, it includes options to save each form as a text file on your disk. California Incorporator runs on IBM and compatible computers—for the details of a special upgrade offer available to purchasers of this book, see the *California Incorporator* order page at the front of this book.

**Important**   Although we've noted fees which are scheduled or likely to increase, all fees (and the addresses of the Secretary of State offices) mentioned in this chapter are subject to change at any time (filing fees often change on the first day of the year; franchise tax amounts can change at any time). To be doubly sure that the fee amounts (and addresses) given in this chapter are current at the time of your incorporation, call the nearest office of the Secretary of State (offices located in Los Angeles, Sacramento, San Diego and San Francisco) just prior to filing your documents.

# Step 1.   Choose a Corporate Name

The first step in organizing your corporation is selecting a name for your corporation which you like and which meets the requirements of state law. Your corporate name is approved by the California Secretary of State when you file your Articles of Incorporation. You are not legally required to include a corporate designator in your corporate name such as "Corporation," "Incorporated," "Limited", or an abbreviation of one of these words ("Corp.," "Inc.," or "Ltd.,") unless, as discussed below, your corporation will include the name of an individual. Most incorporators, of course, will be anxious to use one of these designators precisely because they want others to know that their business is incorporated.

## A. The Importance of Your Corporate Name

Before looking at the legal requirements for choosing a corporate name, let's briefly discuss the importance of choosing the right name for your new corporation. The most significant aspect of choosing a name is that it will, to a large degree, identify the "goodwill" of your business. We don't mean this in any strict legal, accounting or tax sense, but simply that the people you do business with, including your customers, clients, other merchants, vendors, independent contractors, lenders and the business community generally, will identify your business primarily by your name. For this reason, as well as a number of practical reasons such as not wanting to print new stationery, change Yellow Pages or advertising copy, create new logos, purchase new signs, etc., you will want to pick a name that you will be happy with for a long time. So pay particular attention to your choice of a corporate name. As a practical matter, it's likely to become one of your most important assets.

Of course, if you are incorporating an existing business, you'll probably wish to use your current name as your corporate name if it has become associated with your products, services, etc. Many businesses do this by simply adding an "Inc." after their old name (e.g., Really Good Widgets decides to incorporate as Really Good Widgets, Inc.). Using your old name is not required, however, and if you have been hankering after a new one, this is your chance to claim it.

Here are a couple of additional legal points relevant to your choice of a corporate name:

- *Filing your corporate name with the Secretary of State does not guarantee your right to use it.* Contrary to the belief of many people, having your name approved by the California Secretary of State when you file your Articles of Incorporation does not guarantee that you have the absolute right to use it (as explained below, an unincorporated business may already be using it as their trade name or another business may be using it as a trademark or service mark). Consequently, you will probably want to do some checking on your own to be relatively sure that no one else has a prior claim to your proposed corporate name. We discuss special self-help measures you may wish to take prior to deciding on a corporate name in "Performing Your Own Name Search" below.

- *Using a name different than your formal corporate name is allowed.* If you want to adopt a formal corporate name in your Articles which is different from the one which you have used, or plan to use, locally in your business, you can accomplish this by filing a fictitious business name statement with the County Clerk in the counties in which you plan to do business (we explain how to prepare and file this statement in Chapter 6A2).

## B. Secretary of State Name Requirements

The California Secretary of State will not accept your corporate name (and will, therefore, reject your Articles of Incorporation) unless it meets the following requirements:

- Your name must not be the same as, or confusingly similar to, a name already on file with the Secretary of State. The Secretary maintains a list of names of existing California corporations and out-of-state corporations qualified to do business in California, names which have been registered with the Secretary of State by out-of-state corporations, as well as names which have been reserved for use by other corporations. If your name is the same as, or confusingly similar to, any of these, your name will be rejected. We can't give you an exact definition of the phrase "confusingly similar," but, for practical purposes, this restriction simply means that your proposed name cannot be so similar to that of an existing name already on the Secretary of State's list that it will be rejected by this office. For example, if you wish to set up a wholesale house for computer equipment under the name "Compusell, Inc.," and a corporation is already on file with the Secretary of State with the name "Compusel, International, Inc.," your name may be rejected as too similar. (Remember, you don't normally have to add "Inc."

to your name—we include this corporate designator here just for purposes of the example.)

- The name of a person cannot be used as a corporate name without adding a corporate ending to it or some other word or words which show that the name is not that of the individual alone (such as "Incorporated," "Corporation," "Limited," "Company," or an abbreviation of one of these words). This is true even though you can set up a one-person corporation in California. Therefore, "Biff Baxter" would be an invalid corporate name, but "Biff Baxter, Inc.," would be acceptable. As an aside, the Secretary of State recognizes that individuals have special rights to the use of their names in connection with their businesses and, therefore, will normally allow two individuals with the same name to use them in their corporate title without raising the issue of similarity (two Biff Baxter, Inc.'s would be allowed by the Secretary of State).

- A regular profit corporation (the type you will organize) cannot use certain words in its name which are reserved for special types of corporations. Included in these restricted words are the following:

| | | |
|---|---|---|
| Bank | Cooperative | Federal |
| National | Reserve | Trust |
| Trustee | United States | |

- In the (unusual and unlikely) event that you decide to form a close corporation (see Chapter 2A3), your corporate name must include the word "Corporation," "Incorporated," or "Limited," or an abbreviation of one of these words. Again, this book cannot be used to form this special (and unusual) type of California corporation—make sure to have a lawyer modify your forms and stock certificates if you wish to incorporate as a close corporation.

## C. Check to See If Your Proposed Name Is Available

Since your Articles of Incorporation will be rejected if the name you've chosen is not available, you may wish check its availability or reserve it before submitting your Articles to the Secretary of State.

You can check the availability of up to four corporate names by mail by sending a note to the Secretary of State at 1230 J Street, Sacramento, California, 95814.[1] Provide your name and address, a list of up to four proposed corporate names, and a request that each name be checked to see if it is available for use as a corporate name. The Secretary will respond to your written request within one week or two.

**Note** Even if the Secretary indicates by return mail that a corporate name is available, it may not be available when you file your Articles (if someone else actually uses it before you file your papers). To avoid this problem, you can check and reserve a name for a small fee as explained in the next subsection.

**If a Particular Name Is Unavailable** If the use of a particular corporate name is crucial to you and you are told that it is unavailable since it is too close to an existing name already on file with the Secretary of State, there are a few things you can do:

1. Submit a written request for a review of your name's acceptability to the legal counsel's office at the Secretary of State. You should realize that deciding the legal question of whether or not a name is so close to another so as to cause confusion to the public involves looking at a number of criteria contained in a long line of court decisions, including the nature of each trade name user's business (the term "trade name" simply means a name used in conjunction with the operation of a trade or business), the geographical proximity of the two businesses, etc. We cover these issues in more detail below but, for now, we simply note that if you do get into this sort of squabble, you will probably want to see a lawyer who is versed in

the complexities of trade name or trademark law, or do some additional reading on your own.

2. Obtain the written consent of the other corporation already using a similar corporate name to your use of your corporate name.

    **Note**  Make sure to call the Secretary of State (at 1-916-445-0620) and ask a name availability clerk if this written consent procedure will work for you—even with the consent of the other corporation, the Secretary's office will not allow you to use a similar name if they feel the public is likely to be misled (e.g., if the names are very similar in sound, etc.). If you get the go-ahead to use this procedure, ask the name availability clerk for the address of the other corporation and send them your written request for an officer of their corporation to sign, together with an explanatory letter (and/or a preliminary phone call) indicating why you'd like them to agree to your use of your similar name (e.g., because you will be engaged in a different line of business in a different locale).

3. Decide that it's simpler (and less trouble all the way around) to pick another name for your business. We normally recommend this third approach when searching for an available corporate name.

## D. Reserve Your Corporate Name

For a small fee, you can check the availability of up to four names at once and reserve the first available name by mail with the Sacramento office of the Secretary of State. We think it makes sense to do this rather than simply checking to see if your name is available as explained above. If you name is available, it will be reserved exclusively for your use for a period of sixty days. If you cannot file your Articles within this period, you can re-reserve the name by preparing a new reservation letter and paying another fee. Note that a second reservation letter must be received by the Secretary of State at least one day after the first certifi-

cate expires (the law does not allow two consecutive reservations of corporate name—therefore the requests must be separated by at least one day).

The fee to reserve a name by mail for 60 days is $10. Simply use the tear-out form in the Appendix as you follow the instructions and sample form below.

**Warning**  Fees are subject to change. If you want to be doubly sure that this fee amount is current at the time of your incorporation, call the nearest office of the Secretary of State (listed below).

Make sure one of persons who will sign your Articles of Incorporation (one of your initial directors—see Step 2 below) prepares and signs your reservation request letter, since your corporate name will be reserved for use by the individual who signs this letter.

You can also reserve a corporate name in person at any one of the following offices of the Secretary of State:

LOS ANGELES
107 South Broadway, Room 4001
Los Angeles, CA 90012

SACRAMENTO
1230 J Street, Room 100
Sacramento, CA 95814

SAN DIEGO
1350 Front Street, State Building, Room 2060
San Diego, CA 92101

SAN FRANCISCO
455 Golden Gate Avenue, Room 2236
San Francisco, CA 94102

The fee for reserving a name in person is $20. The clerk will ask for *two* $10 checks. If your proposed name is not available, the clerk will only return one $10 check to you.

SAMPLE REQUEST FOR RESERVATION OF CORPORATE NAME

_____
*(date)*

_____
*(your address)*

_____


Secretary of State
Corporate Name Availability
1230 J Street
Sacramento, CA 95814


Secretary of State:

　　　Please reserve the first available corporate name from the list
below for my use. My proposed corporate names, listed in order of
preference, are as follows:

_____
*(list up to four proposed corporate names—the Secretary will use*

_____
*the first available name from this list for your corporation)*

_____



　　　I enclose a check or money order for the required reservation
fee, payable to the "Secretary of State."


Sincerely,


_____
*(your signature)*

_____
*(typed name)*

## E. Perform Your Own Name Search

As we've said, approval by the Secretary of State's office of your corporate name doesn't necessarily mean that you have the legal right to use this name. More specifically, acceptance of your name by the Secretary of State's office simply means that your name does not conflict with that of another corporation already on file with the Secretary of State and that you are presumed to have the legal right to the use of this name for your corporation in California. It is important to realize, however, that other businesses (corporate and noncorporate) may already have the right to use this same name (or one similar to it) as a federal or state trademark or service mark used to identify their goods or services (the Secretary of State does not even check the state trademark/service mark registration lists maintained in the Secretary of State's office when checking to see if your name is available). Also, another business (corporate or noncorporate) may already be presumed to have the legal right to use your name in a particular county if they are using it as trade name (as the name of their business) and have filed a fictitious business name statement with their county clerk.

To underscore the fact that acceptance of a corporate name by the Secretary of State is not determinative of who has this ultimate right, the Secretary's office will send you a notice after you file your Articles which states that the filing of the Articles of Incorporation does not, in itself, authorize the use in California of a corporate name which is in violation of the rights of another person to use the name, including rights in a trade name, rights under state or federal trademark laws or state fictitious business name laws, and rights which arise under principles of common law (the law expressed in court decisions).

Without discussing the intricacies of federal and state trademark, service mark and trade name law, the basic rule is that the ultimate right to use a particular business name will usually be decided on the basis of who was first in time to actually use the name in connection with a particular trade or business, service or product. In deciding who has the right to a name, the similarity of the types of businesses and their geographical proximity are usually taken into account. For example, if you plan to operate the "Sears Bar & Grille, Inc.," you probably won't have a problem at least as far as the well-known retail chain is concerned[2] (but you might if there is another bar or restaurant using the same name in your area, or perhaps even if they are only currently operating in another part of the country but later expand to your area).[3] Similarly, if you find out that your Ukiah car dealership, Bob's Buicks, Inc., is the same as that of an Los Angeles car dealer, you're also probably on safe ground since it is unlikely that the public would be deceived as to the origin of any goods or services. However, you could be challenged (probably successfully), if, in these examples, you incorporated as "Sears Merchandising, Inc.," or operated your car dealership in Ventura. To deal with this rather slippery concept, simply ask yourself whether you, as a hypothetical customer, might reasonably confuse your proposed name with another one that already exists, and thereby deal with the wrong business? If you're honest, you can provide as good a guideline for yourself as any lawyer.

The upshot of this discussion is that it is wise to do a little checking on your own before filing your Articles to see if another business is already using your name as a trade name, service mark or trademark, particularly in the geographical area in which you plan to operate. Obviously, you will not be able to be 100% certain since you can't possibly check all names in use by other businesses. However, you can check obvious sources likely to expose similar names which are not listed as corporate names on the Secretary's list. Here are some suggestions:

- Call the California Secretary of State's trademark/service mark registration section at 916-445-9872 and see if your proposed name is already registered with them for use by another business. They will check up to two names over the phone at no charge.

- Check with the County Clerk in the county or counties in which you plan to do business to see if your name has already been registered by another person or business as a fictitious business name. Most county clerk's will require you to come in and check the files yourself—it takes just a few minutes to do this.

- Go to a public library or special business and government library in your area which carries the federal Trademark Register, a listing of trademark/ service mark names broken into categories of goods and services. This aspect of your search is extremely important. If a name is placed on the Principal Register (the primary federal trademark register) you are deemed to know that it exists and is owned by someone else. Then, if you select a business name that is close to this mark, and use the name in the marketing of your goods or services, you may be liable for trademark infringement, especially if your goods or services are related to the goods or services carrying the registered mark and you are both marketing in the same part of the country. In that event you will probably have to give up your name and maybe even pay damages to the trademark's owner. The moral? Always check the federal and state registers and stay away from names that might be confused with marks on the federal Principal Register.

- To check unregistered trade names (this is true for the majority of names used by unincorporated businesses), use a common sense approach. Check major metropolitan phone book listings, business and trade directories, and other business listings, such as the Dun & Bradstreet business listing. Larger public libraries have phone directories for many major cities within and outside of California.

**Computer Resource Note**   Most of the business name listings mentioned above, including Yellow Pages listings and business directory databases, as well as the federal and state trademark registers, are available as part of several commercial computer databases. For example, the federal and state registers can be accessed through the Trademarkscan® service which is part of the Trademark Research Center forum (Go Traderc) on CompuServe database (call 1-800-848-8990 for subscription information) or the Dialog database (call 1-800-462-3411). If you own, or have access to, a computer and a modem and are already signed up on one of these databases, you can check your proposed name against the names in the federal and state registers in just a few minutes time (for an extra charge for your time while using the Trademarkscan service).

If you want to check further or don't want to do it all yourself, you can pay a private records search company to check federal and state trademarks and service marks as well as local and state-wide business listings. They can check your proposed name against the sources we've listed above including federal and state trademarks and service mark filings, major business directories, metropolitan phone listings, etc.

Alternatively, or in conjunction with your own efforts or search procedures, you can pay a trademark lawyer to oversee or undertake these searches for you. They will take the responsibility of hiring a private search company. In addition, they may provide a legal opinion on the legal issues surrounding, and the relative legal safety of, your use of your proposed corporate name. Normally, this opinion isn't necessary but can be valuable if the search discovers several similar, but not identical, names.

Obviously, the amount of checking and consulting you can do is limited only by the amount of effort or money you are willing to devote to the task and by how safe you need to feel about your choice of a corporate name. In most situations, just following the self-help measures listed above, including, if appropriate, the use of a name search service, will be enough to reassure most small corporations that their choice of a corporate name is a safe one.

## F. Protect Your Name

Once you have filed your Articles of Incorporation, you may wish to take additional steps to protect your name. For example, you may wish to register your corporate name with your local county clerk as a fictitious business name. This provides another form of constructive notice to other businesses that your name is not available for their use. (see Chapter 7A2 for more information on filing a fictitious business name statement). If your name is (or will be) used to identify products which you sell or services that you provide, you may wish to register it with the Secretary of State and the United States Patent and Trademark Office as a trademark or service mark (registration in other states may also be appropriate). While the application procedures are relatively simple and reasonably inexpensive, state and federal trademark and service mark law and procedures, as well as trade name law generally, are beyond the scope of this book. (For information on securing federal and state trademarks and service marks, write the federal Patent and Trademark Office in Washington, do additional reading at your local county law library, or consult an experienced trademark lawyer.)

## Step 2.   Prepare Your Articles of Incorporation

The next step in organizing your corporation is preparing the tear-out Articles of Incorporation contained in the Appendix. You will file this form with the Secretary of State as explained below. Below is a sample of the tear-out Articles of Incorporation.

✓ The parenthetical blanks, i.e., " _(information)_ ," indicate information which you must complete on the tear-out form.

✓ Each circled number (e.g., ❶) refers to a special instruction which provides specific information to help you complete an item. The special instructions immediately follow the sample form.

✓ We suggest you tear out the form in the Appendix and fill in the blanks (using a typewriter with a black ribbon) as you follow the sample form and instructions below.

SAMPLE ARTICLES OF INCORPORATION

_____ *(name of corporation)* _____ ❶

ONE: The name of this corporation is _____ *(name of corporation)* _____ . ❶

TWO: The purpose of this corporation is to engage in any lawful act or activity for which a corporation may be organized under the General Corporation Law of California other than the banking business, the trust company business or the practice of a profession permitted to be incorporated by the California Corporations Code.

THREE: The name and address in this state of the corporation's initial agent for service of process is: _____ *(name and address of initial agent)* _____ . ❷

FOUR: This corporation is authorized to issue only one class of shares of stock which shall be designated common stock. The total number of shares it is authorized to issue is _____ *(number of shares)* _____ ❸ shares.

FIVE: The names and addresses of the persons who are appointed to act as the initial directors of this corporation are:

Name                                        Address

_____        _____

_____        _____

_____        _____

_____        _____

_____        _____

*(full name and business or residence address of each director printed above)* ❹

SIX: The liability of the directors of the corporation for monetary damages shall be eliminated to the fullest extent permissible under California law. ❺

SEVEN: The corporation is authorized to indemnify the directors and officers of the corporation to the fullest extent permissible under California law. ❻

IN WITNESS WHEREOF, the undersigned, being all the persons named above as the initial directors, have executed these Articles of Incorporation.

DATED: _(date of signing)_ ❻        (signature of directors) _____

(print or type name below signature line) _____

_____

_____

_____

_____


The undersigned, being all the persons named above as the initial directors, declare that they are the persons who executed the foregoing Articles of Incorporation, which execution is their act and deed.

DATED: _(date of signing)_ ❻        (signature of directors) _____

(print or type name below signature line) _____

_____

_____

_____

_____

## Special Instructions

❶ Indicate the name of the corporation in the blanks in the heading and in Article ONE. Make sure this name printed is your final choice for a corporate name and that you have checked its availability for corporate use with the Secretary of State and by the other means discussed in Step 1. If you have reserved a corporate name, the name you specify here should correspond exactly to your reserved name (if you have decided not to use your reserved corporate name, that's fine—just make sure to check the availability of the new name indicated here).

❷ Indicate the name and business or residence address of the corporation's initial agent for service of process. This address must be within California. The initial agent for service of process is the person who you wish to authorize to receive legal documents (legal process) for the corporation. Most incorporators will give the name of one of the directors and the principal office of the corporation here as the name and address of the corporation's initial agent. Do not indicate a post office box address in this response.

❸ Indicate the number of authorized shares of the corporation. The traditional long-hand method is to first spell out the number, then indicate the figure in parentheses, e.g., "TWO HUNDRED THOUSAND (200,000)". Since there's no longer a sensible reason for this convention (it made sense in the days of the quill pen), you can either spell out the number or type in a figure in this blank (e.g., "200,000").

Authorized shares are simply those which the corporation can later sell to shareholders, at which time they are referred to as issued shares. There is no magic formula for computing the exact number of authorized shares you should specify—you can authorize as many or as few shares as you wish. However, the number of authorized shares you specify must, of course, be large enough to cover your initial stock issuance. To be sure it is, you may wish to skip ahead to the instructions for preparing the "Issuance of

Shares" resolution in your Minutes in Step 5 of this chapter. After determining the actual number of shares you will issue to all persons and adding a little extra to allow for the future issuance of additional shares (e.g., if 1,000 shares will actually be issued, it is sensible to authorize at least 2,000 shares in your Articles), type the appropriate number here.[4]

❹ Indicate here the full names and business or residence addresses of your initial director(s). Remember: The general rule is that a California corporation must have at least three directors. However, if you will have only two shareholders, you may have only two directors; if you will have only one shareholder, you can have only one director. Of course, you can provide for additional directors above these minimum limits if you wish (see Chapter 2D for further information).

❺ Article SIX uses the language contained in Section 204.5 of the California Corporations Code to eliminate the personal liability of directors for monetary damages to the fullest extent permissible under California law. Article SEVEN uses language contained in Section 317(g) of the California Corporations code to allow the corporation to provide indemnification for the directors and officers beyond the limits expressly permitted by other subsections of Section 317. We have already discussed these special director immunity and indemnification provisions in detail in Chapter 2, Section C2a, "Special California Director Immunity and Indemnification Rules." Here is a brief recap of two central issues related to these Articles:

- The extra director protection afforded by Article SIX relates only to shareholder derivative suits (suits brought by, or in the right of, the corporation for breach of a director's duty of care to the corporation or stockholders), not to third-party lawsuits (suits brought by individual shareholders or outsiders for individual wrongs).

- Article SEVEN authorizes the corporation to provide for additional indemnification elsewhere (e.g., in the corporation's Bylaws or in agreements entered into by the corporation and its directors and officers). We have included broad indemnification rights for directors and officers in Article VII of the Bylaws (see Step 4 below).

❻ There are two sets of date and signature lines which you must fill out at the bottom of your Articles (although somewhat redundant, this is a requirement of California law). Have all of the persons named as initial directors in Article FIVE date and sign the Articles in both places shown. Make sure that their signed and typed names correspond exactly to their names as given in Article FIVE. Use a black-ink pen when signing your Articles—the Secretary of State must be able to photocopy your original Articles.

## A. Prepare Your Cover Letter

A tear-out cover letter for your Articles is included in the Appendix. If you plan to file your Articles in person at one of the offices of the Secretary of State (in Los Angeles, Sacramento, San Diego or San Francisco), you do not need to prepare this letter. However, most incorporators will wish to use this letter since they will be filing their Articles by mail with the Sacramento office of the Secretary of State (as explained below—see Section C).

Below is a sample of the tear-out cover letter for your Articles of Incorporation.

✓ The parenthetical blanks, i.e., " _(information)_ ," indicate information which you must complete on the tear-out form.

✓ Each circled number (e.g., ❶) refers to a special instruction which provides specific information to help you complete an item.

✓ We suggest you tear out the form in the Appendix and fill in the blanks (using a typewriter with a black ribbon or printing neatly with a blank ink pen) as you follow the sample form and instructions below.

### Special Instructions

❶ If you have reserved a corporate name (see Step 1 above), type this optional bracketed sentence shown in the tear-out cover letter, specifying your corporate name reservation number in the blank shown above (we've left space in the tear-out letter for you to include this optional sentence).

❷ The individual and total amounts in the tear-out cover letter reflect the standard fees which must be included when filing your Articles (see Section C, "File Your Articles of Incorporation," below).

❸ One of your initial directors should sign here if you have reserved your corporate name (again, see Step 1). The person who signed your corporate name reservation letter should also sign this cover letter (since your corporate name was reserved for this individual's use).

**Important**   As explained in Chapter 6C1, shortly after incorporating, you will be required to begin estimating and paying your first year corporate franchise taxes. This means you must make another $800 payment (the minimum franchise tax amount) within the first quarter after you file your Articles. Be prepared for this second tax payment.

**Delaying the Filing of Your Articles**   As further explained in Chapter 6C1, you may be able to avoid franchise tax payments for your first tax year by incorporating on a specific date that avoids a short tax year or establishes a very short tax year less than one-half month. California law[5] allows you to request a delayed filing date for your Articles as long as this date is no more than 90 days from the date of receipt of your Articles. If you wish to do this, add a conspicuous sentence to your cover letter asking that your Articles be filed on a specific future date (the delayed date may be a weekend day or a holiday but your Articles must be received at least one business day before the requested future filing date).

SAMPLE COVER LETTER FOR FILING ARTICLES

Secretary of State
Corporate Filing Section
1230 J Street
Sacramento, CA 95814


Re: *(name of corporation)*_____


Dear Secretary of State:

    I enclose an original and two copies of the proposed Articles of
Incorporation of_____*(name of corporation)*_____ .
["This corporate name was reserved with your office pursuant to
Certificate of Reservation # (_____)."❶]


    Also enclosed is payment in the amount of $900.00❷ for the following
fees:

| | |
|---|---|
| Filing Articles of Incorporation | $ 100.00 |
| First year annual franchise tax | 800.00 |
| TOTAL | $ 900.00❷ |

    Please file the original Articles and return the certified copies
to me at the above address.


Very truly yours,


*(name of incorporator)*_____ ❸
*(typed name)*             , Incorporator

## B. Make Copies of Your Articles

After completing the tear-out Articles of Incorporation, make three copies. The tear-out form is your original and will be filed with the Secretary of State's office; two copies will be sent to the Secretary of State's office with the original form to be certified for free and returned to you; the other copy is your file copy (keep this file copy until you receive the certified copies back from the Secretary's office). Make one copy of the completed tear-out cover letter to keep for your records (if you have prepared this letter as explained above). The original tear-out cover letter will be mailed with your Articles of Incorporation to the Sacramento office of the Secretary of State.

Staple the pages of each copy of your Articles together (use one staple in the upper left corner of each copy).

All copies of your Articles should be legible with good contrast.

If you re-type your Articles of Incorporation, please be aware of the following requirements:

- Articles of Incorporation must be typed on one side of a standard 8½" x 11" (letter-sized) page.
- You must leave a 3" square space in the upper right-hand corner of the first page of each copy of your Articles for the Secretary of State's endorse-filed stamp.

## C. File Your Articles of Incorporation

Filing your Articles is a formality. The Secretary of State will file your papers if they conform to law and the proper fees are paid. The Articles are the only formal organizational document that you must file with the Secretary of State (the only other incorporation filing is your Notice of Stock Transaction with the Department of Corporations—see Step 7). You do not file your Bylaws, Minutes of your first meeting, your Shareholder Representation Letters or any of the other incorporation forms or documentation contained in this book with any state agency.

To file your Articles, mail the original tear-out form and two copies, the tear-out cover letter and a check or money order for the total fees (see Section A above) payable to the "California Secretary of State." Send these papers to the Sacramento office of the Secretary of State shown in the heading of the tear-out cover letter.

It normally takes ten business days or so for your Articles to be filed and returned to you by mail (it can take longer during busy filing periods so you may need to be patient).

**Filing Your Articles in Person** You may also file your Articles in person at the Sacramento, Los Angeles, San Diego or San Francisco offices of the Secretary of State if you wish. Again, here are the addresses:

LOS ANGELES
107 South Broadway, Room 4001
Los Angeles, CA 90012

SACRAMENTO
1230 J Street, Room 100
Sacramento, CA 95814

SAN DIEGO
1350 Front Street, State Building
San Diego, CA 92101

SAN FRANCISCO
455 Golden Gate Avenue, Room 2230
San Francisco, CA 94102

There is an additional $15 special handling fee, however, for filing your Articles in person. Also, you must provide the Los Angeles, San Diego or San Francisco office of the Secretary of State with an extra signed copy of your Articles (this copy is in addition to the two copies indicated above). This additional copy will be forwarded by the local office to the Sacramento office of the Secretary of State.

## Step 3.   Set Up a Corporate Records Book (Or Order a Corporate Kit)

### A. Set Up a Corporate Records Book

You will need a corporate records book to keep all your papers in an orderly fashion (Articles, Bylaws, Minutes of your first board meeting and ongoing director and shareholder meetings, stock certificates and stubs, etc.). Setting up and maintaining a neat, well-organized records book is one of your most important tasks—it will serve as a repository for corporate documents and as a formal "paper trail" documenting organizational and ongoing corporate formalities. You should keep your corporate records book at the principal executive office of your corporation at all times.

To set up a corporate records book, you can simply place all your incorporation documents in a three-ring binder. If you prefer, however, you can order a custom designed corporate records book as part of one of the Nolo corporate kits described below.

### B. Nolo Corporate Kits

If you wish to order a Nolo corporate kit, you can do so by completing the order form contained at the back of this book. Each Nolo corporate kit includes:

1. A corporate records book (see description below) with index dividers for Articles of Incorporation, Bylaws, Minutes and Stock Certificates;
2. A metal corporate seal designed to emboss your corporate name and year of incorporation on important corporate documents;

3. Twenty lithographed green and black stock certificates; the name of your corporation is printed on the face of each certificate; and

4. A separately bound Share Transfer Ledger to keep a consolidated record of the names and addresses of your shareholders.[6]

The basic difference between the two kits offered is the style of the corporate records binder itself: The highest-priced kit contains a better quality corporate records binder. Here is a brief description of each:

**The Ex Libris®** uses a higher quality, brown vinyl binder with an integrated slipcase with your corporate name embossed on the spine.

**The Portfolio** features a handcrafted, red and black simulated leather binder with your corporate name embossed in gold on the spine. If you wish to purchase a fancier corporate records book, we think this kit is worth the slightly higher price.

## C. Corporate Seals

A corporation is not legally required to have or use a corporate seal, but many find it handy to do so. A corporate seal is a formal way of indicating that a given document is the duly authorized act of the corporation. It is not normally used on everyday business papers (invoices, purchase orders, etc.) but is commonly employed for more formal documents such as leases, stock certificates, deeds of trust, certifications of board resolutions, and the like. As indicated above, a good quality, reasonably-priced metal pocket seal is available as part of the Nolo corporate kits. Embossed and stamped seals are also available separately through legal stationers for approximately

$40. Most seals are circular in form and contain the name of the corporation, the state and year of incorporation.

## D. Stock Certificates

This book (and the Nolo corporate kits described above) contain stock certificates intended strictly for use by regular profit corporations issuing shares under the California limited offering exemption. The book certificates (and those in the Nolo corporate kits) contain a special legend which is specifically geared to the California limited offering exemption and federal securities law (as discussed in Chapter 3, Sections B and C).[7] This book provides you with ten black and white certificates printed on book quality paper; the corporate kits contain 20 lithographed certificates with green borders and your corporate name printed on each.

**A Precaution** Whether you set up your own corporate records book, order a corporate seal and any special stock certificates separately, or order a complete corporate kit from Nolo Press, you may wish to wait until you have received the certified copies of your Articles back from the Secretary of State's office before you order your corporate seal, special stock certificates or corporate kit. This way, you'll be sure that you really have set up a corporation before you pay for these materials (besides, you need to specify the year of your incorporation when ordering a corporate kit—the year will be embossed on your corporate seal). Of course, if you are committed to forming your corporation and know that you will be filing your Articles before the close of the year, then you're probably safe in ordering these corporate materials ahead of time.

# Step 4.  Prepare Your Bylaws

## A. Fill in the Tear-out Bylaws

After you have received the certified copies of your Articles from the Secretary of State (and ordered a corporate kit if you decided to do so), your next incorporation task is to prepare the tear-out Bylaws contained in the Appendix. Although the Bylaws will be your longest organizational document, you will only have to fill in a few blanks.

Be sure to read the provisions in this document carefully to understand their purpose and effect. Many provisions relating to the duties and responsibilities of your corporation's directors, officers and shareholders and the legal rules for operating your corporation have already been discussed in Chapter 2 this book.

The Bylaws in the Appendix have been carefully drafted and compiled to serve a number of important purposes. First, they reflect specific information central to the organization and operation of your corporation (i.e., number of directors, quorum requirements for meetings, dates of meetings). Second, they restate the most significant provisions of the California Corporations Code that apply to the organization and operation of your corporation. Third, they provide a practical yet formal set of rules for the operation of the corporation.

It should be noted that several alternative models of more and less corporate formality were considered before deciding on provisions relating to the operating rules of the corporation. For example, we decided to include certain minimum requirements such as the holding of an annual meeting of the board of directors, a majority quorum requirement for shareholders' meetings and standard notice of meeting requirements, even though these are not absolutely required by law. On the other hand, we did not require a whole host of other formal rules (e.g., such as special

qualifications for directors; requiring an annual report to be prepared and sent to all shareholders each year—this requirement is waived in Article VI, Section 4 of the Bylaws) believing that most people who run small and moderate sized businesses wish to run their operations without layers of formal operating rules. If you wish to add to, or otherwise modify, the tear-out Bylaws (especially if you want to dispense with the level of formality we provide), please have a lawyer review your changes to ensure compliance with the California Corporations Code.

**Technical Note on Indemnification of Directors and Officers**
We've already discussed California's special indemnification rules in Chapter 2C2, "Special California Director Immunity and Indemnification Rules," and have included special indemnification authorization language in Article Seven of the tear-out Articles (see Step 2 above). Here, in your Bylaws, is where you actually provide for the indemnification of your corporation's directors, officers and other agents (you can also provide for indemnification in separate agreements between the corporation and each of these persons).

Specifically, the indemnification provisions contained in Article VII of the tear-out Bylaws are very broad in scope, requiring the corporation to indemnify (pay back) all directors and officers in all circumstances (e.g., derivative and third-party suits) and for all amounts not prohibited by the Corporations Code. We feel these general provisions will be appropriate for most small corporations. However, you may want to make them even broader by specifically indemnifying employees and all other agents of the corporation as defined by Section 317 of the Corporations Code; by requiring the advancement of expenses by the corporation, etc. Conversely, you may think these provisions are too broad and wish to limit indemnification to particular amounts and circumstances. Further, you might wish to be extra thorough and specifically list all the circumstances where indemnification is required in derivative suits and in third-party actions; protect this language from

future amendments to your Bylaws; specify that past directors, officers and other agents of the corporation shall be indemnified; recite specific provisions of the Corporations Code; refer to contracts between your agents and the corporation; actually indemnify your directors and officers in your Articles or in a contract between your corporation and each person; etc. The point is of course, as with most other legal documents, an almost infinite amount of fine tuning and customization is possible. While we do not believe that this type of customization will normally be needed, if you are interested in any of these additional areas related to indemnification, please see California Corporations Code Sections 204(a)(11) and 317, and consult an experienced corporate lawyer.

**A Quick Reference**   There are only four blanks in the Bylaws which you must fill in. These occur in:

- Heading—show the name of your corporation in the heading of the Bylaws;
- Article II, Section 2—refers to the date and time of your annual shareholder meeting;

- Article III, Section 2—refers to the number of directors who must serve on your Board; and
- Article III, Section 8—refers to the number of directors (out of the total number of directors) who will be required to hold a meeting of your Board (legally, this number is called a "quorum").

Below is a partial sample of the tear-out Bylaws showing these four sections.

✓ The parenthetical blanks, i.e., " _(information)_ ," indicate information which you must complete on the tear-out form.

✓ Each circled number (e.g., ❶) refers to a special instruction which provides specific information to help you complete an item. The special instructions immediately follow the sample form.

✓ We suggest you tear out the form in the Appendix and fill in the blanks as you follow the sample form and instructions.

SAMPLE BYLAWS

of

_____   ❶
*(name of corporation)*

.

.

.

ARTICLE II
SHAREHOLDERS' MEETINGS

### SECTION 1. PLACE OF MEETINGS

All meetings of the shareholders shall be held at the principal executive office of the corporation or at such other place as may be determined by the board of directors.

### SECTION 2. ANNUAL MEETINGS

The annual meeting of the shareholders shall be held each year on _____ , ❷
*(day, month and time of annual shareholders' meeting)*
at which time the shareholders shall elect a board of directors and transact any other proper business. If this date falls on a legal holiday, then the meeting shall be held on the following business day at the same hour.

.

.

.

ARTICLE III
DIRECTORS

### SECTION 1. POWERS

Subject to any limitations in the Articles of Incorporation and to the provisions of the California Corporations Code, the business and affairs of the corporation shall be managed and all corporate powers shall be exercised by, or under the direction of, the board of directors.

### SECTION 2. NUMBER

The authorized number of directors shall be ___*(total number of directors who will serve on your board)*___ ❸ until changed by amendment to this article of these Bylaws.

After issuance of shares, this bylaw may only be amended by approval of a majority of the outstanding shares entitled to vote; provided, moreover, that a bylaw reducing the fixed number of directors to a number less than five (5) cannot be adopted unless in accordance with the additional requirements of Article IX of these Bylaws.

.
.

SECTION 8. QUORUM AND BOARD ACTION

A quorum for all meetings of the board of directors shall consist of  *(number—or percentage of total number—of directors representing a quorum)* ❹ of the authorized number of directors until changed by amendment to this article of these Bylaws.

Every act or decision done or made by a majority of the directors present at a meeting duly held at which a quorum is present is the act of the board, subject to the provisions of Section 310 (relating to the approval of contracts and transactions in which a director has a material financial interest); the provisions of Section 311 (designation of committees); and Section 317(e) (indemnification of directors) of the California Corporations Code. A meeting at which a quorum is initially present may continue to transact business notwithstanding the withdrawal of directors, if any action taken is approved by at least a majority of the required quorum for such meeting.

A majority of the directors present at a meeting may adjourn any meeting to another time and place, whether or not a quorum is present at the meeting.

.
.

CERTIFICATE

This is to certify that the foregoing is a true and correct copy of the Bylaws of the corporation named in the title thereto and that such Bylaws were duly adopted by the board of directors of the corporation on the date set forth below.

Dated: *(date of secretary's signature)* ❺        *(secretary's signature)* ❺ _____

*(typed name)*                                      , Secretary

*(impress corporate seal here)* ❺

## Special Instructions

**❶ Title**   Name of Corporation. Type your corporate name in the heading of the Bylaws. Make sure the name shown here is the same as the name in the certified copies of your Articles.

**❷ Article II, Section 2**   Date and time of Annual Shareholders' Meeting. Indicate the date and time of your annual shareholders' meeting (e.g., "the last Friday in December at 9 AM," "June 15th at 1 o'clock P.M.," etc.).

Your annual directors' meeting is automatically scheduled to be held immediately after this shareholders' meeting (see Article III, Section 7). The date of the corporation's shareholders' meeting is commonly set shortly before or after the close of the corporation's tax year (or tax return filing date) so that the prior year's business can be reviewed and the coming year's business can be discussed and planned. Some incorporators set this date during the last month of the corporation's tax year so that the board of directors may, immediately following the shareholders' meeting, make important year-end tax decisions (for example, fixing the corporation's liability for expenses such as employee bonuses which they wish to deduct in the current year and pay after the start of the next corporate tax year). It's usually best to designate a fixed day rather than a date (e.g., the second Monday of a particular month) to avoid having the meetings fall on a weekend. The Corporations Code requires you to hold this annual shareholders' meeting.

**❸ Article III, Section 2**   Indicate the authorized number of directors of your corporation—this is the total number of directors who will serve on your board. This question should be answered in accordance with the requirements of the Corporations Code set out in Chapter 2D. To sum up these requirements, the general rule is that a California corporation must have at least three directors. However, a corporation with only two shareholders may have only two directors. A one-shareholder corporation may have only one director. Of course, you may provide for more than the minimum number of directors required by law (e.g., if you are the only shareholder in your corporation, you may wish to have your spouse also serve as a director if he or she will participate in management decisions).

**❹ Article III, Section 8**   Quorum for Directors' Meetings: Indicate the number, or percentage of the total number, of directors who must be present at a directors' meeting to constitute a quorum so that business can be conducted (e.g., by specifying "a majority," "one-third," "two," etc.). Although the usual practice is to indicate a "majority" here, under California law you may provide that a quorum be as little as one-third the number of authorized directors or two, whichever is larger. A one-person corporation, however, may (and will) provide for a one-director quorum.

For example, a four-director corporation, under the above minimum rules, may provide for a quorum of two, rather than a majority of three. Applying these rules to a three-director corporation, however, results in a majority quorum of two.

Whatever you decide, you should realize that this section of the Bylaws concerns a quorum, not a vote requirement. Action can be taken by a majority of directors at a meeting at which a quorum is present. For example, if a six-director corporation requires a majority quorum and a meeting is held at which a minimum quorum (four) is present, action can be taken by the vote of three directors, a majority of those present at the meeting.

**❺** Do not date, sign or seal your Bylaws at the bottom of the last page at this time. The corporate Secretary will do this after you hold your first meeting of directors (as explained immediately below in Step 5).

## Step 5. Prepare Minutes of the First Meeting of the Board of Directors

### A. Fill In the Tear-out Minutes of the First Meeting of the Board of Directors

The next step, now that you have filed your Articles and prepared your Bylaws, is to prepare the Minutes of the First Meeting of your Board of Directors. After preparing your Minutes, you will actually hold a meeting as explained in Section B below.

The purpose of your Minutes is to document essential organizational actions taken by your board of directors, including:

- Specifying the principal executive office of the corporation.
- Adopting the Bylaws.
- Electing officers.
- Adopting an accounting period (tax year) for your corporation.

- Authorizing the issuance of the initial shares of stock of the corporation.
- If federal S corporation tax status is desired, approving this election.

Prepare your Minutes by filling in the blanks on the tear-out Minutes of the First Meeting of the Board of Directors contained in the Appendix. There is nothing difficult here, but there are a number of questions that you must answer.

Below is a sample of the tear-out Minutes.

✓ The parenthetical blanks, i.e., " _(information)_ ," indicate information which you must complete on the tear-out form.

✓ Each circled number (e.g., ❶) refers to a special instruction which provides specific information to help you complete an item. The special instructions immediately follow the sample form and are organized in sections which correspond to the various pages and resolutions contained in the Minutes.

✓ We suggest you tear out the form in the Appendix and fill in the blanks as you follow the sample form and instructions below.

SAMPLE MINUTES OF FIRST BOARD MEETING

SAMPLE WAIVER OF NOTICE AND CONSENT TO HOLDING OF
FIRST MEETING OF BOARD OF DIRECTORS

of

_____*(name of corporation)*_____  ❶

     We, the undersigned, being all the directors of __*(name of corporation)*__ ❶, a California corporation, hereby waive notice of the first meeting of the board of directors of the corporation and consent to the holding of said meeting at __*(address of meeting)*__, on __*(date of meeting)*__, at __*(time of meeting)*__ ❷ and consent to the transaction of any and all business by the directors at the meeting including, without limitation, the adoption of Bylaws, the election of officers, the selection of the corporation's accounting period, the designation of the principal executive office of the corporation, the selection of the place where the corporation's bank account will be maintained, and the authorization of the sale and issuance of the initial shares of stock of the corporation.

DATED: __*(date of signing of waiver)*__ ❸

*(signature of director)*_____ ❸
*(print or type name below signature line)*

*(signature of director)*_____
*(print or type name below signature line)*

*(signature of director)*_____
*(print or type name below signature line)*

SAMPLE MINUTES OF FIRST MEETING OF THE BOARD OF DIRECTORS

of

_____(name of corporation)_____ ❶

The board of directors of _____(name of corporation)_____ ❶ held its first meeting at __(address of meeting)__, on __(date of meeting)__, at __(time of meeting)__.❷

The following directors, marked as present next to their names, were in attendance at the meeting and constituted a quorum of the full board:

| ____(name of director)____ | [ ] Present | [ ] Absent ❹ |
| ____(name of director)____ | [ ] Present | [ ] Absent |
| ____(name of director)____ | [ ] Present | [ ] Absent |

On motion and by unanimous vote, ____(name of director)____ ❺ was elected temporary chairperson and then presided over the meeting. ____(name of director)____ ❺ was elected temporary secretary of the meeting.

The chairperson announced that the meeting was held pursuant to written waiver of notice and consent to holding of the meeting signed by each of the directors. Upon a motion duly made, seconded, and unanimously carried, it was resolved that the written waiver of notice and consent to holding of the meeting be made a part of the Minutes of the meeting and placed in the corporation's minute book.

ARTICLES OF INCORPORATION

The chairperson announced that the Articles of Incorporation of the corporation had been filed with the California Secretary of State's office on _____(date of filing of Articles)_____.❻ The chairperson then presented to the meeting a certified copy of the Articles showing such filing and the secretary was instructed to insert this copy in the corporation's minute book.

BYLAWS

A proposed set of Bylaws of the corporation was then presented to the meeting for adoption. The Bylaws were considered and discussed and, upon motion duly made and seconded, it was unanimously

RESOLVED, that the Bylaws presented to this meeting be and hereby are adopted as the Bylaws of this corporation;

RESOLVED FURTHER, that the secretary of this corporation be and hereby is directed to execute a Certificate of Adoption of the Bylaws, to insert the Bylaws as so certified in the corporation's minute book and to see that a copy of the Bylaws, similarly certified, is kept at the corporation's principal executive office, as required by law.

ELECTION OF OFFICERS

The chairperson then announced that the next item of business was the election of officers. Upon motion, the following persons were unanimously elected to the following offices, at the annual salaries, if any as determined at the meeting, shown to the right of their names:

| | | | |
|---|---|---|---|
| President: | *(name of officer)* | $ *(salary)* | ❼ |
| Vice President: | *(name of officer)* | $ *(salary)* | |
| Secretary: | *(name of officer)* | $ *(salary)* | |
| Treasurer: | *(name of officer)* | $ *(salary)* | |

(Chief Financial Officer)

Each officer who was present accepted his or her office. Thereafter, the President presided at the meeting as chairperson, and the Secretary acted as secretary.

CORPORATE SEAL

The Secretary presented to the meeting for adoption a proposed form of seal of the corporation. Upon motion duly made and seconded, it was

RESOLVED, that the form of the corporate seal presented to this meeting be and hereby is adopted as the corporate seal of this corporation, and the secretary of this corporation is directed to place an impression thereof in the space directly next to this resolution.

❽ *impress corporate seal here*

### STOCK CERTIFICATE

The Secretary then presented to the meeting for adoption a proposed form of stock certificate for the corporation. Upon motion duly made and seconded, it was

RESOLVED, that the form of stock certificate presented to this meeting be and hereby is adopted for use by this corporation, and the secretary of this corporation is directed to annex a copy thereof to the Minutes of this meeting.

### ACCOUNTING PERIOD

The chairperson informed the board that the next order of business was the selection of the accounting period of the corporation. After discussion and upon motion duly made and seconded, it was

RESOLVED, that the accounting period of this corporation shall end on _____*(ending date of the accounting period of the corporation)*_____ ❾ of each year.

### PRINCIPAL EXECUTIVE OFFICE

After discussion as to the exact location of the corporation's principal executive office, upon motion duly made and seconded, it was

RESOLVED, that the principal executive office of this corporation shall be located at _____*(address, including city, county and state of principal executive office)*_____ . ❿

### BANK ACCOUNT

The chairperson recommended that the corporation open a bank account with _____*(name of bank(s) and branch office(s))*_____ . ⓫ Upon motion duly made and seconded, it was

RESOLVED, that the funds of this corporation shall be deposited with the bank and branch office indicated just above.

RESOLVED FURTHER, that the Treasurer of this corporation is hereby authorized and directed to establish an account with said bank and to deposit the funds of this corporation therein.

RESOLVED FURTHER, that any officer, employee, or agent of this corporation is hereby authorized to endorse checks, drafts, or other evidences of indebtedness made payable to this corporation, but only for the purpose of deposit.

RESOLVED FURTHER, that all checks, drafts, and other instruments obligating this corporation to pay money shall be signed on behalf of this corporation by any _____ *(number)* _____ ⑫ of the following:

*(name of person authorized to sign checks)* _____ ⑬

*(name of person authorized to sign checks)*

*(name of person authorized to sign checks)*

RESOLVED FURTHER, that said bank is hereby authorized to honor and pay any and all checks and drafts of this corporation signed as provided herein.

RESOLVED FURTHER, that the authority hereby conferred shall remain in force until revoked by the board of directors of this corporation and until written notice of such revocation shall have been received by said bank.

RESOLVED FURTHER, that the Secretary of this corporation be and is hereby authorized to certify as to the continuing authority of these resolutions, the persons authorized to sign on behalf of this corporation, and the adoption of said bank's standard form of resolution, provided that said form does not vary materially from the terms of the foregoing resolutions.

PAYMENT AND DEDUCTION OF ORGANIZATIONAL EXPENSES ⑭

The board next considered the question of paying the expenses incurred in the formation of this corporation. A motion was made, seconded and unanimously approved, and it was

RESOLVED, that the President and the Treasurer of this corporation are authorized and empowered to pay all reasonable and proper expenses incurred in connection with the organization of the corporation, including, among others, filing, licensing, and attorney's and accountant's fees, and to reimburse any persons making any such disbursements for the corporation, and it was

FURTHER RESOLVED, that the Treasurer is authorized to elect to deduct on the first federal income tax return of the corporation the foregoing expenditures ratably over a sixty-month period starting in the month the corporation begins its business, pursuant to, and to the extent permitted by, Section 248 of the Internal Revenue Code of 1986, as amended.

FEDERAL S CORPORATION TAX TREATMENT **⑮**

The board of directors next considered the advantages of electing to be taxed under the provisions of Subchapter S of the Internal Revenue Code of 1986, as amended. After discussion, upon motion duly made and seconded, it was unanimously

RESOLVED, that this corporation hereby elects to be treated as a Small Business Corporation for federal income tax purposes under Subchapter S of the Internal Revenue Code of 1986, as amended.

RESOLVED FURTHER, that the officers of this corporation take all actions necessary and proper to effectuate the foregoing resolution, including, among other things, obtaining the requisite consents from the shareholders of this corporation and executing and filing the appropriate forms with the Internal Revenue Service within the time limits specified by law.

QUALIFICATION OF STOCK AS SECTION 1244 STOCK **⑯**

The board next considered the advisability of qualifying the stock of this corporation as Section 1244 Stock as defined in Section 1244 of the Internal Revenue Code of 1986, as amended, and of organizing and managing the corporation so that it is a Small Business Corporation as defined in that section. Upon motion duly made and seconded, it was unanimously

RESOLVED, that the proper officers of the corporation are, subject to the requirements and restrictions of federal, California and any other applicable securities laws, authorized to sell and issue shares of stock in return for the receipt of an aggregate amount of money and other property, as a contribution to capital and as paid-in surplus, which does not exceed $1,000,000.

RESOLVED FURTHER, that the sale and issuance of shares shall be conducted in compliance with Section 1244 so that the corporation and its shareholders may obtain the benefits of that section.

RESOLVED FURTHER, that the proper officers of the corporation are directed to maintain such records as are necessary pursuant to Section 1244 so that any shareholder who experiences a loss on the transfer of shares of stock of the corporation may determine whether he or she qualifies for ordinary loss deduction treatment on his or her individual income tax return.

AUTHORIZATION OF ISSUANCE OF SHARES ❼

The board of directors next took up the matter of the sale and issuance of stock to provide capital for the corporation. Upon motion duly made and seconded, it was unanimously

RESOLVED, that the corporation sell and issue the following number of its authorized common shares to the following persons, in the amounts and for the consideration set forth under their names below. The board also hereby determines that the fair value to the corporation of any consideration for such shares issued other than for money is as set forth below:

| Name | Number of Shares | Consideration | Fair Value |
|------|------------------|---------------|------------|
| _____ | _____ | _____ | $ _____ |
| _____ | _____ | _____ | $ _____ |
| _____ | _____ | _____ | $ _____ |
| _____ | _____ | _____ | $ _____ |
| _____ | _____ | _____ | $ _____ |
| _____ | _____ | _____ | $ _____ |

RESOLVED FURTHER, that these shares shall be sold and issued by this corporation strictly in accordance with the terms of the exemption from qualification of these shares as provided for in Section 25102(f) of the California Corporations Code.

RESOLVED FURTHER, that the appropriate officers of this corporation are hereby authorized and directed to take such actions and execute such documents as they may deem necessary or appropriate to effectuate the sale and issuance of such shares for such consideration.

Since there was no further business to come before the meeting, upon motion duly made and seconded, the meeting was adjourned.

_____
(signature of secretary)
_____
(typed name of Secretary)          , Secretary ❽

## Special Instructions

### Waiver of Notice and Consent to Holding of First Meeting of Board of Directors

This form is included as the first page of the tear-out Minutes in the Appendix. This page is necessary in order to dispense with formal director notice requirements that apply to special board meetings (see Article III, Section 7 of your Bylaws). Here are the special instructions associated with this page of your Minutes:

### ❶ Name of Corporation

Indicate the name of your corporation in the heading to this page and in the first blank of the first paragraph.

### ❷ Address, Date and Time of Meeting

Indicate the address, date and time of your first directors' meeting (e.g., at *555 Ramdos Drive, Silicon Valley, California* on *March 15th, 199x* at *10 A.M.*). Normally, you will show the address of the corporation here as the place of your board meeting. As you'll see in Section B below, we think it's wise for your first meeting to be more than just a "paper" meeting. In other words, if you have more than one director, you should actually sit down with the other directors at the place, date and time indicated here to review and agree to the provisions in your completed Minutes.

### ❸ Signatures of All Directors and Date of Waiver

Have each director sign his name and make sure to complete the date line on the waiver of notice page. **Note** If you have more than one director, the date shown can be the date the first director signs the form.

## Title Page

The next page of your Minutes (page 2) contains the title of the document and begins by reciting the facts necessary for you to hold your meeting, repeating the name of your corporation and the address, date and time of the meeting given above. Fill in these five blanks as explained just above.

### ❹ Present and Absent Directors

Show the names of all your directors in these blanks. You will check the appropriate box to the right of each name when you hold your first board meeting (see Section B below) to show whether each director is present at, or absent from, the meeting. Although we suggest that all of your directors be present at your first meeting, only a quorum of the board (as specified in Article III, Section 8 of your Bylaws) actually need attend the meeting.

### ❺ Temporary Chairperson and Secretary

These blanks relate to a minor, but logically necessary, formality. Since you have not yet elected officers, these blanks show the names of the directors who you name as temporary chairperson and secretary of your first meeting (the corporate President and Secretary normally serve in these capacities). Type (or print) the name of one of your directors as your temporary chairperson in the first blank and another director as your temporary secretary in the second. If your corporation has only one director, you will, naturally, enter this person's name in both these blanks.

### Articles of Incorporation Resolution

This is the first resolution of your Minutes and appears just after the introductory material on your title page (page 2) referred to above. This resolution serves as a formal record of the date of filing of your Articles of Incorporation and indicates the first day of the legal existence of your corporation.

### ❺ Date of Filing of Articles

Type the date on which your Articles were filed by the Secretary of State—this is the "endorsed-filed" date stamped on the first page of the certified copies of your Articles of Incorporation (see Step 2 above for further information on filing your Articles).

### Bylaws Resolution

This resolution is included in your Minutes to show the formal adoption of your Bylaws by the directors. The Bylaws require you to keep your corporate records book (and a copy of your Bylaws) at the principal executive office of the corporation. You will establish the location of this office in a separate minute resolution discussed below.

### Election of Officers Resolution

This resolution is included for you to elect the officers of your corporation and to authorize any officer salaries you feel appropriate.

When filling in these blanks, remember the following points (for a further discussion, Chapter 2E):

- Under California law you must fill the offices of President, Secretary and Treasurer (referred to in the California Corporations Code as the "Chief Financial Officer").
- You are not required to elect a Vice President although many incorporators will wish to do so.
- One person may be elected to all, or any number of, these officer positions. For example, in a one-person corporation, this individual will be elected as President, Secretary and Treasurer (and Vice President, if this person wants to add this optional title to her name). Although less common, the

same rule applies if you have more than one person in your corporation.

*Example:* Joan, Gary and Matthew form their own corporation. Since it's really Joan's business (her spouse Gary and her brother Matthew are simply investing as shareholders), Joan fills the officer positions of President, Secretary and Treasurer.

- An officer need not be a director or shareholder in your corporation (although, for small corporations, the officer usually will be both).

### ❼ Election of Officers and Optional Officers' Salaries

Show the name of your President, Secretary and Treasurer (Chief Financial Officer) and any salary you wish to authorize for each officer. If you wish to fill the optional officer position of Vice President, show the name of the person who will fill this office.

For all the officers, filling in the salary blank is optional. Specifically, many corporations will not wish to provide for officer salaries (and will not fill in these blanks) because the individuals who will actively work for the corporation, whether they are also directors, officers or shareholders, will not be paid a salary as an officer, per se, but in some other capacity related to the particular business of the corporation.

*Example:* Betty Bidecker is a 75% shareholder and the President and Treasurer of her incorporated software publishing company. Bix Bidecker, her spouse, is a 25% shareholder and the Vice President and Secretary of the corporation. Rather than being paid for serving in any officer capacity, both are paid annual salaries as executive employees of the corporation: Betty as the Publisher, Bix as the Associate Publisher.

If you do provide for officer salaries, remember, salaries should be reasonable in view of the actual duties performed by the officer and should be comparable to compensation paid for similar skills in similar businesses (see Chapter 2C3 for a further discussion of this issue). Don't be overly concerned here: If you are active in your business and can afford to pay yourself a large salary because of the profitability of your corporation, your salary will most likely be reasonable in view of your material participation in your corporation's productivity and, generally, in view of the trend towards paying higher corporate salaries in most key corporate positions these days.

## Corporate Seal Resolution

This resolution is included in your Minutes to show acceptance of the form of corporate seal you will use.

## ❽ Impression of Corporate Seal

Stamp or impress the corporate seal in the space provided to the right of this resolution. As discussed in Step 3 of this chapter, although you are not legally required to have a corporate seal, an impression of the corporate seal is often expected on formal corporate documents (e.g., bank account or loan authorizations, certifications of board resolutions, etc.). We assume most incorporators will wish to purchase a corporate seal—see Step 3 above if you wish to order a corporate seal as part of one the corporate kits offered by Nolo Press. If you don't buy a corporate seal, it's perfectly alright to leave this resolution in your Minutes unused (without a corporate seal impression made to the right of this resolution).

## Stock Certificate Resolution

This resolution is included in your Minutes to show acceptance of the form of stock certificate you will use (either the certificates included in the Appendix of this book or those which you have purchased on your own as part of one of corporate kits ordered from Nolo Press—see Step 3 above—or purchased separately).

## Accounting Period Resolution

This resolution allows you to specify the accounting period of your corporation. You should normally select this period with the help of your corporate tax advisor (see Chapter 4D for a discussion of the rules which apply to selecting a corporate accounting period and tax year).

## ❾ Ending Date of Corporate Accounting Period

Indicate the date (month and day) of the end of your corporation's accounting period in this blank. For example, if you choose a calendar year accounting period for your corporation, respond by typing the ending date as "December 31."

You should realize that the California Franchise Tax Board and the IRS will look to your initial tax returns to determine the ending date of your corporate accounting period and tax year: If your first corporate tax returns are submitted for a period ending on July 30th, this date will be taken as the end date of your corporate tax year. In other words, you are not bound by this initial minute resolution (although we do expect your answer here to reflect your reasonable expectations for your ultimate accounting period and tax year).

After you file your initial returns, you will usually need the consent of the IRS and the California Franchise Tax Board to change your tax year. For further information on filing your initial returns and fixing your corporate tax year, see Chapters 4D and 6B8.

## Principal Executive Office Resolution

This resolution allows you to formally specify the "principal executive office" of your corporation. This is a term used in the Corporations Code to indicate the legal address of the corporation. We expect you to indicate your corporation's principal place of business (your active address where all or most of your business is carried out) as its legal principal executive office. Although not required, we expect most incorporators to indicate a principal executive office within California (see Article I, Section 1 of the tear-out Bylaws).

### ⑩ Full Address of Principal Executive Office

Indicate the street address, including the city, county and state (California), of the principal executive office of your corporation (e.g., "1212 Market Street, River City, Humboldt County, California"). **Note** Although not required by law (see Article I, Section 1 of your Bylaws), we assume most incorporators will indicate a principal executive office within California. In any case, do not use a post office box address here—please show a complete street address.

### Bank Account Resolution

This resolution authorizes the opening of the corporations bank account(s) with one or more banks, showing the names of individuals authorized to sign checks and the number of signatures required on corporate checks. Typically, you will also have to fill out, and impress the corporate seal on, a separate bank account authorization form provided by your bank. Banks customarily require your corporation to have a federal employer identification number. This number is obtained by filing form SS-4 with the IRS (Chapter 6B2). All corporations will also need to obtain a state employer number and make deposits of state and federal withholding and employment taxes with an authorized bank as explained more fully in Chapter 6.

### ⑪ Name of Banks(s) and Branch Office(s)

Type the name(s) of the bank(s) and branch office(s) where the corporation will maintain its accounts (e.g., "Second Multistate Savings; West Covina branch").

### ⑫ Number of Signatures on Corporate Checks

Indicate the number of individual signatures which will be required on each corporate check. For example, if you wish to have your President and Secretary sign all corporate checks, type "two" here in this blank.

### ⑬ Names of Individuals Who May Sign Checks

Indicate the names of individuals who are authorized to sign checks on behalf of your corporation. For example, although you may only require one authorized signature on corporate checks, you may wish to allow both your corporate Treasurer (who will normally sign checks) and your President (when necessary) to sign corporate checks. Generally, you will show the name of one or more officers or key employees here (such as your salaried in-house bookkeeper). Simply type the names of the appropriate individual(s) in these blanks.

### ⑭ Payment and Deduction of Organizational Expenses Resolution (Optional)

This resolution is optional. If you do not wish to use this resolution, do not include this tear-out page in your completed Minutes.

*Whether to Include This Resolution in Your Minutes* Many incorporators will wish to include this resolution in their Minutes to allow the corporation to reimburse the incorporators for, and have the corporation pay and deduct over a period of time, the expenses incurred in organizing the corporation under Section 248 of the Internal Revenue Code (without a specific election to deduct these expenses over a specified period of time, such a deduction is normally not possible). Note that you must implement this federal tax election by attaching a statement to your first federal corporate income tax return indicating that you are choosing to amortize organization expenses, providing a description of the expenses together with other required details. Check with your tax advisor for help in deciding whether to use this resolution (and for help in preparing the statement to send to the IRS).

### ⑮ Federal S Corporation Tax Treatment Resolution (Optional)

This resolution is optional. If you do not wish to use this resolution, do not include this tear-out page in your completed Minutes.

*Whether to Include This Resolution in Your Minutes* The decision to include this resolution in your Minutes involves several tax factors discussed in Chapter 4C—please review this material. If you decide to elect federal S corporation tax status, include this resolution in your Minutes.

### ⑯ Section 1244 Stock Resolution (Optional)

This resolution is optional. If you do not wish to use this resolution, do not include this tear-out page in your completed Minutes.

*Whether to Include This Resolution in Your Minutes* Most incorporators will wish to have their stock treated as Section 1244 stock (so that any future stock losses may be deductible as "ordinary losses"—see Chapter 4E for a further discussion). If you do wish this tax treatment, include this resolution in your Minutes. Note the necessity of keeping ongoing records to insure that you will be able to meet the requirements of Section 1244—your tax advisor can help you maintain these records.

### Authorization of Issuance of Shares Resolution

This resolution authorizes your corporation to issue its initial shares to your shareholders after the meeting of your board (throughout the book, we refer to this resolution as your "stock issuance resolution).

**Note** This resolution in your Minutes does not result in the issuance of shares—it simply authorizes the appropriate corporate officers to issue shares to the shareholders after the meeting. You will actually issue shares as part of Step 8 below.

### ⑰ Share Issuance Information

In this resolution, you provide information relating to your initial stock issuance. Specifically, for each shareholder you should indicate:

- the name of the shareholder;
- the number of shares to be issued to this person;
- the description of payment the shareholder will make for the shares (legally this payment is referred to as the "consideration" for the shares—we use this legal term in this column of the stock issuance resolution); and
- the fair value of the payment for shares to be made by the shareholder (either the amount of cash paid or the fair market value of any noncash payment). Section 409(e) of the California Corporations Code requires the board to make this determination of fair value to the corporation of all noncash consideration for which shares are issued.

Please read the accompanying review box before filling in the blanks for each of these items in the stock issuance resolution in the tear-out Minutes.

**Joint Shareholder Note** As we explain in Step 8A below, many incorporators (particularly spouses) will purchase their shares jointly (e.g., as community property, in joint tenancy, etc.). If you plan to own shares jointly with your spouse or another person, show both names in the shareholder name blank for these shares.

*Example:* If Steve Marconi and Katherine Marconi will jointly purchase 1,000 shares for $1,000, they would fill in the blanks in the stock issuance resolution as shown below.

**Note**   You do not need to indicate here how the joint owners will take title to their shares (e.g., as community property—see Step 8 below). You will do this when you fill out your stock certificates.

### Stock Issuance Examples

Here are some examples to help you fill in the blanks on your stock issuance resolution:

### Issuance of Shares for Cash
If a shareholder will pay cash for her shares, simply type "Cash" for the consideration and the dollar amount of the cash payment as the fair value of the payment for this person's shares.

### Issuance of Shares for Specific Items of Property

If a shareholder will purchase shares by transferring property to the corporation (we are referring to specific items of property here such as a computer system, a truck, a patent or copyright; not the complete assets of a business—this latter situation is dealt with in the next example), be as specific as you can when entering the consideration (e.g., "1987 Ford pickup, vehicle ID #__") and show the fair market value (in the case of a vehicle, bluebook value is a good measure) of the property as the fair value of the payment.

SAMPLE AUTHORIZATION OF ISSUANCE OF SHARES

| Name | Number of Shares | Consideration | Fair Value |
|------|------------------|---------------|------------|
| Steve Marconi and Katherine Marconi | 1,000 | Cash | $1,000 |
| | | | |
| | | | |
| | | | |

## REVIEW NOTES

Before filling in the blanks in your stock issuance resolution, we suggest that you re-read Chapter 3 to make sure you understand the requirements for issuing your shares in compliance with the California limited offering exemption and federal securities laws. Let's review a few points mentioned in Chapter 3 (and in other preceding chapters and steps) regarding the issuance of your shares:

- Make sure that the total number of shares to be issued to all shareholders is not greater than the number of shares authorized to be issued in Article Four of your Articles of Incorporation—Article Four places an upper limit on the number of shares which you can actually issue (see Step 2, instruction 3).

- We assume that you are issuing your shares in compliance with and under the terms of the California limited offering exemption (25102(f) of the Corporations Code)—(see Chapter 3B). Under this exemption (and under California law generally), you may issue shares for any legal consideration which includes:

  - cash
  - tangible or intangible property actually received by the corporation
  - debts cancelled (the cancellation of a note reflecting money owed by the corporation to the shareholder), and
  - labor done or services actually rendered to the corporation, or for its benefit, or in its formation

  You *cannot* issue shares in return for the performance of future services by a shareholder nor can you issue shares in return for promissory notes (a promise by the shareholder to pay for the shares later) unless certain conditions related to adequate security for the notes are met (see Chapter 2F). We assume you will check with a lawyer before issuing shares in return for such notes. Furthermore, most small corporations will not be in a position to issue shares for labor done or services rendered since they are just getting started.

- As a matter of common sense, and to avoid unfairness or fraud, issue your shares for the same price per share to all initial shareholders. Make sure to place a fair value on the assets or other property or services being given in return for the shares. If you are transferring the assets of an existing business to your corporation in return for shares (if you are incorporating a prior business), we suggest that you have an accountant or other qualified appraiser make a written determination of the value of these assets. You may also wish to have a balance sheet prepared for the prior business, showing the assets and liabilities being transferred to your corporation (you can attach this balance sheet to the Bill of Sale which you can prepare as part of Step 8 below to document this type of transfer). Be realistic in your determination of fair value of all noncash payments for shares, particularly if you will be issuing shares in return for speculative or intangible property such as the goodwill of a business, copyrights, patents, etc. You don't want to "short-change" other shareholders who have put up cash or tangible property of determinative value.

### Issuance of Shares for Assets of a Prior Business

If a shareholder will transfer his part, or full, interest in a prior business to the corporation in return for shares (e.g., if you are incorporating a prior business), then you should not refer to the specific assets of the business when describing the consideration to be paid by each prior business owner. Instead, simply describe the interest in the prior business which will be transferred by each owner.

*Example:* If two business owners will be incorporating their pre-existing partnership, "Just Partners," the following simple description in the consideration blank would be appropriate for each shareholder (each prior business owner):

"One-half interest in assets of the partnership 'Just Partners,' as more fully described in a Bill of Sale to be prepared and attached to these Minutes."

This Bill of Sale can be prepared as part of Step 8 below. Each partner can show one-half of the dollar value of these assets (e.g., one-half of their book value as reflected on a current balance sheet) as the *fair value* of the payment to be made by each shareholder.

### Issuance of Shares for Cancellation of Indebtedness

If shares will be issued for the cancellation of indebtedness owed by the corporation to a shareholder, a description of the debt should be given as the *consideration* for the shares (e.g., "cancellation of a promissory note dated ___"). The *fair value* of the payment to be made by this shareholder should be the dollar amount of the remaining unpaid principal amount due on the debt plus any unpaid accrued interest. Ideally, a copy of the note or other written evidence of the debt should be attached to your Minutes.

This type of transaction isn't typical since, as we've said earlier, a newly-formed corporation will not normally owe shareholders any amounts except, perhaps, by way of small advances made to help meet

organizational costs which will be reimbursed by the corporation directly (see the Payment and Deduction of Organizational Expenses Resolution above).

### Issuance of Shares for Past Services

If you will be issuing shares to a shareholder in return for past services actually rendered the corporation,[8] indicate the date and name of the person who has provided the services as the *consideration* to be paid by this shareholder (e.g., "Services rendered the corporation by Bob Beamer, January 5 to February 15, 19__"). The *fair value* of the payment to be made by this shareholder should be the fair market value of the services performed by this shareholder. A bill from the shareholder to the corporation showing the amount due for these services should be attached to your Minutes. Remember, you cannot issue shares for services which have not yet been performed.

### ⑱ Signature of Secretary

Have your corporate Secretary sign at the bottom of the last page of the Minutes and type his name just under the signature line.

## B. Hold the First Meeting of the Board of Directors

After preparing your Minutes, we suggest you actually hold a meeting with all your directors present (although only a quorum is required to attend, we think this it is sensible to have as many as many directors present as possible). Each director should review and agree to the resolutions contained in your Minutes. As a reminder, make sure to do the following:

1. Date, and have each director sign, the Waiver of Notice Form (see Section A above, instruction 3);

2. Indicate which directors were present and absent by checking the appropriate box to the right of each director's name in your printed Minutes (Section A, instruction 4);

3. Have the corporate Secretary sign the last page of the Minutes (Section A, instruction 18).

## C. Consolidate Your Papers

After printing your Minutes, make sure to do the following before going on to Step 6 below:

- Have your Secretary sign, date and seal the "Certificate" section at the end of your Bylaws.
- Set up a corporate records book with (at least) the following four sections:
  - Articles of Incorporation
  - Bylaws
  - Minutes of Meetings
  - Stock Certificates

  You can use a simple three-ring binder for this purpose. If you have ordered a Nolo Press corporate kit as explained in Step 3 above, it will include a corporate records book divided into these sections.
- Place your Minutes and attachments (copies of your Articles endorsed-filed by the California Secretary of State, Bylaws certified by your corporate Secretary, a sample stock certificate, any copies of notes cancelled, bills for services rendered, balance sheet for a prior business, etc.) in your corporate records book.
- Keep your corporate records book at the corporation's principal executive office. An important part of corporate life is keeping your records properly, so be sure to document future corporate transactions (by preparing standard Minutes of annual director and shareholder meetings) and place copies of corporate Minutes and other documents in your corporate records book.

CONGRATULATIONS! You have now completed the Minutes of your first meeting. We explain how to accomplish your last major organizational task, complying with the formalities of the California limited offering stock exemption and issuing your shares, in Steps 6, 7 and 8. Stay with us, you're just a few steps away from completing your incorporation.

## Step 6. Prepare Shareholder Representation Letters

This step of the book shows you how to prepare shareholder representation letters (included as a tear-out form in the Appendix) to document your compliance with the California limited offering exemption when issuing your initial shares. This step, together with Steps 7 and 8 of this chapter, are the formal steps which you must take to issue your shares. You will not receive the consideration (payment) for shares or issue them to your shareholders until Step 8 below.

To review the requirements of the limited offering exemption and the importance of having each shareholder sign a shareholder's representation letter, please read Chapter 3B. If you have any questions concerning your eligibility for this exemption or how to fill in any of the blanks associated with this form after reviewing Chapter 3 and the instructions below, consult a lawyer.

## A. Steps You Should Have Already Taken

Before preparing shareholder representation letters, make sure that you have done the following:

- Made a reasonable inquiry to see if each shareholder will be purchasing shares for his own account. If an individual will be buying the shares for resale or for someone else's account, you will not want to issue shares to this individual. The fact that a shareholder represents in writing that he is buying for his own account may not be enough—the corporation should assure itself of the truth of this representation.

- Made sure that you have disclosed all facts concerning the finances and business of the corporation and of the terms and conditions of your proposed stock issuance to all prospective shareholders. You should provide this disclosure in writing and be able to prove that full disclosure was made to all shareholders—remember, state and federal securities laws require you to disclose all material facts (see Chapter 3, Sections B and C).

## B. Prepare Shareholder Representation Letters

You need to prepare a shareholder representation letter for each of your initial shareholders (this includes each person, such as a spouse, who will jointly own shares in your corporation). So, to start this step, tear out the printed shareholder representation letter in the Appendix and make a copy to fill out for each of your prospective shareholders (the persons who are to receive shares according to the stock issuance resolution in your Minutes, prepared as part of Step 5 above).

**Joint Shareholder Note** If any of your shares will be owned jointly (e.g., if a husband and wife will take ownership to their shares jointly as community property or in joint tenancy, see Step 8B below), you will need to complete a separate shareholder representation letter for each of the joint owners. So, when making copies of the tear-out form, make sure to make an additional copy to complete for each joint owner of shares.

Below is a sample of the tear-out Shareholder Representation Letter contained in the Appendix. Complete a separate letter for each person who will be an initial shareholder in your corporation according to the sample form and instructions below. (Remember to complete a separate letter for any joint owners of shares in your corporation—again, see Step 8B below for an discussion of joint ownership of shares).

- ✓ The parenthetical blanks, i.e., " _(information)_ ," indicate information which you must complete on the tear-out form.

- ✓ Each circled number (e.g., ❶) refers to a special instruction which provides specific information to help you complete an item. The special instructions immediately follow the sample form.

- ✓ Tear out the form in the Appendix and fill in the blanks (using a typewriter with a black ribbon or printing neatly with a blank ink pen) as you follow the sample form and instructions below.

**REVIEW NOTES**

As a brief review, let's look at the most important reasons for preparing a representation letter for each prospective shareholder. As in Chapter 3B, we use the terms "shareholder" and "purchaser" (of shares) interchangeably.

- The California limited offering exemption requires each purchaser of shares to represent that she is purchasing the shares for her own account and not for resale.

- Each purchaser of California limited offering shares should document in writing the fact that she fits within one of the six shareholder suitability categories discussed in detail in Chapter 3B2.

- If a purchaser relying on the limited offering exemption cannot meet one of these tests based on her own relationship to the corporation, its directors or officers, or because of her financial savvy or qualifications (see Categories 1-4 and Category 6), then she should designate, in writing, a professional advisor who has sufficient business or financial experience to protect the shareholder's interests (Category 5). Again, please review these specific categories in Chapter 3B2 before reaching any conclusions on this important aspect of the limited offering exemption.

- In addition to California law, your corporation must comply with federal securities law. Most small, closely-held corporations will wish to rely on the federal "private offering" stock exemption when issuing their initial shares (see Chapter 3C).

Reliance on this exemption can be made more secure by documenting the fact that the shareholders have received a full disclosure of all material facts and have had an opportunity to ask questions and receive answers concerning the terms and conditions of the stock issuance. The shareholder representation letter accomplishes this.

SAMPLE SHAREHOLDER REPRESENTATION LETTER

To:

___*(name of corporation)*_____ ❶

___*(address)*_____

___*(city, state, zip)*_____

 

      I, ___*(name of shareholder)*___, ❷ in connection with my purchase of a/an _____ ❷ interest in ___*(number of shares)*___ ❷ common shares of the corporation named above, hereby make the following representations:

      A. I am a suitable purchaser of these shares under the California limited offering exemption because:

*[Check the box to the left of one of the following clauses which describes how you qualify as a suitable purchaser of shares under the California limited offering exemption. The number and name of the limited offering suitability category associated with each clause is indicated above each clause in the sample below.]* ❸

Category 1. Inside Shareholder:

      1. [ ] I am a director, officer or promoter of the corporation, or because I occupy a position with the corporation with duties and authority substantially similar to those of an executive officer of the corporation.

Category 2. Existing Relationship:

      2. [ ] I have a pre-existing personal and/or business relationship with the corporation, or one or more of its directors, officers or controlling persons, consisting of personal or business contacts of a nature and duration which enables me to be aware of the character, business acumen and general business and financial circumstances of the person (including the corporation) with whom such relationship exists.

Category 3. Sophisticated Shareholder:

      3. [ ] I have the capacity to protect my own interests in connection with my purchase of the above shares by reason of my own business and/or financial experience.

Category 4. Major Shareholders:

 4. [  ] I meet one of the investment, net worth or individual income requirements provided for in Sections 260.102.13(e) and 260.102.13(g) of Title 10 of the California Code of Regulations and I meet one of the additional requirements provided for in Sections 260.102.13(e)(1)-(3) of this Title.

Category 5. Reliance on Professional Advisor:

 5(a). [  ] I have the capacity to protect my own interests in connection with my purchase of the above shares by reason of the business and/or financial experience of _____ *(name of professional advisor)* ❸ whom I have engaged and hereby designate as my professional advisor in connection with my purchase of the above shares.

 5(b). REPRESENTATION OF PROFESSIONAL ADVISOR

 _____ *(Name of professional advisor)* ❸ hereby represents:

 (1) I have been engaged as the professional advisor of _____ *(name of shareholder)* ❸ and have provided him or her with investment advice in connection with the purchase of _____ *(number of shares)* ❸ common shares in _____ *(name of corporation)* ❸.

 (2) As a regular part of my business as a/an _____ *(profession)* ❸, I am customarily relied upon by others for investment recommendations or decisions and I am customarily compensated for such services, either specifically or by way of compensation for related professional services.

 (3) I am unaffiliated with and am not compensated by the corporation or any affiliate or selling agent of the corporation, directly or indirectly. I do not have, nor will I have (a) a relationship of employment with the corporation, either as an employee, employer, independent contractor or principal; (b) the beneficial ownership of securities of the corporation, its affiliates or selling agents, in excess of 1% of its securities; or (c) a relationship with the corporation such that I control, am controlled by, or am under common control with the corporation, and, more specifically, a relationship by which I possess, directly or indirectly, the power to direct, or cause the direction, of the management, policies or actions of the corporation.

Dated: _*(date of signing)*_ ❸        _*(signature of professional advisor)*_
                                        *(typed name of advisor)*

Category 6. Relative of Another Suitable Shareholder:

I am the spouse, relative, or relative of the spouse of another purchaser of shares and I have the same principal residence as this purchaser.❸

❹B. I represent that I am purchasing these shares for investment for my own account and not with a view to, or for, sale in connection with any distribution of the shares. I understand that these shares have not been qualified or registered under any state or federal securities law and that they may not be transferred or otherwise disposed of without such qualification or registration pursuant to such laws or an opinion of legal counsel satisfactory to the corporation that such qualification or registration is not required.❺

❹C. I have not received any advertisement or general solicitation with respect to the sale of the shares of the above-named corporation.

❹D. I represent that, before signing this document, I have been provided access to, or been given, all material facts relevant to the purchase of my shares, including all financial and written information about the corporation and the terms and conditions of the stock offering and that I have been given the opportunity to ask questions and receive answers concerning any additional terms and conditions of the stock offering or other information which I, or my professional advisor if I have designated one, felt necessary to protect my interests in connection with the stock purchase transaction.

Dated: _(date of signing)_          ❻          _(signature of shareholder)_ _____ ❻
                                                 _(typed name of shareholder)_

## Special Instructions

❶ Insert the name of your corporation and street address of the principal executive office of the corporation in these blanks.

❷ Print or type the name of the shareholder in the first blank in this paragraph. In the second blank, indicate the percentage of interest the shareholder will receive in the shares (in most cases, you will simply show a "full" interest here—see the next paragraph if the shares will be co-owned). In the third blank, show the number of shares which will be issued individually or jointly to the shareholder.

Let's look a little closer at the second blank in this paragraph. If the shareholder will be taking title to her shares individually (without any co-owners), insert "full" here to show that the shareholder will receive a full interest in the shares. If you are issuing a block of shares jointly to two shareholders (whether in joint tenancy or tenancy in common or as part of a business partnership), then you will show an "undivided half" interest here to indicate that the shareholder for whom you are preparing the letter will receive a half-interest in the block of shares together with another co-owner. (For a discussion of ways to take title to shares and the basic characteristics of each type of ownership, see Step 8B below.)

*Example:* Gregg Walker and his friend and business associate Frank Federman form their own corporation. Gregg will own 500 shares individually. Frank will take title to his 500 shares jointly with his wife, Tracy Federman (for legal and tax reasons, the Federmans will take title to their shares in joint tenancy—again, see Step 8B below). In this instance, the corporation would prepare three shareholder representation letters: one for Gregg; one for Frank and one for Tracy. Here's how this paragraph would be prepared for each shareholder:

### Shareholder Letter 1 (Gregg Walker)

"I,____*Gregg Walker*____, in connection with my purchase of a/~~an~~____*full*____ interest in ____*500*____ common shares of the corporation named above, hereby make the following representations:"

### Shareholder Letter 2 (Frank Federman)

"I, ____*Frank Federman*____, in connection with my purchase of ~~a/~~an ____*undivided half*____ interest in ____*500*____ common shares of the corporation named above, hereby make the following representations:"

### Shareholder Letter 3 (Tracy Federman)

"I,____*Tracy Federman*____, in connection with my purchase of ~~a/~~an ____*undivided half*____ interest in ____*500*____ common shares of the corporation named above, hereby make the following representations:"

❸ Complete Section A of the letter. The purpose of this section is to indicate that the shareholder for whom this letter is prepared fits within one of the shareholder suitability categories of the limited offering exemption. Check the box to the left of one of the six suitability clauses in this section to show how the shareholder meets the requirements of the limited offering exemption.

*Example:* If you are preparing a letter for a director or officer of your corporation, check box 1 to show that the shareholder fits within the exemption as an Inside Shareholder (Category 1).

If you are preparing a letter for a spouse of one of these directors or officers (and the spouse shares the same principal residence as the director or officer), check the box next to Category 6 to show that this shareholder is a Relative of Another Suitable Shareholder (Category 6).

**Note** You only need to check one box for each shareholder. However, if a shareholder fits within more than one suitability category, you can check each box that applies if you wish.

We have designed this section of the letter to correspond to the six categories of suitable shareholders under the limited offering which are discussed in Chapter 3, Section B2, Categories 1-6 (box 5 in this section is a special case which we discuss below). In the sample letter above, we have added the name of the suitability category associated with each clause just above the beginning of each clause. We do not repeat our discussion of these technical categories here. Again, we assume you will refer back to Chapter 3B when choosing a box for each shareholder representation letter.

Let's look a little closer at Box 5(a). This box would be checked for a shareholder who is relying on the financial or business experience of a professional advisor to protect his interests in the stock purchase transaction. In this case, you and your professional advisor need to complete the separate page in the tear-out shareholder representation letter which contains Sections 5(a) and 5(b). To do this, check box 5(a) and indicate the name of the professional advisor on the blank line in this paragraph. Then complete all the blanks in Section 5(b) by typing the name of the shareholder who is being represented, the number of shares the shareholder will purchase, and the name of the corporation in the appropriate blanks in paragraph (1) of 5(b). The advisor should show her profession in paragraph 2 of 5(b) (see the accompanying box, "Who Can Be A Professional Advisor?") and sign and date the advisor representation at the bottom of Section 5(b) (type the advisor's name directly under the signature line here).

❹ Paragraphs B, C and D of each shareholder letter contain important representations and disclosures which each shareholder must make. Make sure each shareholder reads these paragraphs and understands their effect before she signs the letter (see Chapter 3, Sections B and C for further information on these representations).

❺ The stock certificates in the Appendix of this book (and those contained in the corporate kits offered by Nolo Press (see Step 3 above and the corporate kit order page at the back of the book) contain a legend which alerts your shareholders to the restrictions contained in this paragraph. If you order other stock certificates, you will have to specify the exact language of any legend you wish to add to your certificates.

❻ Each shareholder should sign and date his representation letter. Remember, if you have checked Category 5 for any shareholder, make sure the shareholder has his professional advisor date and sign the Representation of Professional Advisor section of the letter. Make a copy of each completed letter to place in your corporate records book and give each shareholder the completed original.

## Step 7. Prepare and File Notice of Stock Transaction Form

When issuing your initial shares under the California limited offering exemption, you must prepare and file a "Notice of Transaction Pursuant to Corporations Code Section 25102(f)." This form must be filed with any one of the offices of the California Department of Corporations within 15 calendar days "after the first sale of the securities in the transaction in this state." Your "first sale" of shares should occur when the corporation first receives payment from any shareholder for any of your initial shares.

**Technical Note**   Legally, the first sale occurs "when the issuer [corporation] has obtained a contractual commitment in this state to purchase one or more of the securities [shares] the issuer intends to sell in connection with the transaction." We assume that you have not entered in any such pre-issuance commitment (such as a shareholder's subscription agreement). If you follow the steps in this chapter in sequence, you will receive all of the payments for your

## WHO CAN BE A PROFESSIONAL ADVISOR?

Attorneys, certified public accountants (CPAs), persons licensed or registered as broker-dealers, agents, investment advisors, and banks and savings and loan associations have been specifically designated by the regulations to the limited offering exemption as qualified to act as professional advisors. This list is not exhaustive and you may also rely on and designate a person as a professional advisor, a person "who, as a regular part of such person's business, is customarily relied upon by others for investment recommendations or decisions, and who is customarily compensated for such services, either specifically or by way of compensation for related professional services."

Professional advisors must be "unaffiliated" with, and not be directly or indirectly compensated by, the corporation or by any of the corporation's affiliates or selling agents. Paragraph (3) of Section 5(b) of the professional advisor's representation—repeats the specific language of the regulations related to these requirements and asks the professional advisor to represent that he meets these requirements. For a further discussion of this category under the limited offering exemption, see Chapter 3B2.

shares (consideration) in return for the issuance of all of your shares as part of Step 8 below. To be absolutely sure, however, we ask you to prepare and file the Notice of Stock Transaction form now, before you sell your shares. This way you will be certain to mail your notice form to the Department of Corporation in advance of the 15-day deadline.[9]

A few additional points before you prepare the notice form:

- You should only prepare and file this form after you are sure of all of the details of your initial stock issuance (who will purchase your shares, the type and amount of payment to be received, etc.). Of course, at this stage in your incorporation, this should be no problem, as the details of your stock issuance should be contained in the stock issuance resolution of your Minutes, prepared as part of Step 5 of this chapter (your stock issuance information is also contained in your shareholder representation letters, prepared as part of Step 6, above).

- The information provided in this notice form should relate to your entire initial stock issuance transaction. No subsequent notices need to be filed with the state for sales of shares in connection with the same "transaction." Remember, you will need to obtain a permit or seek another exemption (file another notice with the help of a lawyer) for any subsequent issuances of shares.

- If you decide to file a federal notice form with the SEC under one of the rules of Regulation D or Section 4(6) of the federal Securities Act notifying them of your initial stock offering, you can dispense with the notice form shown here and send the Department of Corporations a copy of your federal notice form instead, together with a cover letter and the proper filing fee (see Section 260.102.14 of Title 10 of the California Code of

Regulations for further information). As we indicate in Chapter 3C, we don't expect most small closely-held corporations to make this federal filing, and we therefore assume that you will have to file the California notice form discussed in this section. Also, this California notice form is not required if none of your shares are purchased in California. We assume, however, that all or most of your shares will be purchased in this state by California residents (see Chapter 3A for a brief discussion of some of the technicalities involved with out-of-state sales of shares).

## A. Prepare Your Notice of Stock Transaction Form

A tear-out "Notice of Transaction Pursuant to Corporations Code Section 25102(f)" for filing with the California Department of Corporations is included in the Appendix. Fill out the Notice form according to the sample form and instructions below.

✓ The parenthetical blanks, i.e., " _(information)_ ," indicate information which you must complete on the tear-out form.

✓ Each circled number (e.g., ❶) refers to a special instruction which provides specific information to help you complete an item.

✓ We suggest you tear out the form in the Appendix and fill in the blanks (using a typewriter with a black ribbon or printing neatly with a blank ink pen) as you follow the sample form and instructions below.

**Note on Form Revisions** The Appendix contains the most recent version of this form as of the date of this printing of the book (currently form version 10/84). The official number of this form is 260.102.14(c). As forms occasionally change, you may want to call the Department of Corporations to be sure the 10/84 version of the notice form is current at the time of your stock issuance (or is still being accepted for filing). To do this, call one of the offices of the Department of Corporations listed below. If they are not accepting this version of the form, ask the clerk to send you one or two copies of the most recent Notice form.

### Department of Corporations Telephone Numbers

| | |
|---|---|
| Los Angeles | 213-736-2741 |
| Sacramento | 916-445-7205 |
| San Diego | 619-237-7341 |
| San Francisco | 415-557-3787 |

### Special Instructions

❶ **Top of Form** Ignore the blanks at the upper-left and -right portions of the form; the blanks at the upper-left will be filled out by the Department of Corporations and the blank at the upper right is only for corporations that have previously qualified securities with the Department and have been issued a Department File Number.

❷ **Heading** Circle the appropriate fee which you must submit with the Notice. You will compute this amount as part of Section B below. Just remember to come back and circle the right fee amount later.

SAMPLE NOTICE OF STOCK TRANSACTION FORM

(Department of Corporations Use Only) Department of Corporations File No., if any

Fee Paid $ _(leave these lines blank)_ ❶          _(leave this line blank)_ ❶

Receipt No. _____          (Insert File Number(s) of Previous Filings
                                             Before the Department, if any)

❷ FEE:  $25.00   $35.00   $50.00   $150.00   $300.00
(Circle the appropriate amount of fee.
See Corp. Code Section 25608(c))

COMMISSIONER OF CORPORATIONS
STATE OF CALIFORNIA

NOTICE OF TRANSACTION PURSUANT TO CORPORATIONS CODE SECTION 25102(f)

A. Check one:  Transaction under [**X**]❸ Section 25102(f)   ( ) Rule 260.103.

1. Name of Issuer: _____ _(name of corporation)_ ❹ _____

2. Address of Issuer: _(address of principal executive officer)_ ❺ _____
                        Street              City      State     ZIP

   Mailing Address: _(mailing address if different)_ ❺ _____
                        Street              City      State     ZIP

3. Area Code and Telephone Number: _(phone number of corporation)_ ❻ ____

4. Issuer's state (or other jurisdiction) of incorporation or organization: California❼

5. Title of class or classes of securities sold in transaction: Common Stock❽

6. The value of the securities sold or proposed to be sold in the transaction, determined in accordance with Corp. Code Section 25608(g) in connection with the fee required upon filing this notice, is (fee based on amount shown in line (iii) under "Total Offering"):

|  | California | Total Offering |  |
|---|---|---|---|
| (a) (i) in money | $_____ | $_____ | ❾ |
| . . .(ii) in consideration other than money | $_____ | $_____ | |
| . . (iii) total of (i) and (ii) | $_____ | $_____ | |

(b) ❿ ( ) Change in rights, preferences, privileges or restrictions of or
          on outstanding securities.  ($25.00 fee)   (See Rule 260.103)

7. Type of filing under Securities Act of 1933, if applicable: __None ⓫_____

8. Date of Notice: _(date of signing)_ ⓬ _____          _(name of corporation)_ ⓬ _____
                                                                    Issuer

( )   Check if issuer already has a          _(signature of officer or director)_ ⓬ ____
      consent to service of process          Authorized Signature on behalf of issuer
      on file with the Commissioner.         _(typed name of officer or director)_ ⓬ ____
                                             Print name and title of signatory

Name, Address and Phone number of contact person:
      _(typed name, address and phone number of signer above)_ ⓬ _____

Instruction: Each issuer (other than a California corporation) filing a notice under Section 25102(f) must file a consent to service of process (Form 260.165), unless it already has a consent to service on file with the Commissioner.

260.102.14(c)  (10/84)

❸ **Item A**   Check the box titled "Section 25102(f)" so that this line reads "Transaction under (**X**) Section 25102(f)"—this means that the form is being used to provide notice of your stock issuance under the California limited offering exemption.

❹ **Item 1**   Type the name of your corporation exactly as it appears in your Articles of Incorporation.

❺ **Item 2**   Type the address of the principal executive address of your corporation (this is the address specified in the Principal Executive Office resolution of your Minutes prepared in Step 5 above). Make sure to provide a full street address (no P.O. boxes), including the city, state and zip code. If you use a mailing address different from your principal executive office, show this address on the second line of this item.

❻ **Item 3**   Type the telephone number of the corporation, including the area code.

❼ **Item 4**   Type "California" in this blank to indicate California as the state of your incorporation.

❽ **Item 5**   Type "Common Stock" in this blank to indicate that you are issuing only one class of common shares. Of course, we assume here that you have used the tear-out Articles of Incorporation in the Appendix of this book (these Articles are prepared as part of Step 2 and provide for one class of common shares).

❾ **Item 6(a)**   In these blanks, show the value of the shares which you will sell to your shareholders. As we explain in the accompanying technical note box, for most small closely-held corporations, the value of the corporation's initial shares is the same as the value of the cash or noncash payments which will be made for the shares.

You have already prepared a list of the fair value of the payments to be made by your shareholders in the Stock Issuance Resolution prepared as part of your Minutes in Step 5 of this chapter. Consequently, you can simply add up the cash payment and noncash payment amounts from the Fair Value column of your stock issuance resolution and place these totals in the blanks here. (Note that we assume that the "fair value" figures in your stock issuance resolution do, in fact, reflect the "actual value" of any nonmonetary consideration to be received for your shares).

Here's how to fill in each of the blanks in this section of the form:

- Indicate the total amount of all cash payments to be made by your California shareholders in the California column of blank 6(a)(i).
- Indicate the total value of all noncash payments to be made by your California shareholders in the California column of blank 6(a)(ii) —again, the actual value of any noncash payments made by your shareholders is shown in the stock issuance resolution in your Minutes).
- Total the above amounts and place the result in the California column of blank 6(a)(iii).
- If, as we assume, all your initial shareholders will be California shareholders, simply carry over the three California amounts to the corresponding row of the Total Offering column in Item 6(a). If you will sell shares outside of California, add the out-of-state cash and noncash figures to the California figures and place these totals in the corresponding rows in the "Total Offering" column. Then provide a new overall total in the blank 6(a)(iii) of the Total Offering column.

The calculations here are really quite easy and are best demonstrated with an example or two.

*Example 1:* You plan to issue a total of 30,000 initial shares for cash and property totalling $30,000: $10,000 in cash; $20,000 as the fair value of all the property to be transferred for shares. All your prospective shareholders are California residents. You would fill out this item in the Notice form as follows:

|  | California | Total Offering |
|---|---|---|
| (a) (i) in money | $ _10,000_ | $ _10,000_ |
| . . .(ii) in consideration other than money | $ _20,000_ | $ _20,000_ |
| . . (iii) total of (i) and (ii) | $ _30,000_ | $ _30,000_ |

*Example 2:* Assume the same facts as the previous example except that 5,000 shares will also be issued to an out-of-state shareholder in return for $5,000 cash. In this case, the Total Offering column figures will be changed to reflect this out-of-state amount as follows:

|  | California | Total Offering |
|---|---|---|
| (a) (i) in money | $ _10,000_ | $ _15,000_ |
| . . .(ii) in consideration other than money | $ _20,000_ | $ _20,000_ |
| . . (iii) total of (i) and (ii) | $ _30,000_ | $ _35,000_ |

**⑩ Item 6(b)** Ignore this box ("Change in rights, preferences, privileges or restrictions of or on outstanding securities"). It applies to other types of transactions than the kind we are talking about here.

**⑪ Item 7** In answer to the "Type of filing under Securities Act of 1933, if applicable," type "None." This question relates to the federal securities laws. If you are actually registering your stock offering or filing a notice with the SEC (with the help of a lawyer), the attorney who is helping you with your federal filing will indicate "Registered" or show the number of the rule under which the federal filing was made on the separate Notice form he is preparing for you. Please see Chapter 3C for a discussion of the federal securities laws.

**⑫ Item 8** Type the name of the corporation on the line with the word "Issuer" under it; the name of a corporate officer or director who will sign your Notice form (on the line marked "Print name and title of

signatory") ; and this person's name, address and phone number as the "contact person" for your corporation in the blanks indicated in the sample Notice form. (The contact person is the person the Department will notify in the event there are any questions concerning your Notice form).

**Important Note** Make sure to complete the date and signature lines in this part of the form on all copies of your Notice form: these are the lines marked "Date of Notice" and "Authorized Signature on behalf of issuer."

Ignore the printed parenthetical blank "( )" under Item 8 on your Notice form which reads "Check if issuer already has a consent to service of process on file with the Commissioner." As the official instructions at the bottom of the form indicate, California corporations do not need to file a consent to service of process with the Department.

## TECHNICAL NOTE ON THE VALUE OF YOUR SHARES

The reason you must supply the information in Item 6(a) of the Notice form is to arrive at a total value figure for all of the securities (shares) you are issuing under the limited offering exemption, which will then be used to compute the filing fee for your Notice form (as explained in Step 7B below). As you might guess, there are legal guidelines for determining the fair value of your shares.[10] The assumption we have made in the above instructions on filling in these blanks on your Notice form is that the value of your shares is (1) the actual price to be paid for the shares (if the shares are purchased for cash) or (2) the actual value of any consideration other than money (noncash consideration such as property) to be received for the shares. This is the legal rule which will apply to most, if not all, privately-held corporations for purposes of determining the fair value of their shares when computing the Notice form filing fee. However, under the legal rules footnoted below, if the value of your shares when issued is greater than the actual cash price or value of the noncash made for the shares, then this higher figure should be used when filling in these blanks on the Notice form and computing your filing fee.

NOTE   It is very unlikely that this alternative rule will apply to you since your corporation's initial shares should have no value in and of themselves (e.g., there's no market for such shares). In other words, in the absence of outside market pressures driving up share values or outside investors vying for your initial shares, these shares should only be worth the actual amount paid for them by your shareholders.

## B. Determine the Notice Form Filing Fee

After you have completed your Notice form, compute the fee which you must submit with the notice. The fee is based upon the total value of the securities to be sold as shown on line 6(a)(iii) of your printed form in the "Total Offering" column, according to the following fee schedule:

| Value of Securities Proposed to Be Sold (from "Total Offering" column, line 6(a)(iii)) | Filing Fee |
| --- | --- |
| $25,000 or less | $25 |
| $25,001 to $100,000 | $35 |
| $100,001 to $500,000 | $50 |
| $500,001 to $1,000,000 | $150 |
| Over $1,000,000 | $300 |

Many small corporations will issue their initial shares for less than $25,000 and will therefore pay the minimum filing fee of $25. Go back to the heading of the Notice form at this point and circle the appropriate fee amount on your tear-out Notice (and on any copies you may have made—see instruction 2, Section A above).

**Warning** Again, please realize that fees, like forms, are subject to change. You may want to check with one of the offices of the Department of Corporations listed above to make sure the above fee schedule reflects the current fees.

## C. File Your Notice Form

Once you have completed your the tear-out Notice form as explained above, make two copies. Sign and date all copies of the final form. Mail *two* copies and a stamped self-addressed envelope (addressed to the person who signed your Notice forms, c/o your corporation) together with a check made payable to "California Department of Corporations" for the amount of the filing fee (computed as explained above) to:

> Department of Corporations
> 1115 11th Street
> Sacramento, CA 95814

**Note** Although you can file this notice in person at any branch office of the Department (Los Angeles, San Francisco or San Diego), we assume most incorporators will find this mailing to the main Sacramento office the most convenient means of making this filing.

Within a week or so, you should receive a copy of your Notice from the Department of Corporations, file-stamped by the Department. Place this copy in your corporate records book.

# Step 8. Issue Shares of Stock

The final step in your incorporation process is issuing the initial shares of your corporation to your shareholders. Issuing shares of stock is an essential step in your incorporation process and, as a general (and we think important) rule, you should not begin doing business as a corporation until you have completed this step (see Chapter 21).

Ten blank, ready-to-use stock certificates are included in the Appendix at the back of this book. They are specifically designed for use by corporations issuing their initial shares under the California limited offering exemption. If you want to order specially printed certificates for your corporation, you can do so by ordering one of the corporate kits offered by Nolo Press (see the order form at the back of the book). Each kit contains 20 custom-printed stock certificates. (For a further discussion on choosing the right certificates, see Step 3 above.

---

**A FEW REMINDERS WHEN YOU ISSUE SHARES**

- All of your initial shares should be sold for the same price per share. For example, if someone pays the corporation $1,000 cash for ten shares, then another person selling the corporation a machine worth $10,000 should receive 100 shares.

- Your corporation cannot issue more shares than the number of shares authorized by your Articles of Incorporation. (As we've said in Step 2 above, it's common for corporations to authorize more shares in their Articles than they will actually issue here.)

- Of course, by now you know that you must issue your initial shares under the California limited offering exemption when following the procedure contained in this book. See Chapter 3B to refresh yourself on these rules.

---

## A. If Applicable, Comply With California's Bulk Sales Law

Before discussing the details of your stock issuance, we must make a slight detour to mention a pre-stock issuance formality that may apply to some readers—compliance with California's Bulk Sales Law. [11]

Generally, this law applies to you if:

- You are transferring more than half the value of the inventory and equipment of an unincorporated business located in California to your new corporation (if you are incorporating an existing sole proprietorship or partnership);

- The value of the business assets being transferred is $10,000 or more; [12] *and*

- The business being incorporated is a restaurant or is engaged in the principal business of selling inventory from stock (such as a retail or wholesale business, including a business that manufactures what it sells).

If not all of the above conditions apply to your incorporation, you can ignore this section and go on to Section B below.

Even if you do meet all three conditions, you may still be eligible from an exemption from most of the provisions of California's bulk sales law. The most important exemption available to incorporators of a small business is the following: [13]

You are exempt from further compliance with the bulk sales act if your corporation:

- Assumes the debts of the unincorporated business;
- Is not insolvent after the assumption of these debts; and
- Publishes and files a notice to creditors within 30 days of the transfer of assets (normally, the assets are transferred when shares are issued to the initial shareholders).

**Note**   If your corporation is not eligible for this or another exemption from the bulk sales provisions, the publication and filing procedures must be accomplished at least 12 business days *prior* to the transfer of business assets.

To comply with this exemption to the bulk sales law, call a local legal newspaper. The paper will send you a notice of bulk transfer form to prepare and will publish and file this form with the county recorder's and tax collector's offices for a fee.

## BACKGROUND TO THE BULK SALES PROVISIONS

The purpose of the Bulk Sales provisions in California and other states is to prevent business owners from secretly transferring the "bulk" of the assets of their business to another person or entity in an attempt to avoid creditors and to prevent schemes whereby the prior business owners "sell out" (usually to a relative at bargain prices) and come back into the business through a back door later on. Of course, we assume you are simply changing the form of your unincorporated business, not trying to convince others that you are disassociated from their prior business (and its debts). In other words, if the bulk sales law applies to you, you should be complying with its notice and filing procedures only as formalities. If, on the other hand, your unincorporated business will have debts outstanding at the time of its incorporation and your corporation does not plan to, or may have difficulty in, assuming and promptly paying these debts as they become due, then compliance with the bulk sales procedures is more than a mere formality and you should see a lawyer.

RECORDING REQUESTED BY:

AND WHEN RECORDED MAIL TO:

Name

Address

City, State, Zip

*Space Above This Line for Recorder's Use*

## NOTICE TO CREDITORS OF BULK SALE

[SECS. 6103(c)(10), (11), 6105 U.C.C.]

Escrow No. _____

     Notice is hereby given to creditors of the within named seller that a sale that may constitute a bulk sale has been or will be made.

     The individual, partnership, or corporate names and the business addresses of the seller are:

     As listed by the seller, all other business names and addresses used by the seller within three years before the date such list was sent or delivered to the buyer are: (If "none," so state)

     The address to which inquiries about the sale may be made, if different from the seller's address: (if "same," so state)

     The individual, partnership, or corporate names and the business addresses of the buyer are:

     The assets sold or to be sold are described in general as:

and are located at:

     The date or prospective date of the bulk sale was/is _____ ,
at _____ .

     The buyer has assumed or will assume in full the debts that were incurred in the seller's business before the date of the bulk sale.

Dated: _____ , 19 _____

_____
(Signature of Buyer)

_____
(Type or Print Name)

*This form is provided at no charge as an accommodation to our customers. Any questions concerning its use should be referred to an attorney.*

California Newspaper Service Bureau, Inc.

**Note** There are various notice forms that fit specific provisions of the bulk sales law. To rely on the exemption above, make sure to prepare and have the newspaper publish and file a Notice to Creditors under Section 6013(c)(10) of the Uniform Commercial Code. This notice will usually include a heading indicating that it is a Bulk Sale and Assumption form. In any case, it must include a clause stating, or to the effect that, "the buyer has assumed or will assume in full the debts that were incurred in the seller's business before the date of the bulk sale."

Below is a sample notice to creditors from under Section 6103(c)(10) of the bulk sales law.

**If You Don't Comply** The penalty for failure to comply with the requirements of the bulk sales law is that a claimant against the prior business can collect the amount owed from the corporation. Of course, if the unincorporated business does not owe any money or have potential liabilities, or if you are sure that your corporation will pay any outstanding debts and claims as they become due, you may not be concerned with this penalty. Even in these cases, we recommend that incorporators to whom the bulk sales law applies do attend to these simple publication and filing formalities. Besides helping you avoid claims in the future, doing so is additional proof that you have perfected the separate legal existence of your corporation.

## B. Taking Title To Stock

In the next section you will actually fill out your stock certificates. Before you do, however, a few words about how to take title to your shares are in order. If all shareholders will take title to stock in their own names, individually, you can skip most of this section. However, if joint ownership is involved, read this section carefully.

Taking title to stock, essentially, means putting the owner's name on the ownership line of the stock certificate. Here's how to do it:

**Sole Ownership** Type the owner's name on the ownership line. That's all there is to it.[14]

People sometimes wish to hold shares of stock jointly with another person. There are several common ways to do this, including co-owning shares in joint tenancy, as community property, or as tenancy in common. Let's briefly look at each of these forms of joint ownership.

**Joint Tenancy** This form of ownership is often used by family members wishing to co-own property since upon the death of one joint owner (joint tenant), the survivor takes full title to the shares without the necessity of the property going through probate. Joint tenancy avoids probate because when one person dies, the property is viewed by law as automatically belonging to the other co-owner. During life each joint tenant (assuming there are two) is viewed as owning half of the stock. Although joint tenancy property cannot be willed to a third party, it can be sold or transferred during the life of a co-owner (such a sale terminates the joint tenancy and turns the co-ownership into tenancy in common—see the discussion below). The fact that a joint tenancy can be ended unilaterally by a joint tenant means that there is no guarantee that the surviving joint tenant(s) will end up owning all the property. Joint tenancy ownership is created by using the word "as joint tenants," or "in joint tenancy," on the ownership line (e.g., "Carolyn Kimura and Sally Sullivan, as joint tenants"). It is also common, but not legally necessary in California, to add the words "with right of survivorship" (e.g., "Carolyn Kimura and Sally Sullivan, as joint tenants with right of survivorship").

**Estate Planning Note** As an estate planning measure, the use of an intervivos trust (living trust) allows the beneficiary of the trust to receive title to the shares upon the death of the shareholder and also keeps the shares outside of probate. In other words, some share-holders may wish to transfer their shares to this type of trust for the benefit of another person rather than taking title to their shares in joint tenancy with the other person (married shareholders may also wish to transfer shares—held as community property as explained below—to this type of trust). If you do transfer your shares to a trust, you will need to make out new share certificates showing the trust as the owner of the transferred shares. For more details on this and other estate planning techniques, see *Plan Your Estate,* by Clifford (Nolo Press).

**Community Property**  Community property ownership[15] can only be used by a husband and wife. Although spouses can use other joint ownership forms such as joint tenancy, community property ownership is normally preferred when the stock is in fact purchased with community property (property purchased with money or property earned by either spouse during a marriage). The reason for this is that when property passes to another person upon the death of the owner, the property is given a "stepped-up" basis equal to its value at the time of the owner's death. If the property is held jointly by two people, the normal rule is that only the deceased owner's half-interest in the property is given this increased basis. However, if the property is held jointly as community property, both co-owners' half-interests (the deceased and the surviving spouse's interests) will be given this stepped-up basis. This additional increase in basis will result in increased tax savings when the property is later sold or transferred. If this benefit is important to you when taking title to your shares and you have further questions, please check with your tax advisor.

*Example 1:* If you have a $1,000 basis in your shares (because you paid $1,000 for them) and you later sell the shares for $10,000, your taxable income resulting from the sale will be $9,000.

*Example 2:* If your basis in these shares is stepped-up to $5,000, the taxable income resulting from the sale is reduced to $5,000 ($10,000-$5,000).

As a result, if a married person plans to purchase shares in your corporation, he or she will probably wish to take title to the shares jointly (in the names of both spouses) as community property.[16] To signify this type of co-ownership, the spouses should use the phrase "as community property" after their names (e.g., "Mai Chang and Lee Chang, as community property").

**Tenancy in Common**  The third common category of co-ownership is tenancy in common. Each co-owner holds an equal interest in the property and can sell, transfer, or will his or her interest to a third person at any time. This form of co-ownership does not have the special probate or income tax benefits associated with joint tenancy property or community property mentioned above. Typically, unrelated people who wish to purchase property together take title in this fashion. However, in the context of your stock issuance, it is unlikely that two unrelated persons will wish to co-own shares. More likely, each unrelated person will wish to separately purchase and hold title to his or her own shares. However, if, for some reason, shareholders do wish to jointly own stocks as tenants in common, the co-owners should use the phrase "as tenants in common" after their names (e.g., "Reuben Ruiz and Herman Grizwold, as tenants in common").

**Warning—Gifts Are Taxable**  It is important to realize that adding another person's name to your shares without receiving money or property of fair value for doing so constitutes a gift, and gift taxes may have to be paid. For example, if the separate property of one spouse is used to purchase shares that will be held as the community property of both spouses or if a person buys shares with his own money but decides to take title to the shares in joint tenancy with another person, a gift has occurred.[17]

**NUMBER** ❶

SHARES ❷

**INCORPORATED UNDER THE LAWS OF CALIFORNIA**

Common Shares

*(name of corporation)* ❸

THE SHARES REPRESENTED BY THIS CERTIFICATE HAVE NOT BEEN REGISTERED OR QUALIFIED UNDER ANY FEDERAL OR STATE SECURITIES LAW. THEY HAVE BEEN ACQUIRED FOR INVESTMENT PURPOSES AND NOT WITH A VIEW TOWARD RESALE AND MAY NOT BE OFFERED FOR SALE, SOLD, TRANSFERRED, OR PLEDGED WITHOUT REGISTRATION AND QUALIFICATION PURSUANT TO SUCH LAWS OR AN OPINION OF LEGAL COUNSEL SATISFACTORY TO THE CORPORATION THAT SUCH REGISTRATION AND QUALIFICATION IS NOT REQUIRED.

*This Certifies that* _____ *(name of shareholder)* ❹ _____ *is the owner of* _____ *(number of shares)* ❺ _____ *fully paid and nonassessable Shares of the above Corporation transferable only on the books of the Corporation by the holder hereof in person or by duly authorized Attorney upon surrender of this Certificate properly endorsed.*

*In Witness Whereof, the Corporation has caused this Certificate to be signed by its duly authorized officers and to be sealed with the Seal of the Corporation.*

Dated _____ *(date of issuance)* ❻

_____ *(signature of president)* ❻
, *President*

_____ *(signature of secretary)* ❻
, *Secretary*

❼

---

Certificate Number _____

For _____ *(number of shares)* _____ Shares

Issued To:

_____ *(name of shareholder)*

_____ *(address of shareholder)*

Dated _____ *(date of issuance)* _____ 19 _____ ❶

---

From Whom Transferred ❽

Dated _____ 19 _____

| No. Original Shares | No. Original Certificate | No. of Shares Transferred |
|---|---|---|
|  |  |  |

---

Received Certificate Number _____

For _____ *(number of shares)* _____ Shares

This _____ *(date of issuance)* _____ day of _____ 19 _____

_____ *(signature of shareholder)*

SIGNATURE

## C. Fill Out Your Stock Certificates and Stubs

Fill in the blanks on the tear-out stock certificates contained in the Appendix at the back of the book (or on the specially printed certificates you have ordered (see Step 3). This book contains ten certificates (each Nolo corporate kit contains 20 certificates). The appropriate information on the stock certificate stubs should also be completed. Simply follow the directions on the sample stock certificate which we provide below. The circled numbers in the blanks on the sample certificate refer to the special instructions below.

Each stock certificate should represent the number of shares the corporation is issuing to a particular shareholder (or, if issuing joint shares, to the joint owners of the shares). If shares are owned jointly, only fill out one stock certificate for the joint owners, showing both names and the manner of taking title to the shares on the ownership line (as explained below).

### Special Instructions

❶ Complete the left and right portions of the stub as indicated on the sample stub.

**Note**  The date of issuance and shareholder signature lines on the stubs will be filled out when you distribute your stock certificates (Section E below). If you've ordered one of corporate kits offered by Nolo Press, fill out each separate stub page in your kit in the same manner (these stub pages are already numbered).

Number each certificate and its associated stub. Each person you issue stock to gets one certificate no matter how many shares she purchases (joint owners of shares, of course, get one certificate for their jointly owned shares). The stock certificates issued by the corporation should be consecutively numbered, and should be issued in consecutive order. This is impor-

tant since it enables the corporation to keep track of who owns its shares.

*Example:* If you plan to issue stock to four people (no matter how many shares each person will receive), the certificates should be numbered 1 through 4. Thus, if Jack pays $10,000, Sam $5,000, Julie $2,500 and Ted transfers a computer with a fair market value of $1,000 for their shares, assuming the price of the shares is established at $50 per share, Jack receives a certificate for 200 shares, Sam receives one for 100 shares, Julie one for 50 shares and Ted a certificate for 20 shares. Obviously this means you should issue four certificates, numbered 1 through 4 (it doesn't matter who gets the certificate numbered #1, #2, etc.).

The fixing of a price per share amount is arbitrary. In the above example it would be just as easy and sensible to establish a price per share amount of $25 with each shareholder receiving a stock certificate representing twice as many shares. Along these lines, these shareholders would not want to fix the price per share amount in this example at $15 per share, since this would result in their receiving fractional shares—a permissible but unnecessarily complex method of issuing your shares.

❷ Type in the number of shares which each certificate represents. The number of shares each person is entitled to receive is indicated in the stock issuance resolution of your Minutes.

❸ Type the name of the corporation exactly as it appears in your Articles of Incorporation.

❹ Type the name of the shareholder. If the stock certificate will be held by two persons, indicate both persons names here and the form of co-ownership here (for example, "Mai Chang and Lee Chang, as community property" or "Carolyn Kimura and Sally Sullivan, as joint tenants"). See Section B above for a discussion on taking title to jointly owned shares.

❺ Again, show the number of shares represented by each stock certificate. Simply type or spell out a number here. The number shown here should be the same number indicated in special instruction 2, above.

❻ You will type in the date of issuance and obtain the signature of your President and Secretary on each certificate when you distribute your shares as part of Section E below.

❼ An impression of the corporate seal should be placed at the bottom of each stock certificate.

❽ The transfer sections (both here, on the stub, and on the back of each certificate) should be left blank. They are to be used only if, and when, the stock certificates are later transferred by the original shareholders. If you've ordered a corporate kit from Nolo Press, this also applies to the transfer sections on the separate stub pages and on the back of the printed stock certificates which are included as part of each kit.

After filling out the stock certificates and stubs, place the completed stubs in consecutive order in the stock certificate section of your corporate records book. These stubs represent your corporation's share register.

**Note** You'll need to neatly cut the stub away from the top of the stock certificate (along the dotted line) if you are using the certificates provided in the Appendix at the back of this book. It's easier to do this if you first tear out the entire page.

If you've ordered a corporate kit from Nolo Press, do not detach the completed stub pages in the stock certificate section of your corporate kit. Each kit contains a separate "Stock Transfer Ledger (Share Register)." Fill out one line on the left side of each page for each shareholder in the appropriate alphabetical box (the columns at the extreme right are used for transfers of the original shares).

## D. Prepare a Bill of Sale and/or Receipts for Your Shareholders

After filling out your stock certificates, you may wish to prepare receipts and, if incorporating a prior business, a bill of sale for your shareholders before actually distributing your stock certificates. You are not legally required to prepare these forms but we think it's generally good business to do so (and a sensible precaution to avoid later confusion as to who paid what for shares in your corporation).

A tear-out Bill of Sale and separate receipts are contained in the Appendix to this book. This paperwork allows the corporation and each shareholder to have a written statement of the details of each person's stock issuance transaction. Simply tear-out the appropriate forms from the Appendix, make copies, and prepare these forms according to the sample forms and instructions below.

### 1. Prepare a Bill of Sale for Assets of a Business (If Incorporating a Prior Business)

If you are incorporating a prior business (you are transferring the assets of an unincorporated business to your corporation in return for the issuance of shares to the prior owners), you may wish to prepare the tear-out Bill of Sale in the Appendix. If not, skip to Section D2 below.

**Note on the Transfer of Real Property or Leases** If you are transferring real property or a lease to your corporation, you will have to prepare and execute new corporate ownership papers, such as deeds, leases, assignments of leases. etc. (the assignment of a lease will usually only occur as part of the transfer of a pre-existing business to the corporation). An excellent *California* guide to transferring property interests and preparing new deeds (with tear-out forms) is *The Deeds Book*, by Randolph (Nolo Press). When it comes to rental property, you should talk to the landlord about having a new lease prepared showing the corporation as the new tenant. (An alternative is to have the prior tenants assign the lease to the corporation; however, read your lease carefully before trying to do this as many leases are not assignable without the landlord's permission.)

If the property being transferred is mortgaged, then you will most likely need the permission of the lender to transfer the property. If your real property note agreement contains a "due on sale or transfer" clause, you may even be required to refinance your deed of trust (mortgage) if rates have gone up substantially since the existing deed of trust was executed. This, of course, may be so undesirable that you decide not to transfer the real property to the corporation, preferring to keep it in the name of the original owner and lease it to the corporation. Also, don't forget that the transfer of real property to your corporation may trigger a Proposition 13 reassessment of the property; check with your tax advisor before completing a real property transfer to your corporation.

Prepare and execute these new ownership papers, lease documents, etc., before you give the prior property owners their shares (this will be done as part of Section E below).

Below is a sample of the tear-out Bill of Sale form with instructions.

✓ The parenthetical blanks, i.e., " _(information)_ ," indicate information which you must complete on the tear-out form.

✓ Each circled numbers (e.g., ❶) refers to a special instruction below which provides specific information to help you complete an item.

✓ We suggest you tear out the form in the Appendix and fill in the blanks as you follow the sample form and instructions below.

As indicated in the form, attach to the Bill of Sale an inventory of the assets of the prior business which will be transferred to the corporation. If you have any questions, your tax advisor can help you with the preparation of this inventory and in deciding on the options offered in this form.

## Special Instructions

❶ Type (or print) the names of the prior business owners.

❷ Show the name of your corporation.

❸ Enter the total number of shares to be issued to all prior owners of the business in return for the transfer of the business to the corporation.

**Example**: If Patricia and Kathleen will each receive 2,000 shares in return for their respective half-interests in their pre-existing partnership (which they are now incorporating), they would indicate 4,000 shares here.

❹ Use this line to show any assets of the prior business that are not being transferred to the corporation (e.g., you may wish to continue to personally own real property associated with your business and lease it to your new corporation). For most businesses being incorporated, all prior business assets will be transferred to the corporation and you should type "No Exceptions" here.

**Note**　As indicated in this paragraph of the bill of sale, you should attach a current inventory showing the assets of the prior business transferred to the corporation.

❺ Indicate the name of the prior business being transferred to the corporation. For sole proprietorships and partnerships not operating under a fictitious business name, the name(s) of the prior owners may simply be given here (e.g., "Heather Langsley and Chester Treacher").

❻ Show the full address of the prior business.

❼ This paragraph indicates that your corporation will assume the liabilities of the prior business. This will be appropriate for the incorporation of most small businesses. If your corporation will not assume any of the liabilities of the prior business (see Chapter 4J and Section 8A above for a discussion of some of the issues here), then you will need to re-type the tear-out Bill of Sale, omitting this paragraph.

In the blank in this paragraph, list any liabilities of the prior business which will not be assumed by the corporation. Normally your new corporation will assume all liabilities of the prior business and you should indicate "No Exceptions" here.

SAMPLE BILL OF SALE FOR ASSETS OF A BUSINESS

This is an agreement between:

_____*(name of prior business owner)*_____ ❶

_____*(name of prior business owner)*_____ ❶

herein called "transferor(s)," and _____*(name of corporation)*_____, ❷ a California corporation, herein called "the corporation."

In return for the issuance of _____*(number of shares)*_____ ❸ shares of stock of the corporation, transferor(s) hereby sell(s), assign(s), and transfer(s) to the corporation all right, title, and interest in the following property:

All the tangible assets listed on the inventory attached to this Bill of Sale and all stock in trade, goodwill, leasehold interests, trade names, and other intangible assets [except _____*(any nontransferred assets shown here)*_____ ❹] of _____*(name of prior business)*_____ ❺, located at _____*(address of prior business)*_____ ❻.

In return for the transfer of the above property to it, the corporation hereby agrees to assume, pay, and discharge all debts, duties, and obligations that appear on the date of this agreement on the books and owed on account of said business [except _____*(any unassumed liabilities shown here)*_____ ❼]. The corporation agrees to indemnify and hold the transferor(s) of said business and their property free from any liability for any such debt, duty, or obligation and from any suits, actions, or legal proceedings brought to enforce or collect any such debt, duty, or obligation.

❽ The transferor(s) hereby appoint(s) the corporation as representative to demand, receive, and collect for itself any and all debts and obligations now owing to said business and hereby assumed by the corporation. The transferor(s) further authorize(s) the corporation to do all things allowed by law to recover and collect any such debts and obligations and to use the transferor's(s') name(s) in such manner as it considers necessary for the collection and recovery of such debts and obligations, provided, however, without cost, expense, or damage to the transferor(s).

Dated: _____*(date)*_____ ❾       _____*(signature of prior business owner)*_____ ❾
                                      *(typed name)*            , Transferor

                                      _____*(signature of prior business owner)*_____ ❾
                                      *(typed name)*            , Transferor

                                      _____*(signature of prior business owner)*_____ ❾
                                      *(typed name)*            , Transferor

Dated: _____*(date)*_____ ❾       _____*(name of corporation)*_____ ❾
                                      Name of Corporation

                                By:   _____*(signature of President)*_____ ❾
                                      *(typed name)*            , President

                                      _____*(signature of Treasurer)*_____ ❾
                                      *(typed name)*            , Treasurer

❽ This paragraph is included in the tear-out Bill of Sale to indicate that your corporation is appointed to collect for itself any debts and obligations (accounts receivable) owed to the prior business which are being transferred to the corporation.

❾ Type the name of the corporation on the line indicated. Don't fill out the other blanks yet. You should date the form and have the prior business owners (transferors) and the President and Treasurer of the corporation sign the Bill of Sale when you distribute the stock certificates to the prior business owners (as explained in Section E below).

## 2. Prepare Receipts for Your Shareholders

You may wish to prepare one or more receipts for your shareholders (for preparing a bill of sale to document the transfer of the assets of a business in return for shares, see the previous subsection). In the Appendix, we have included tear-out receipts for the following types of payment made by a shareholder:

• Cash
• Cancellation of Indebtedness
• Specific Items of Property
• Services Rendered the Corporation

Let's look at each of these transactions and the associated receipt form below. Obviously, you will need to make copies of each receipt to be prepared for more than one shareholder (e.g., you will want to make two additional copies of the cash receipt form if you will be issuing shares in return for cash payments to be made by three shareholders).

✓ The parenthetical blanks, i.e., " _(information)_ ," indicate information which you must complete on the tear-out receipts.

✓ Each circled number (e.g., ❶) refers to a special instruction below which provides specific information to help you complete an item.

✓ We suggest you tear out the receipt in the Appendix and fill in the blanks as you follow the sample form and instructions below.

**Dating and Signing the Receipts**  Fill in the date and signature lines on your receipts when you distribute your stock certificates in return for the payments made by each of your shareholders (Section E below).

**Joint Shareholder and Joint Payments Note**  If you will issue shares to joint owners (see Section B above), you may, if you wish, show the names of both joint owners on the signature line in the sample receipt forms below (although a receipt showing the name of just one of the joint owners is sufficient). Again, this issue of whether a shareholder will take title to shares individually or jointly with another shareholder is primarily the concern of the shareholder, not the corporation. Of course, if two shareholders jointly contribute an item of property in return for the issuance of two separate blocks of individually owned shares, then you will wish to prepare a separate receipt for each of these shareholders. The particular details of each transaction will usually determine the most appropriate way to prepare the receipt form (normally, you will wish to make out the receipt in the name of the shareholder making the payment).

_Example 1:_ Teresa and Vernon Miller will pay $1,000 for 1,000 shares which they will take title to jointly as community property. You make out a receipt in the name of the shareholder who writes the check (if the funds are written from a joint checking account, you will naturally make the receipt form in the name of both spouses).

_Example 2:_ Mike and his brother, Burt, transfer a jointly owned lathe with a value of $5,000. Each will receive 250 shares. You make out a separate receipt for each brother, showing the transfer of a one-half interest in the lathe in return for the issuance of 250 shares.

## a. Receipt for Cash Payment

If shares are issued for cash, it is best to pay with a personal check (made payable by the shareholder to the corporation) since the shareholder's cancelled check can serve as an additional proof of payment. Here is a sample of the tear-out cash receipt form.

### Special Instructions

❶ Fill in the amount of cash being paid by the shareholder in this blank.

❷, ❸, ❺ and ❼ Type the name of the shareholder, the number of shares which will be issued to this shareholder, the name of your corporation and the name of your Treasurer in the appropriate blank as shown on the sample form.

❹ and ❻ After receiving payment from the shareholder (Section E below), your Treasurer should date and sign each cash receipt on the lines indicated.

---

SAMPLE RECEIPT FOR CASH PAYMENT

Receipt of $___(amount of cash payment)___ ❶ from ___(name of shareholder)___ ❷ representing payment in full for ___(number of shares)___ ❸ shares of the stock of this corporation is hereby acknowledged.

Dated: ___(date of payment)___ ❹

Name of Corporation: ___(name of corporation)___ ❺

By: ___(signature of Treasurer)___ ❻

___(typed name)___, Treasurer ❼

## b. Receipt for Cancellation of Indebtedness

If shares are issued in return for the cancellation of indebtedness owed by the corporation to a shareholder (as we've said, this is not a common means of payment for newly-formed corporations), you can prepare this tear-out receipt form shown below to document this type of stock issuance transaction. Attach a photocopy of the cancelled debt instrument (if you have one such as a promissory note, written loan agreement, etc.) to the receipt.

## Special Instructions

❶ and ❷  Insert the number of shares being issued to this shareholder and the name of the shareholder in these blanks.

❸  Indicate the date of the original loan made by the shareholder to the corporation.

❹  Show the total of the outstanding principal amount and accrued and unpaid interest (if any) owed on the loan in this blank.

❺ and ❻  Indicate the date of cancellation of the note in the date line on the receipt—this will be the date you actually distribute the shares. Provide this date and have the shareholder sign the receipt as part of Section E below.

---

SAMPLE FORM FOR CANCELLATION OF INDEBTEDNESS

The receipt of _____(number of shares)_____ ❶ shares of this corporation to _____(name of shareholder)_____ ❷ for the cancellation by _____(name of shareholder)_____ ❷ of a current loan outstanding to this corporation, dated _____(date of loan)_____ ❸, with a remaining unpaid principal amount and unpaid accrued interest, if any, totalling $_____(loan balance)_____ ❹ is hereby acknowledged.

Dated: _____(date of cancellation of loan)_____ ❺

_____(signature of shareholder)_____ ❻
(typed name of shareholder) ❷

## c. Receipt For Specific Items of Property

If specific items of property are being transferred to the corporation by a shareholder (other than the assets of an existing business—in this latter case, see Section D1 above), you may wish to prepare a receipt (bill of sale) for the property before issuing shares to the shareholder. Make sure that the property has first been delivered to the corporation and that any ownership papers ("pink slip" for a vehicle) have been signed over to the corporation. If you are transferring real property interests to your corporation, see the "Note on the Transfer of Real Property or Leases" in Section D1 above.

Below is a sample receipt (bill of sale) to document this type of stock transaction for one or more of your shareholders.

## Special Instructions

❶, ❷ and ❸  Show the number of shares being issued to this shareholder, the name of the corporation and the name of the shareholder in these blanks.

❹ Provide a short description in this space of the property being transferred to the corporation by this shareholder. This description should be brief but specific (e.g., make, model, and serial numbers of the property, vehicle ID and registration number for vehicles, etc.).

❺ and ❻  The date of the sale will be the date you distribute the stock certificate in return for the delivery of the property to the corporation. Complete this date line and have the shareholder (the transferor of the property) sign the receipt when you distribute your shares as part of Section E below.

---

SAMPLE BILL OF SALE FOR ITEMS OF PROPERTY

In consideration of the issuance of _____(number of shares)_____ ❶ shares of stock in and by _____(name of corporation)_____, ❷ _____(name of shareholder)_____ ❸ hereby sells, assigns, conveys, transfers, and delivers to the corporation all right, title and interest in and to the following property:

(Description of Property)❹

Dated: _____(date of sale)_____ ❺

_____(signature of shareholder)_____ ❻
(name of shareholder)❸, Transferor

### d. Receipt for Services Rendered the Corporation

If you are transferring shares in return for past services performed by a shareholder for the corporation (remember, you cannot issue shares in return for the performance of services which will be performed in the future by a shareholder—see Chapter 2F), prepare the tear-out form as explained below and have the shareholder date and sign a bill for these services as "Paid in Full" showing the date of payment (the date you distribute the shares in return for these services—Section E below).

**Note** As we've said, this is not a common type of stock issuance transaction for newly-formed corporations since (1) most work done for the corporation will occur after your stock issuance and (2) most contractors or other professionals who have performed services will want cash (not shares of stock) as payment for their services. However, if one of the principals of your closely-held corporation has performed services for the corporation prior to your stock issuance, this type of stock issuance transaction may make sense. Of, course, to avoid unfairness to your other stockholders, you will want to make sure that the shareholder charges no more than the prevailing rate for the services performed. For a further discussion of this type of payment for shares, see the "Stock Issuance Resolution" section in Step 5 of this chapter.

### Special Instructions

❶ ❷ and ❸ Show the name of the corporation, the name of the shareholder and the number of shares this person will receive in the blanks.

❹ Provide a short description in this space of the past services performed by the shareholder (e.g., the date(s), description and value of (amount billed for) past services performed by the shareholder).

❺ and ❻ When you distribute the shares in return for the past services (Section E below), provide the date of issuance of the shares and have the shareholder sign the receipt on the lines indicated above.

---

SAMPLE RECEIPT FOR SERVICES RENDERED

In consideration of the performance of the following services actually rendered to, or labor done for, ___(name of corporation)___ ❶, ___(name of shareholder)___ ❷, the provider of such services or labor done, hereby acknowledges the receipt of ___(number of shares)___ ❸ shares of stock in ___(name of corporation)___ ❶ as payment in full for these services:

*(Description of Past Services)*❹


Dated: ___(date of issuance)___ ❺


___(signature of shareholder)___ ❻
*(name of shareholder)*❸

## E. Distribute Your Stock Certificates

Now that you've filled in your stock certificates and prepared receipts for your shareholders (and a bill of sale if you are incorporating a prior business), issue your shares by distributing your stock certificates to your shareholders. Distribute your shares after receiving payment from each shareholder. When completing this step, make sure to do the following:

- Have each shareholder (or, if two persons take title to the shares, the joint shareholders) sign their stock certificate stub. Indicate the date of stock issuance on each stub.

- Date each stock certificate and have your President and Secretary sign each one (impress your corporate seal in the circular space at the bottom of each certificate). If you have ordered a corporate kit from Nolo Press, write the date of issuance in the "Time Became Owner" column for each shareholder in the Stock Transfer Ledger (Share Register) included with each kit.

- Complete the date and signature lines on your receipts (and bill of sale for the assets of a business if you have prepared this form) as explained in Section D above. Give each shareholder a copy of his or her receipt(s) and/or a copy of the bill of sale (if you have prepared one to document the transfer of the assets of a business to the corporation).

- Make sure to place all your completed stock stubs and completed copies of all receipts, bills of sale, and any attachments (inventory of assets of the prior business, cancelled notes, paid-in-full bill for services, etc.) in your corporate records book.

- If you have not already done so, make sure to prepare and file your Notice of Stock transaction with the California Department of Corporations (Step 7 of this chapter). Remember, you are required to file this Notice form within 15 calendar days of your sale of stock. For a fuller explanation, see Step 7 above.

**A Suggestion**  If you have stock certificates left over after filling out and distributing the certificates for your initial limited offering stock issuance, we suggest you tear them up and throw them away. Remember, future stock issuances or transfers may require a permit from the California Commissioner of Corporations, and you will need to consult a lawyer to ensure compliance with state and federal securities laws.

CONGRATULATIONS!

You have now completed your last incorporation step! There is one last point we wish to make which is central to the operation of your newly-formed corporation. One of the reasons you decided to form a corporation was to limit your personal liability in business affairs. So, from now on, whenever you sign a document on behalf of the corporation, be certain to do so in the following manner:

_(name of corporation)_
By : _(signature of corporate officer)_
  _(typed name)_, _(corporate title, e.g., President)_

If you fail to sign documents this way (on behalf of the corporation in your capacity as a corporate officer or director), you may be leaving yourself open to personal liability for corporate obligations. This is but one example designed to illustrate a basic premise of corporate life: From now on, it is extremely important for you to maintain the distinction between the corporation which you've organized and yourself (and the other principals of the corporation). As we've said, the corporation is a separate legal "person" and you want to make sure that other people, businesses, the IRS and the courts respect this distinction (see Chapter 21 for a further discussion).

**One Final Request**  Please read and follow the post-incorporation procedures contained in Chapter 6.

## Endnotes

[1]You can check available names by phone if you establish a pre-paid account. Call the Secretary of State at 916-323-3433 for information.

[2]Although the law generally affords individuals a preferential right to use their names in connection with their businesses, we'll use this opportunity to mention an exception to this rule and to general principles of trademark law under state "dilution of trademark" statutes. Specifically, even if you use your own surname in your corporate name and even though your products, services and geographical area of operation and marketing are unrelated to those of another business, if your corporate name contains a word or phrase which is the same or similar to the name of their mark, they can seek to enjoin (stop) you from using your name on the theory that your use will dilute the value of their mark. Without going into the technicalities here, our best advice, again, is to use common sense. If your proposed corporate name contains a word of phrase which is the same as a known mark, you may wish to add a word or phrase to your corporate name to make it clear that you are unaffiliated with the company that owns the mark (e.g., in the example in the text, the owners might decide to incorporate under the full name of the owner as "John P. Sears Bar & Grille, Inc."). This issue will not arise for most incorporators. If it does, we suggest you check with a trademark lawyer.

[3]Also, in an age where a huge number of service businesses—muffler shops, smog checks, eyeglass stores, house cleanup services, etc.—are being purchased nationally by large franchise chains, service businesses should be careful that their local name is not in conflict with a national name which may later move into their area.

[4]Authorizing additional shares here beyond the actual amount you plan to issue can be helpful should you wish to implement a stock bonus or option plan in the future (of course, corporate and tax formalities will have to be complied with in implementing plans of this type and, in all cases, future stock issuances will have to meet the requirements of the state and federal securities laws). If you don't authorize additional shares now and wish to increase the authorized number of shares stated in your Articles at a later date, you will have to prepare a special Amendment to your Articles of Incorporation and file it with the Secretary of State.

[5]See California Corporations Code § 110.

[6]Legal stationers and suppliers also sell corporate kits containing bylaws, minutes of the first meeting, printed stock certificates, as well as a corporate seal and a three-ring binder bearing the corporate name. These forms contain blanks which you must type in yourself. This book includes tear-out Bylaws and Minutes as well as other essential incorporation documents (Articles, California Stock Issuance Notice, shareholder representation letters, corporate name reservation and Articles cover letters, etc.). Consequently, the less expensive kits advertised at the back of the book contain all the "extras" you should need. Also, you should realize that the Bylaws and Minutes contained in these other kits are often generic or minimal in nature and will not correspond to our forms or the specific instructions contained in this book.

[7]In the unusual event that you have decided to set up your corporation as a "close" corporation (see Chapter 2A3) or if you will not be relying on the California limited offering exemption when offering and issuing your shares (e.g., you will obtain a permit for your shares or rely on the California small offering exemption—see Chapter 3B), you cannot use the stock certificates contained in this book (or the stock certificates included as part of the Nolo corporate kits). In either of these special situations, therefore, you will need to order special certificates with different stock certificate legends printed on their face. The lawyer who you will consult for special help in these situations can order the proper certificates for you.

[8]Note that we are also referring here to shares issued in return for "labor done," another category of consideration for shares specified in the Corporations Code (Chapter 2G). Our guess is that "labor done" is meant to distinguish contracting-type services performed for the corporation (construction of a building, etc.) as opposed to organizational or administrative type services. Since we see no real distinction between these types of services, we include this type of labor in our discussion here. Again, it is unlikely that you will issue shares to persons who have performed work for the corporation (unless they are close friends or business associates who will be active participants in your corporation)—contractors prefer money, not shares, as payment for services rendered.

[9]The limited offering exemption statute indicates that a failure to file this notice form within the time limit specified

by law will not result in your loss of the ability to rely on this exemption (perhaps in recognition of the fact that, in real life, we don't always get things done on time). However, if you don't file the notice on time, you must file the notice form within 15 business days after a demand by the Department, paying the fees which would have been due if you issued your shares under a permit procedure (a more costly process). While this may be of some comfort to you if you send in the notice form late, such a late filing is, in the opinion of some legal commentators, still a violation of the California securities laws and may subject you to other penalties. Our conclusion: Keep things simple and file this notice form before the specified deadline.

[10]Release 73-C of the Commissioner in conjunction with Section 25608(g) of the Corporations Code indicates that the value of securities (your initial shares) in this context is:

(1) the price to be paid for the shares (money) or the actual value of any consideration other than money to be received for the shares; or

(2) the value of the shares when issued; whichever is greater.

[11]See Division 6 of the California Commercial Code, starting with Section 6101.

[12]An exemption from the provisions of the bulk sales law also applies if the value of the assets being transferred is more than $5 million.

[13]Other exemptions to full compliance with the bulk sales act law exist. Again, see Division 6 of the California Commercial Code for specifics.

[14]Often a married person will take title to stock in his or her name alone. This is perfectly legal, even if community property is used to buy the shares. The other (nonlisted) spouse has a half interest in the stock even if the spouse's name doesn't appear, and can enforce this interest against the named spouse if necessary (i.e., at death or divorce). The names that appear on the certificates are of concern primarily to the shareowners, not the corporation.

[15]Definitions of community and separate property are discussed in detail (along with instructions on how to transfer separate property to community property and vice versa) in California Marriage and Divorce Law, by Warner, Ihara & Elias (Nolo Press).

[16]In earlier years many people placed property in joint tenancy to avoid probate. This is no longer necessary for spouses to do, as probate law has been simplified to the point that community property can be transferred to a surviving spouse easily and quickly. However, remember that each spouse is free to leave their half share of community property to anyone they wish. If they leave it to someone other than their surviving spouse, probate will normally be required.

[17]Broadly speaking, property up to a value of $10,000 can be given to an individual each year tax-free. If you wish to make a gift of stock worth more than this, see an accountant or an attorney.

# CHAPTER 6

# After Your Corporation Is Organized

At this point the organization of your corporation should be complete. As you know, operating any business, regardless of its size, involves paying attention to paperwork. In this chapter, we show you how to take a few final, necessary steps associated with organizing your corporation and how to comply with the various ongoing state and federal tax requirements which may apply to your corporation. We also discuss other formalities related to hiring employees and conducting corporate business. Due to the individual nature of each corporation and its business, it is not possible to discuss every tax for which your corporation may be liable. Rather, this discussion is intended to be a general guide to routine tax obligations that every corporation faces. Most of the tax forms we discuss below can be obtained from the IRS or California Franchise tax board (or your tax advisor).

## A.  Final Formalities After Forming Your Corporation

### 1.  File California Annual Domestic Stock Corporation Statement

Shortly after you have filed your Articles of Incorporation, you will receive an Annual Statement of Domestic Stock Corporation from the California Secretary of State's office. This form must be filled out and sent back to the Secretary within 90 days of the date your Articles were filed together with a small filing fee. The purpose of this form is to provide the public with current information as to the corporation's principal executive office, its directors and officers, etc.

Each year you will receive a new Domestic Stock Corporation Statement which must be filled out and returned by the due date indicated. If there has been no change in the information given in the last statement, the corporation need only indicate that no changes have occurred. In addition to filing each annual statement, the corporation may file a new statement any time during the year that the information contained in the last annual statement becomes inaccurate (new directors or officers, new executive office, etc.), and must file a new statement whenever the name or address of the corporation's agent for service of process is changed.

If the corporation fails to file the initial or annual statements within the appropriate time limits, it is subject to a fine and a possible suspension of corporate powers. Enough said: Make sure to follow this simple formality.

### 2.  File and Publish Fictitious Business Name Statement (If Appropriate)

We've already discussed the significance of fictitious business name statements in Chapter 5, Step 1A. To recap, if your corporation is to do business under a name other than the exact corporate name given in your Articles of Incorporation, you must file and publish a fictitious business name statement in the county of the corporation's principal place of business. For instance, if the name stated in your Articles is "Acme Business Computers, Inc.," and you plan to do business under the acronym, "ABC, Inc.," you should file and publish a Fictitious Business Name Statement. Remember, if you are the first to file this statement for a particular name in a particular county and if you actually engage in business in this county under this name, you are presumed to have the exclusive right to use this name in connection with your business in this county. Although this presumption can be overcome

## FOR MORE INFORMATION

An excellent source of legal information on starting a small business, generally, is The Legal Guide for Starting and Running a Small Business by Steingold (Nolo Press). Another excellent sourcebook of practical information, including financial ledgers and worksheets, is Small Time Operator, by Kamaroff (Bell Springs Publishing). See the back of the book for ordering information.

We suggest all incorporators obtain IRS Publication 509, Tax Calendars, prior to the beginning of each year. This pamphlet contains tax calendars showing the dates for corporate and employer filings during the year.

Further information on withholding, depositing, reporting and paying federal employment taxes can be found in IRS Publication 15, Circular E, Employer's Tax Guide, and the Publication 15 Supplement, as well as IRS Publication 937, Business Reporting. Further federal tax information can be found in IRS Publication 542, Tax Information on Corporations, and Publication 334, Tax Guide for Small Business.

Helpful information on accounting methods and bookkeeping procedures is contained in IRS Publication 538, Accounting Period and Methods, and Publication 583, Information for Business Taxpayers. These publications can be picked up at your local IRS office (or ordered by phone—call your local IRS office or try the toll-free IRS forms and publications request telephone number 1-800-TAX-FORM).

For information on withholding, contributing, paying and reporting California employment taxes, obtain the California Employer's Tax Guide (Publication DE 44) and Employer's Guide (Publication DE 4525—for unemployment and disability tax information) from your local California Employment Tax District Office.

(because another business has been using the same or a similar name first), this can be a helpful legal presumption.

The law (Section 17900, and following, of the California Business and Professions Code) requires that this statement be filed not later than 40 days from the time you start to transact business under your fictitious name. Also, you can be barred from using the courts to sue another business or person involving a transaction or contract in which you used your fictitious name until you first file and publish this statement.

To file and publish your fictitious business name statement, do the following:

1. Obtain a Fictitious Business Name Statement and instructions from a legal newspaper or from your local county clerk's office. If you haven't already done so (as suggested in Chapter 5, Step 1), you should check the county clerk's files (on microfiche display or a computer terminal, available for your use) to make sure that another business is not already using your fictitious name in the county.

2. Prepare the statement, following the instructions which apply to corporations.
   Note  If your fictitious business name (not your formal corporate name) includes a corporate designator such as "Incorporated," "Inc.," "Corporation," or "Corp.," you may have to provide proof that you are a corporation (by showing the county clerk a certified copy of your Articles).

3. File the original statement with the county clerk of the county in which the principal executive office of the corporation is located, paying the current filing fee. Obtain a file-endorsed copy of the statement from the county clerk.

4. Mail a copy of the statement to a qualified legal newspaper of general circulation in the county of the corporation's principal place of business for publication of your fictitious name statement and for filing of an affidavit of publication with the county clerk (including, of course, the newspaper's fee for this service). The newspaper will publish the statement once a week for four successive weeks and should file an affidavit of publication with the County Clerk for you. If you wish to make this filing yourself, follow the instructions accompanying the statement.

5. Place a copy of the endorsed-filed fictitious business name statement and endorsed-filed affidavit of publication in your corporate records book.

6. Make a note in your corporate records book to file another statement five years after your original filing (as explained in the instructions). The county clerk will not notify you of this renewal date.

7. Make similar filings (and publications of the statement), if you wish, in other counties in which you plan to use this name.

## 3. File Final Papers on Prior Business

If you have incorporated a pre-existing business (transferred the assets of a business to the corporation in return for shares), the prior business owners should file all papers needed to terminate their prior business (including final sales tax and employment tax returns, if appropriate (see Chapter 4J for a discussion of issues to consider when incorporating a prior business). Of course, you should close your previous business bank accounts and open up the corporate bank accounts indicated in the bank account resolution of your Minutes. In addition, if the old business holds any licenses or permits, these may need to be cancelled and new licenses or permits taken out in the name of the corporation (see Section D below).

## 4. Notify Creditors and Others of Dissolution of Prior Business

If you have incorporated a prior business or transferred its assets to the corporation, you should notify the creditors of the prior business and other interested parties (e.g., suppliers, others with whom you have open book accounts or lines of credit, etc.), in writing, of the termination and dissolution of the prior business and the fact that it is now a corporation.

If the prior business was a partnership, you should use the following notification procedure (nonpartnership businesses can simply send out a notification letter as discussed in 4 below).

1. Obtain at least two copies of a Notice of Dissolution of a Partnership form from a legal newspaper.
2. Fill out the Notice following the instructions on the form.
3. Send the completed Notice to a legal newspaper(s) circulated in the place or places at which the partnership business was regularly carried on with the request that they publish the Notice at such place(s) and file an affidavit of publication with the county clerk within 30 days after such publication. Include publication and filing fees with your request. Place copies of the notice form and the endorsed-filed affidavit of publication in your corporate records book.
4. Notify creditors (and other interested parties) by mail of the dissolution of the partnership (or other type of business). This notice should be in letter form, addressed and sent to each creditor, and contain the same information as that included in the published Notice (you will want to modify the information in the letter to show that it is directed to a particular individual or business, rather than the general public). You will want to indicate that your prior business has been dissolved and that you are now doing business as a corporation under your new corporate name. You should, of course, indicate your new corporate address if you have changed the location of your principal place of business. Place a copy of each letter in your corporate records book.

# B. Tax Forms—Federal

## 1. S Corporation Tax Election

If you have decided to elect federal S corporation tax status, and have included an authorizing resolution in your Minutes, you must make a timely election by filing IRS form 2553 and the consents of your shareholders (see Chapter 4C). If you haven't made your election yet (and haven't consulted a tax advisor as to the timing of the election—see Chapter 7B), call your advisor now and make sure the S corporation election form is sent in on time—you don't want to miss the deadline for this election.

Tax Year Note   Remember, S corporations must generally select a calendar tax year unless they are eligible to elect a fiscal tax year under IRS rules and regulations (see Chapter 4D). You will want to check with your tax advisor at this time and, if appropriate, make a timely election of a corporate fiscal tax year as well.

## 2. Federal Employer Identification Number

As soon as possible after your Articles are filed, your corporation must apply for a federal Employer Identification Number (EIN) by filling out IRS Form SS-4 and sending it to the nearest IRS center.[1] If you are incorporating a pre-existing sole proprietorship or partnership, you will need to apply for a new EIN. This number is needed for the employment tax returns and deposits discussed below.

## 3. Employee's Withholding Certificates

Each employee of the corporation must fill out and furnish the corporation with an Employee's Withholding Exemption Certificate (IRS Form W-4) on or before commencing employment. Obtain the most recent version of Form W-4. This form is used in determining the amount of income taxes to be withheld from the employee's wages.

Generally, any individual who receives compensation for services rendered the corporation subject to the control of the corporation, both as to what shall be done and how it should be done, is considered an employee. All shareholders of the corporation who receive salaries or wages for services as directors, officers, or nontitled personnel are considered employees of the corporation and must furnish a W-4.[2] Be careful of trying to avoid the payment of employment taxes by classifying people as "independent contractors." The law in this area is fuzzy, and the IRS (and the California Employment Development Department which oversees state unemployment taxes—see Section C3 below) are often obstinate. For more information, see IRS Publication 937.

## 4. Income and Social Security Tax Withholding

The corporation must withhold federal income tax and Social Security tax (FICA) from wages paid to each employee. These, as well as other employment taxes, are withheld and reported on a calendar-year basis, regardless of the tax year of the corporation, with returns and deposits being submitted on a quarterly or more frequent basis.

The amount of federal income tax withheld is based upon the employee's wage level, marital status and the number of allowances claimed on the employee's W-4.

Social Security taxes are withheld at a specific rate on an employee's wage base (the rate and wage-base figures change constantly). The corporation is required to make matching Social Security tax contributions for each employee.

## 5. Quarterly Withholding Returns and Deposits

The corporation is required to prepare and file a Withholding Return (IRS Form 941) for each quarter of the calendar year showing all income and Social Security taxes withheld from employees' wages as well as matching corporation social security tax contributions.

The corporation is required to deposit federal income and Social Security taxes on a monthly (or more frequent) basis in an authorized commercial or federal reserve bank. Payment for undeposited taxes owed at the end of a calendar quarter must be submitted with the quarterly return. Consult IRS Publication 15 for specifics.

## 6. Annual Wage and Tax Statement

The corporation is required to furnish two copies of the Wage and Tax Statement (IRS Form W-2) to each employee if income tax has been withheld from this person's wages or would have been withheld if the employee had claimed no more than one withholding exemption on his W-4. This form must show total wages paid and amounts deducted for income and social security taxes. A special six-part W-2 should be used in California to show state income tax and disability insurance contributions in addition to the required federal withholding information. W-2 forms must be furnished to employees no later than January 31 following the close of the calendar year.

The corporation must submit the original of each employee's previous year's W-2 form and an annual Transmittal of Income and Tax Statement (Form W-3) to the Social Security Administration on or before the last day of February following the close of the calendar year.

## 7. Federal Unemployment Tax

Most corporations are subject to the federal unemployment tax provisions. Under the tax statutes, your corporation is subject to paying Federal Unemployment Tax (FUTA) if, during the current or preceding calendar year, the corporation:

1. Paid wages of $1,500 or more during any calendar quarter, or
2. Had one or more employees for some portion of at least one day during each of 20 different calendar weeks. These 20 weeks do not have to be consecutive.

FUTA taxes are paid by the corporation and are not deducted from employees' wages. The FUTA tax is determined by the current rate and employee wage base and is paid by the corporation (as usual, rates and wage-base figures are subject to change). The corporation receives a credit for a percentage of this tax for California unemployment taxes paid or for having been granted a favorable experience rating by the state.

Generally, the corporation must deposit the tax in an authorized commercial or federal reserve bank within one month following the close of the quarter. For help in computing your quarterly FUTA tax liability, see instructions in IRS Publication 15. An annual FUTA return (IRS Form 940) must be filed by the corporation with the nearest IRS center by January 31 following the close of the calendar year for which the tax is due. Any tax still due is payable with the return.

## 8. Corporate Income Tax Return

A regular business corporation must file an annual Corporation Income Tax Return (IRS Form 1120) on or before the 15th day of the third month following the close of its tax year. A two-page Short-Form Corporation Income Tax Return (IRS Form 1120-A) is available for use by smaller corporations with gross receipts, total income and total assets of $500,000 or less. The corporation's tax year must correspond with the corporation's accounting period (the period for which corporate books are kept as specified in your Minutes) and is established by the first income tax return filed by the corporation. For a discussion of special corporate tax year requirements for S corporations and personal service corporations, see Chapter 4D.

Your first corporate first tax year may be a short year of less than twelve months. For example, if the corporate accounting period selected in the Minutes is the calendar year, January 1 to December 31, and the corporate existence began on March 13 (the date the Articles were filed), the corporation would establish its calendar tax year and report income for its first tax year by filing its first annual return on or before March 15 of the following year.

Note that this first return would be for the short year, March 13 to December 31. If the Minutes select a fiscal tax year, say from July 1 to June 30, and the corporate existence begins on May 1, the first return would be filed on or before August 15 for the first short year of May 1 to June 30.

## 9. S Corporation Income Tax Return

Even though federal S corporations are, for the most part, not subject to the payment of corporate income taxes, such corporations must file an annual U.S. Small Business Corporation Income Tax Return (IRS Form 1120S) on or before the 15th day of the third month following the close of the tax year for which the S corporation election is effective.

## 10. Corporate Employee and Shareholder Returns

Corporate employees and shareholders report employment and dividend income on their annual individual income tax returns (IRS Form 1040). S corporation shareholders report their pro rata share of undistributed corporate taxable income on Form 1040, Schedule E (as noted in Chapter 4C, S corporation shareholders may be required to estimate and pay taxes on this undistributed taxable income during the year).

## 11. Estimated Corporate Income Tax Payments

Corporations that expect to owe federal corporate income taxes at the end of their tax year (and most will), are required to make estimated tax payments. Estimated tax payments must be deposited in an authorized commercial or federal reserve bank. Both the due date and amount of each installment are computed by a formula based upon the corporation's income tax liability.

To determine corporate estimated tax liability and the date and amount of deposits, obtain IRS Form 1120-W. This form is to be used for computational purposes only and should not be filed with the IRS.

## C. Tax Forms—State

## 1. Corporate Estimated Tax Return

As already mentioned, a California profit corporation is required to pay an annual California franchise tax based upon its annual net taxable income, and must always pay the minimum annual franchise tax each

year. The corporation is required to estimate its franchise tax liability each year and make advance franchise tax payments each quarter. At least the minimum annual amount must be submitted with the corporation's first-quarter estimated tax payment each year.

Important   Don't confuse your first installment payment obligation with the initial franchise tax payment submitted with your Articles (Chapter 5, Step 2). The $800 franchise tax fee paid when filing Articles is for the privilege of doing business as a corporation only. Within the first quarter after incorporating, you are required to pay another $800 as an estimated tax payment—this represents the minimum franchise taxes owed for your first corporate tax year.

Further, if this first corporate tax year is a short year, another $800 minimum payment for your second tax year will be due shortly thereafter. For example, if your Articles are filed on December 9th and your corporation selects a calendar tax year, you will owe $800 for the first short tax year ending December 31st and another $800 for the second tax year beginning on January 1st. Both these payments are above and beyond the initial $800 paid when the corporation's Articles were filed with the Secretary of State.

Delaying the Start of Corporate Existence   To avoid paying franchise taxes for a short first tax year, you can ask the Secretary of State to file your papers on a specific day after receipt of your Articles, as explained in Chapter 5, Step 2. For example, you can mail your Articles to the Secretary of State at the beginning of December and ask in your cover letter that the Articles be filed on January 1st—by doing this you avoid being taxed for the first short tax year that would otherwise occur in December.

Exception for Very Short First Tax Years   There is a second way to avoid paying franchise taxes for a short first tax year: If you corporation has a first tax year less than one-half month and the corporation is inactive during this period, a state corporate tax return is not required and no franchise taxes are owed for the first tax year. For example, if a corporation selects a calendar tax year and files its Articles on December 20th, as long as the corporation is inactive during this period, it owes no franchise taxes for the first short tax year of December 20th-31st. The maximum number-of-days duration of this one-half month period varies depending upon the length of the month involved[3]— call the Franchise Tax Board in Sacramento for further information if you want to establish a short first tax year of less than one-half month.

## 2. Annual Corporate Franchise Tax Return

Your corporation must submit an annual California Corporate Franchise Tax Return (Form 100) on or before the 15th day of the third month following the close of its tax year. Payment must be submitted with the return for any portion of the tax due which wasn't estimated and paid during the year, as explained above.

## 3. Employer Registration Forms

All California corporations with employees (individuals who perform services for wages or fees) must register with the California Employment Development Department within 15 days of becoming subject to the California personal income tax withholding provisions and the California Unemployment Insurance Code (most are subject to these provisions immediately)— so, if you have employees, register right now if you haven't done so. Registration forms can be obtained by calling the nearest California Employment Tax District Office. If you are incorporating a pre-existing business, you'll need to re-register with the Employment Development Department (even though you may be given the same account number). See the Employer's Guide mentioned in the introduction to

this chapter and contact your local Employment Tax District Office for more information.

Caution   As noted in Section B3 above, be careful about classifying people who perform services for your corporation as "independent contractors." The EDD is particularly aggressive when it comes to collecting state unemployment taxes from businesses and this office routinely investigates employee complaints and conducts field audits to monitor compliance with California's Unemployment Insurance Code provisions.

## 4. State Withholding Allowance Certificate

Although the corporation can use the information contained in the federal W-4 form to compute the amount of state personal income taxes to be withheld from employees' wages, it is required to make a special California Withholding Allowance Certificate (DE-4) available to all its employees. Use of this form by the employee is optional. If not used, the corporation withholds state personal income tax from an employee's wages in accordance with the allowances on her federal W–4.

## 5. Personal Income Tax Withholding

The amount withheld by the corporation from employee wages for state personal income tax is based on tax tables which take into account the marital status, claimed allowances, and wages of the employee. These tables automatically allow for applicable exemptions and the standard deduction.

## 6. California Unemployment and Disability Insurance

California unemployment insurance contributions are paid by the corporation at its employer contribution rate shown on the Quarterly Withholding Return (DE-3) discussed below. Employer contributions are payable on the current employee wage-base amount.

The employer contribution rates vary and, except for new businesses, are based upon the employer's experience rating for each year. Experience ratings vary depending upon the extent of unemployment benefits paid to former employees of the corporation.[4]

Disability insurance contributions are paid by the employee.

## 7. Withholding Returns

A corporation is required in most cases to file Monthly Withholding Returns (Form DE-3M) with the state, indicating California personal income tax withholding and disability and unemployment tax contributions for each employee.

The corporation must file a Quarterly Withholding Return (Form DE-3) reporting personal income tax withholding and disability and unemployment insurance contributions for the previous quarter and pay any balance not already paid with Monthly Returns. For more specific information, consult the California Employer's Guide available from your local Employment Tax District Office as mentioned in the introduction to this chapter.

## 8. Annual Wage and Tax Statement

The corporation should prepare a six-part combined federal/state Annual Wage and Tax Statement, Form W-2, as discussed in Section B6 above. One copy must be filed with the state as explained below.

## 9. Annual Reconciliation of Income Tax Withholding

The corporation must file a completed Reconciliation of Income Tax Withheld Form (Form DE-43 or DE-43A) together with one copy of each employee's W-2 form, copies of California unemployment insurance filings and a total listing of all personal income tax withheld with the California Employment Development Department on or before February 28 following the close of each calendar year.

## 10. Sales Tax Permits and Returns

Subject to a few exceptions, every corporation which has gross receipts from the sale of personal property (e.g., merchandise sold to customers) in California must apply for a Seller's Permit by filing an application (Form BT-400) with the nearest office of the California Board of Equalization. This form also provides for registration as an employer with the Employment Development Department.[5] No fee is required in applying for and obtaining the Sales Tax permit.

Some applicants may be required to post a bond or other security for payment of future sales taxes (if you indicate that you plan to do a very small amount of resale business, this deposit amount may be waived). A separate permit is required for each place of business at which transactions relating to sales tax are customarily entered into with customers. Sales tax is added to the price of certain goods and is collected from the purchaser.

Wholesalers, as well as retailers, must obtain a permit. A wholesaler, however, is not required to collect sales tax from a retailer who holds a valid Seller's Permit and who buys items for resale to customers, provided a resale certificate is completed in connection with the transaction.

Sellers must file periodic sales and use tax returns, reporting and paying sales tax collected from customers. A seller must keep complete records of all business transactions, including sales, receipts, purchases, and other expenditures, and have them available for inspection by the board at all times.

## D. Licenses and Permits

Many businesses, whether operating as corporations or not, are required to obtain state licenses or permits before commencing business. Licenses and permits are usually based upon one or more requirements relating to registration, experience, education, examination scores, and adequate bonding.

Your corporation should obtain all proper licenses before commencing corporate operations. Even if you are incorporating an already licensed business, you must comply with any corporate license requirement in your field. Some businesses must obtain licenses in the name of the corporation, while others must obtain them in the name of supervisory corporate personnel. For specific information relating to corporate licensing requirements, check with a local Department of Consumer Affairs office.[6] They will either refer you to one of their boards or to an appropriate outside agency.

## E. Workers' Compensation Insurance

With some exceptions, all employees of a corporation, whether officers or otherwise, are required to be covered by Workers' Compensation Insurance. Rates vary depending on the salary level and risk associated with an employee's job. Generally, if all of the officers are the only shareholders of the corporation, they do not have to be covered by Workers' Compensation. Also, if directors are only paid travel expenses for attending meetings, they may be exempt from coverage (although flat per-meeting payments will generally make them subject to coverage)—this is a blurry area so check with your local State Compensation Insurance Commission office for names of carriers, rates and extent of required coverage in all cases.

## F. Private Insurance Coverage

Corporations, like other businesses, should carry the usual kinds of insurance to prevent undue loss in the event of an accident, fire, theft, etc. Although the corporate form may insulate shareholders from personal loss, it won't prevent corporate assets from being jeopardized by such eventualities. Basic commercial coverage should be obtained and often includes coverage for autos, inventory, personal injuries on premises, etc. Additional coverage for product liability, directors' and officers' liability and other specialized types of insurance may also be appropriate (of course, these policies may be more difficult, i.e., costly, for a closely-held corporation to obtain). Many smaller companies elect to have a large deductible to keep premium payments down. Obviously, there are a number of options to consider when putting together your corporate insurance package. The best advice here is to talk to a few experienced commercial insurance brokers and compare rates and areas and extent of coverage before deciding. Look for someone who suggests ways to get essential coverage for an amount you can live with—not someone who wants to sell you a policy that will protect you from all possible risks. In the first place, this type of policy really doesn't exist. Secondly, even if it did, you probably wouldn't want to pay the price. ■

## Endnotes

[1]You can fax your SS-4 form to the IRS by calling 1-606-292-5760. The IRS should call back within a day or two with your assigned number.

[2]Directors, with certain exceptions, are not considered employees if they are paid only for attending board meetings. However, if they are paid for other services or are salaried employees of the corporation, they will be considered employees whose wages are subject to the employment taxes discussed below—check with the IRS and your local state Employment Tax District office.

[3]FTB rules say that a short tax year will be ignored if, in the case of a 28-day month, the Articles were filed on the 15th of the month or later; if Articles were filed during a 29- or 30-day month, they must have been filed on the 16th or later; and for a 31-day month, on the 17th or later. Double-check these requirements with the FTB prior to filing Articles if you wish to avoid payment of franchise taxes for a short (one-half month or less) initial corporate tax year.

[4]An aside: While officers are employees for purposes of unemployment insurance contributions, unemployment benefits may be denied to them if they are laid off or terminated by the corporation if the corporation pays them any "fringes" while they are not working (e.g., profit-sharing, pension benefits, etc.). Also, if the officers and directors are the only shareholders of the corporation, they won't be eligible for benefits unless the corporation is subject to paying federal unemployment taxes (see Section B7 of this chapter). Check with your local Employment Tax District Office about this when you first contact them.

[5]The State Board of Equalization also collects an annual environmental fee from corporations doing business in California with 50 or more employees. Corporations with 50 to 100 employees pay $100 per year. Call the Excise Tax Division of the Board in Sacramento for more information.

[6]The California License Handbook, published by the California Department of Commerce, is a comprehensive guide to California license requirements, as well as a thorough sourcebook on California's regulatory agencies and the red tape involved in doing business in California. Call the Department of Commerce, Office of Small Business in Sacramento (1-916-445-6546) to order this publication.

# Lawyers and Accountants

# A.  Lawyers

As we've mentioned previously, consulting an experienced attorney prior to incorporating, to review your incorporation papers and suggest any specific modifications you may need to make in view of the unique needs surrounding your incorporation, is often a good idea. Reviewing your incorporation papers with an attorney is a sensible way to insure that all of your papers are up-to-date and meet your specialized needs.

A consultation with a lawyer to review the forms and organizational aspects of your incorporation is quite different than having him do, or redo, it all for you. The lawyer should have experience in small business incorporations, should be prepared to answer your specific, informed questions, and should review, not rewrite (unless absolutely necessary), the forms you have prepared.

Throughout this book we have flagged areas of potential complexity where a degree of customization may be warranted. If any of these loom large to you, go over them with an experienced lawyer before filing your Articles of Incorporation. For example, the following areas will specifically require a lawyer's (or other professional's) services if they arise in the process of your incorporation:

- One of your proposed shareholders needs (or wishes) to specifically designate and to rely on the advice of a lawyer, accountant or other professional advisor in order to be eligible as a suitable shareholder (Category 5) under the California limited offering exemption—Chapter 5, Step 6, and Chapter 3B.
- You wish to add customized stock buy-out provisions to your Bylaws or prepare a special shareholders' buy/sell agreement for the repurchase of shares in your corporation—Chapter 5, Step 4.
- In the unusual event that you wish to form a California statutory close corporation, you will need a lawyer's help in preparing a special close corporation shareholders' agreement and in adding the required close corporation provisions to your Articles of Incorporation and stock certificates—Chapter 5, Step 2, and Chapter 2A3.

Assuming you do decide to consult a lawyer, you may well ask, "What type of lawyer should I consult?" The best lawyer to choose is someone whom you both personally know and trust and who has lots of experience advising small businesses. The next best is usually a small business expert whom a friend (with her own business experience) recommends. If you make some calls, you can almost always find someone via this excellent, "word of mouth" approach. Far less preferable, although occasionally necessary as a last resort, is to select names from the phone book and begin calling. As part of doing this, you may also call a local bar association referral service for a recommendation. We don't advise this approach as many referral services are operated on a strict rotating basis—you'll get the name of the next lawyer who says he handles small businesses (experienced lawyers with plenty of business are rarely on these lists in the first place). Also realize that there is a growing movement to private (and highly suspect) referral services that often refer people to themselves—watch out for these.

When you call a prospective lawyer (not just her law office), you can probably get a good idea of how the person operates by paying close attention to the way your call is handled. Is the lawyer available, or is your call returned promptly? Is the lawyer willing to spend at least a few minutes talking to you to determine if she is really the best person for the job? Do you get a good personal feeling from your conversation? Oh, and one more thing: Be sure to get the hourly rate the lawyer will charge set in advance.[1] If you are using this book, you will probably not be impressed by someone who charges $350 per hour to support an office on top of the tallest building in town.

**Looking Up the Law Yourself**  Many incorporators may wish to research legal information not covered in this book on their own. County law libraries are open to the public (you will not be asked to produce a bar card before being helped) and are not difficult to use once you understand how the information is categorized and stored. They are an invaluable source of corporate and general business forms, corporate tax procedures and information, etc. Research librarians will usually go out of their way to help you find the right statute, form or background reading on any corporate or tax issue. If you are interested in doing self-help legal research, an excellent source of information on how to break the code of the law libraries is *Legal Research: How to Find and Understand the Law*, by Elias and Levinkind (Nolo Press). Also, you may wish to obtain a copy of the California Corporations Code to look up Code sections yourself (an edition published by West Publishing Co. is available through Nolo Press).

## B. Accountants and Tax Advisors

As you already know, organizing and operating a corporation involves a significant amount of financial and tax work, and many important decisions need to be made. Again, we have flagged areas of special consideration involving financial planning and specific corporate tax issues throughout the manual. A few of the more central questions and issues are listed below:

- Should you elect federal S corporation tax status?—Chapter 4C.
- Are you eligible for Section 351 tax-free exchange treatment of your incorporation?—Chapter 4, Section F.
- Do you need help in selecting your corporate tax year?—Chapter 5, Step 7
- Do you wish to set up IRS qualified fringe benefit packages for yourself and other employees?—Chapter 4G.

- Will you rely on an accountant or other professional in setting up your corporate books (double-entry journals and general ledger) and in making ongoing corporate and employment tax filings?—See the discussion below and Chapter 6, Sections B and C.
- Do you need to obtain a valuation of the assets of a prior business being transferred to your corporation in return for shares?—Chapter 5, Step 8.

Generally, although we tend to use the terms tax advisor, financial consultant and accountant interchangeably, you may prefer to refer these initial incorporation considerations to a certified public accountant with corporate experience. For general assistance and advice, a qualified financial planner may also be very helpful.

Once your initial incorporation questions have been answered, your corporation set up and your books established, you may want to have routine tax filings and bookkeeping tasks performed by corporate personnel or independent contractors who have been trained in bookkeeping and tax matters (in many instances trained or recommended by the accountant you have previously consulted). Most corporations will have at least their annual corporate returns handled by their accountant or other tax return preparer.

For future financial advice, you may wish to contact an officer in the corporate department of the bank where you keep your corporate account(s). Banks are an excellent source of financial advice, particularly if they will be corporate creditors—after all, they will have a stake in the success of your corporation. Further, the Small Business Administration can prove to be an ideal source of financial and tax information and resources (as well as financing in some cases).

Whatever your arrangement for financial or tax advice and assistance, you may wish to order the IRS publications listed in the "For More Information" box in Chapter 6 to familiarize yourself with some of the tax and bookkeeping aspects of operating a corporation.[2]

When you select an accountant, bookkeeper, financial advisor, etc., the same considerations apply as when selecting a lawyer. Choose someone you know or whom a friend with business experience recommends. Be as specific as you can regarding the services you wish performed and find someone with experience in corporate taxation and with corporate and employee tax returns and requirements. ■

## Endnotes

[1]Rules of the State Bar require a lawyer to provide you with a written fee agreement in advance if the fee for services will exceed certain a certain amount (or in contingency fee cases).

[2]Two excellent self-help sources, referred to earlier in this book, are *How to Write a Business Plan,* by McKeever, and *Small Time Operator,* by Kamaroff, available from Nolo Press.

# $A$PPENDIX

# Tear-Out Forms

Request for Reservation of Corporate Name

Cover Letter for Filing Articles

Articles of Incorporation

Bylaws

Waiver of Notice and Consent to Holding of First Meeting of Board of Directors

Minutes of First Meeting of the Board of Directors

Notice of Transaction Pursuant to Corporations Code Section 25102(f)

Stock Certificates

# REQUEST FOR RESERVATION OF CORPORATE NAME

Secretary of State
Corporate Name Availability
1230 J Street
Sacramento, CA 95814

Secretary of State:

    Please reserve the first available corporate name from the list below for my use. My proposed corporate names, listed in order of preference, are as follows:

_____

_____

_____

_____

    I enclose a check or money order for the required reservation fee, payable to the "Secretary of State."

Sincerely,

ARTICLES OF INCORPORATION

of

_____

ONE: The name of this corporation is _____
_____ .

TWO: The purpose of this corporation is to engage in any lawful act
or activity for which a corporation may be organized under the General
Corporation Law of California other than the banking business, the trust
company business or the practice of a profession permitted to be
incorporated by the California Corporations Code.

THREE: The name and address in this state of the corporation's
initial agent for service of process is: _____
_____
_____ .

FOUR: This corporation is authorized to issue only one class of
shares of stock which shall be designated common stock. The total number
of shares it is authorized to issue is _____
_____ shares.

FIVE: The names and addresses of the persons who are appointed to
act as the initial directors of this corporation are:

Name                                  Address

_____          _____

_____          _____

_____          _____

_____          _____

_____          _____

SIX: The liability of the directors of the corporation for monetary damages shall be eliminated to the fullest extent permissible under California law.

SEVEN: The corporation is authorized to indemnify the directors and officers of the corporation to the fullest extent permissible under California law.

IN WITNESS WHEREOF, the undersigned, being all the persons named above as the initial directors, have executed these Articles of Incorporation.


Dated: _____    _____

                               _____

                               _____

                               _____

                               _____


The undersigned, being all the persons named above as the initial directors, declare that they are the persons who executed the foregoing Articles of Incorporation, which execution is their act and deed.


Dated: _____    _____

                               _____

                               _____

                               _____

                               _____

COVER LETTER FOR FILING ARTICLES

Secretary of State
Corporate Filing Section
1230 J Street
Sacramento, CA 95814


Re: _____


Dear Secretary of State:

      I enclose an original and two copies of the proposed Articles of
Incorporation of _____ .

      Also enclosed is payment in the amount of $900.00 for the following
fees:

|  |  |
|---|---|
| Filing Articles of Incorporation | $ 100.00 |
| First year annual franchise tax | 800.00 |
| TOTAL | $ 900.00 |

      Please file the original Articles and return the certified copies
to me at the above address.


Very truly yours,



_____
                              , Incorporator

BYLAWS

of

_____

ARTICLE I
OFFICES

SECTION 1. PRINCIPAL EXECUTIVE OFFICE

The location of the principal executive office of the corporation shall be fixed by the board of directors. It may be located at any place within or outside the state of California. The secretary of this corporation shall keep the original or a copy of these bylaws, as amended to date, at the principal executive office of the corporation if this office is located in California. If this office is located outside California, the bylaws shall be kept at the principal business office of the corporation within California. The officers of this corporation shall cause the corporation to file an annual statement with the Secretary of State of California as required by Section 1502 of the California Corporations Code specifying the street address of the corporation's principal executive office.

SECTION 2. OTHER OFFICES

The corporation may also have offices at such other places as the board of directors may from time to time designate, or as the business of the corporation may require.

ARTICLE II
SHAREHOLDERS' MEETINGS

SECTION 1. PLACE OF MEETINGS

All meetings of the shareholders shall be held at the principal executive office of the corporation or at such other place as may be determined by the board of directors.

SECTION 2. ANNUAL MEETINGS

The annual meeting of the shareholders shall be held each year on

_____ ,

at which time the shareholders shall elect a board of directors and transact any other proper business. If this date falls on a legal holiday, then the meeting shall be held on the following business day at the same hour.

## SECTION 3. SPECIAL MEETINGS

Special meetings of the shareholders may be called by the board of directors, the chairperson of the board of directors, the president, or by one or more shareholders holding at least 10 percent of the voting power of the corporation.

## SECTION 4. NOTICES OF MEETINGS

Notices of meetings, annual or special, shall be given in writing to shareholders entitled to vote at the meeting by the secretary or an assistant secretary or, if there be no such officer, or in the case of his or her neglect or refusal, by any director or shareholder.

Such notices shall be given either personally or by first-class mail or other means of written communication, addressed to the shareholder at the address of such shareholder appearing on the stock transfer books of the corporation or given by the shareholder to the corporation for the purpose of notice. Notice shall be given not less than ten (10) nor more than sixty (60) days before the date of the meeting.

Such notice shall state the place, date, and hour of the meeting and (1) in the case of a special meeting, the general nature of the business to be transacted, and that no other business may be transacted, or (2) in the case of an annual meeting, those matters which the board at the time of the mailing of the notice, intends to present for action by the shareholders, but, subject to the provisions of Section 6 of this Article, any proper matter may be presented at the annual meeting for such action. The notice of any meeting at which directors are to be elected shall include the names of the nominees which, at the time of the notice, the board of directors intends to present for election. Notice of any adjourned meeting need not be given unless a meeting is adjourned for forty-five (45) days or more from the date set for the original meeting.

## SECTION 5. WAIVER OF NOTICE

The transactions of any meeting of shareholders, however called and noticed, and wherever held, are as valid as though had at a meeting duly held after regular call and notice, if a quorum is present, whether in person or by proxy, and if, either before or after the meeting, each of the persons entitled to vote, not present in person or by proxy, signs a written waiver of notice or a consent to the holding of the meeting or an approval of the minutes thereof. All such waivers or consents shall be filed with the corporate records or made part of the minutes of the meeting. Neither the business to be transacted at the meeting, nor the purpose of any annual or special meeting of shareholders need be specified in any written waiver of notice, except as provided in Section 6 of this Article.

SECTION 6. SPECIAL NOTICE AND WAIVER OF NOTICE REQUIREMENTS

Except as provided below, any shareholder approval at a meeting, with respect to the following proposals, shall be valid only if the general nature of the proposal so approved was stated in the notice of meeting, or in any written waiver of notice:

a. Approval of a contract or other transaction between the corporation and one or more of its directors or between the corporation and any corporation, firm, or association in which one or more of the directors has a material financial interest, pursuant to Section 310 of the California Corporations Code;

b. Amendment of the Articles of Incorporation after any shares have been issued pursuant to Section 902 of the California Corporations Code;

c. Approval of the principal terms of a reorganization pursuant to Section 1201 of the California Corporations Code;

d. Election to voluntarily wind up and dissolve the corporation pursuant to Section 1900 of the California Corporations Code;

e. Approval of a plan of distribution of shares as part of the winding up of the corporation pursuant to Section 2007 of the California Corporations Code.

Approval of the above proposals at a meeting shall be valid with or without such notice, if it is by the unanimous approval of those entitled to vote at the meeting.

SECTION 7. ACTION WITHOUT MEETING

Any action that may be taken at any annual or special meeting of shareholders may be taken without a meeting and without prior notice if a consent, in writing, setting forth the action so taken, shall be signed by the holders of outstanding shares having not less than the minimum number of votes that would be necessary to authorize or take such action at a meeting at which all shares entitled to vote thereon were present and voted.

Unless the consents of all shareholders entitled to vote have been solicited in writing, notice of any shareholders' approval, with respect to any one of the following proposals, without a meeting, by less than unanimous written consent shall be given at least ten (10) days before the consummation of the action authorized by such approval:

a. Approval of a contract or other transaction between the corporation and one or more of its directors or another corporation, firm or association in which one or more of its directors has a material financial interest, pursuant to Section 310 of the California Corporations Code;

b. To indemnify an agent of the corporation pursuant to Section 317 of the California Corporations Code;

c. To approve the principal terms of a reorganization, pursuant to Section 1201 of the California Corporations Code; or

d. Approval of a plan of distribution as part of the winding up of the corporation pursuant to Section 2007 of the California Corporations Code.

Prompt notice shall be given of the taking of any other corporate action approved by shareholders without a meeting by less than a unanimous written consent to those shareholders entitled to vote who have not consented in writing.

Notwithstanding any of the foregoing provisions of this section, and except as provided in Article III, Section 4 of these bylaws, directors may not be elected by written consent except by the unanimous written consent of all shares entitled to vote for the election of directors.

A written consent may be revoked by a writing received by the corporation prior to the time that written consents of the number of shares required to authorize the proposed action have been filed with the secretary of the corporation, but may not be revoked thereafter. Such revocation is effective upon its receipt by the secretary of the corporation.

## SECTION 8. QUORUM AND SHAREHOLDER ACTION

A majority of the shares entitled to vote, represented in person or by proxy, shall constitute a quorum at a meeting of shareholders. If a quorum is present, the affirmative vote of the majority of shareholders represented at the meeting and entitled to vote on any matter shall be the act of the shareholders, unless the vote of a greater number is required by law and except as provided in the following paragraphs of this section.

The shareholders present at a duly called or held meeting at which a quorum is present may continue to transact business until adjournment notwithstanding the withdrawal of enough shareholders to leave less than a quorum, if any action is approved by at least a majority of the shares required to constitute a quorum.

In the absence of a quorum, any meeting of shareholders may be adjourned from time to time by the vote of a majority of the shares represented either in person or by proxy, but no other business may be transacted except as provided in the foregoing provisions of this section.

## SECTION 9. VOTING

Only shareholders of record on the record date fixed for voting purposes by the board of directors pursuant to Article VIII, Section 3 of these bylaws, or, if there be no such date fixed, on the record dates given below, shall be entitled to vote at a meeting.

If no record date is fixed:

a. The record date for determining shareholders entitled to notice of, or to vote, at a meeting of shareholders, shall be at the close of business on the business day next preceding the day on which notice is given or, if notice is waived, at the close of business on the business day next preceding the day on which the meeting is held.

b. The record date for determining the shareholders entitled to give consent to corporate actions in writing without a meeting, when no prior action by the board is necessary, shall be the day on which the first written consent is given.

c. The record date for determining shareholders for any other purpose shall be at the close of business on the day on which the board adopts the resolution relating thereto, or the 60th day prior to the date of such other action, whichever is later.

Every shareholder entitled to vote shall be entitled to one vote for each share held, except as otherwise provided by law, by the Articles of Incorporation or by other provisions of these bylaws. Except with respect to elections of directors, any shareholder entitled to vote may vote part of his or her shares in favor of a proposal and refrain from voting the remaining shares or vote them against the proposal. If a shareholder fails to specify the number of shares he or she is affirmatively voting, it will be conclusively presumed that the shareholder's approving vote is with respect to all shares the shareholder is entitled to vote.

At each election of directors, shareholders shall not be entitled to cumulate votes unless the candidates' names have been placed in nomination before the commencement of the voting and a shareholder has given notice at the meeting, and before the voting has begun, of his or her intention to cumulate votes. If any shareholder has given such notice, then all shareholders entitled to vote may cumulate their votes by giving one candidate a number of votes equal to the number of directors to be elected multiplied by the number of his or her shares or by distributing such votes on the same principle among any number of candidates as he or she thinks fit. The candidates receiving the highest number of votes, up to the number of directors to be elected, shall be elected. Votes cast against a candidate or which are withheld shall have no effect. Upon the demand of any shareholder made before the voting begins, the election of directors shall be by ballot rather than by voice vote.

SECTION 10. PROXIES

Every person entitled to vote shares may authorize another person or persons to act by proxy with respect to such shares by filing a proxy with the secretary of the corporation. For purposes of these bylaws, a "proxy" means a written authorization signed or an electronic transmission authorized by a shareholder or the shareholder's attorney in fact giving another person or persons power to vote with respect to the shares of the shareholder. "Signed" for the purpose of these bylaws means the placing of the shareholder's name or other authorization on the proxy (whether by manual signature, typewriting, telegraphic, or electronic transmission or otherwise) by the shareholder or the shareholder's attorney in fact. A proxy may be transmitted by an oral telephonic transmission if it is submitted with information from which it may be determined that the proxy was authorized by the shareholder, or his or her attorney in fact.

A proxy shall not be valid after the expiration of eleven (11) months from the date thereof unless otherwise provided in the proxy. Every proxy shall continue in full force and effect until revoked by the person executing it prior to the vote pursuant thereto, except as otherwise provided in Section 705 of the California Corporations Code.

ARTICLE III
DIRECTORS

SECTION 1. POWERS

Subject to any limitations in the Articles of Incorporation and to the provisions of the California Corporations Code, the business and affairs of the corporation shall be managed and all corporate powers shall be exercised by, or under the direction of, the board of directors.

SECTION 2. NUMBER

The authorized number of directors shall be _____ .

After issuance of shares, this bylaw may only be amended by approval of a majority of the outstanding shares entitled to vote; provided, moreover, that a bylaw reducing the fixed number of directors to a number less than five (5) cannot be adopted unless in accordance with the additional requirements of Article IX of these bylaws.

## SECTION 3. ELECTION AND TENURE OF OFFICE

The directors shall be elected at the annual meeting of the shareholders and hold office until the next annual meeting and until their successors have been elected and qualified.

## SECTION 4. VACANCIES

A vacancy on the board of directors shall exist in the case of death, resignation, or removal of any director or in case the authorized number of directors is increased, or in case the shareholders fail to elect the full authorized number of directors at any annual or special meeting of the shareholders at which any director is elected. The board of directors may declare vacant the office of a director who has been declared of unsound mind by an order of court or who has been convicted of a felony.

Except for a vacancy created by the removal of a director, vacancies on the board of directors may be filled by approval of the board or, if the number of directors then in office is less than a quorum, by (1) the unanimous written consent of the directors then in office, (2) the affirmative vote of a majority of the directors then in office at a meeting held pursuant to notice or waivers of notice complying with this Article of these bylaws, or (3) a sole remaining director. Vacancies occurring on the board by reason of the removal of directors may be filled only by approval of the shareholders. Each director so elected shall hold office until the next annual meeting of the shareholders and until his or her successor has been elected and qualified.

The shareholders may elect a director at any time to fill a vacancy not filled by the directors. Any such election by written consent other than to fill a vacancy created by the removal of a director requires the consent of a majority of the outstanding shares entitled to vote.

Any director may resign effective upon giving written notice to the chairperson of the board of directors, the president, the secretary or to the board of directors unless the notice specifies a later time for the effectiveness of the resignation. If the resignation is effective at a later time, a successor may be elected to take office when the resignation becomes effective. Any reduction of the authorized number of directors does not remove any director prior to the expiration of such director's term in office.

## SECTION 5. REMOVAL

Any or all of the directors may be removed without cause if the removal is approved by a majority of the outstanding shares entitled to vote, subject to the provisions of Section 303 of the California Corporations Code. Except as provided in Sections 302, 303 and 304 of the

California Corporations Code, a director may not be removed prior to the expiration of the director's term of office.

The Superior Court of the proper county may, on the suit of shareholders holding at least 10 percent of the number of outstanding shares of any class, remove from office any director in case of fraudulent or dishonest acts or gross abuse of authority or discretion with reference to the corporation and may bar from re-election any director so removed for a period prescribed by the court. The corporation shall be made a party to such action.

SECTION 6. PLACE OF MEETINGS

Meetings of the board of directors shall be held at any place, within or without the State of California, which has been designated in the notice of the meeting or, if not stated in the notice or if there is no notice, at the principal executive office of the corporation or as may be designated from time to time by resolution of the board of directors. Meetings of the board may be held through use of conference telephone or similar communications equipment, as long as all directors participating in the meeting can hear one another.

SECTION 7. ANNUAL, REGULAR AND SPECIAL DIRECTORS' MEETINGS

An annual meeting of the board of directors shall be held without notice immediately after and at the same place as the annual meeting of the shareholders.

Other regular meetings of the board of directors shall be held at such times and places as may be fixed from time to time by the board of directors. Call and notice of these regular meetings shall not be required.

Special meetings of the board of directors may be called by the chairperson of the board, the president, vice president, secretary, or any two directors. Special meetings of the board of directors shall be held upon four (4) days' notice by mail, or forty-eight (48) hours' notice delivered personally or by telephone or telegraph. A notice or waiver of notice need not specify the purpose of any special meeting of the board of directors.

If any meeting is adjourned for more than 24 hours, notice of the adjournment to another time or place shall be given before the time of the resumed meeting to all directors who were not present at the time of adjournment of the original meeting.

SECTION 8. QUORUM AND BOARD ACTION

A quorum for all meetings of the board of directors shall consist of _____ of the authorized number of directors until changed by amendment to this article of these bylaws.

Every act or decision done or made by a majority of the directors present at a meeting duly held at which a quorum is present is the act of the board, subject to the provisions of Section 310 (relating to the approval of contracts and transactions in which a director has a material financial interest); the provisions of Section 311 (designation of committees); and Section 317(e) (indemnification of directors) of the California Corporations Code. A meeting at which a quorum is initially present may continue to transact business notwithstanding the withdrawal of directors, if any action taken is approved by at least a majority of the required quorum for such meeting.

A majority of the directors present at a meeting may adjourn any meeting to another time and place, whether or not a quorum is present at the meeting.

SECTION 9. WAIVER OF NOTICE

The transactions of any meeting of the board, however called and noticed or wherever held, are as valid as though undertaken at a meeting duly held after regular call and notice if a quorum is present and if, either before or after the meeting, each of the directors not present signs a written waiver of notice, a consent to holding the meeting, or an approval of the minutes thereof. All such waivers, consents, and approvals shall be filed with the corporate records or made a part of the minutes of the meeting. Waivers of notice or consents need not specify the purpose of the meeting.

SECTION 10. ACTION WITHOUT MEETING

Any action required or permitted to be taken by the board may be taken without a meeting, if all members of the board shall individually or collectively consent in writing to such action. Such written consent or consents shall be filed with the minutes of the proceedings of the board. Such action by written consent shall have the same force and effect as a unanimous vote of the directors.

SECTION 11. COMPENSATION

No salary shall be paid directors, as such, for their services but, by resolution, the board of directors may allow a reasonable fixed sum and expenses to be paid for attendance at regular or special meetings. Nothing contained herein shall prevent a director from serving the corporation in any other capacity and receiving compensation therefor. Members of special or standing committees may be allowed like compensation for attendance at meetings.

# ARTICLE IV
## OFFICERS

### SECTION 1. OFFICERS

The officers of the corporation shall be a president, a vice president, a secretary, and a treasurer who shall be the chief financial officer of the corporation. The corporation also may have such other officers with such titles and duties as shall be determined by the board of directors. Any number of offices may be held by the same person.

### SECTION 2. ELECTION

All officers of the corporation shall be chosen by, and serve at the pleasure of, the board of directors.

### SECTION 3. REMOVAL AND RESIGNATION

An officer may be removed at any time, either with or without cause, by the board. An officer may resign at any time upon written notice to the corporation given to the board, the president, or the secretary of the corporation. Any such resignation shall take effect at the date of receipt of such notice or at any other time specified therein. The removal or resignation of an officer shall be without prejudice to the rights, if any, of the officer or the corporation under any contract of employment to which the officer is a party.

### SECTION 4. PRESIDENT

The president shall be the chief executive officer and general manager of the corporation and shall, subject to the direction and control of the board of directors, have general supervision, direction, and control of the business and affairs of the corporation. He or she shall preside at all meetings of the shareholders and directors and be an ex-officio member of all the standing committees, including the executive committee, if any, and shall have the general powers and duties of management usually vested in the office of president of a corporation and shall have such other powers and duties as may from time to time be prescribed by the board of directors or these bylaws.

### SECTION 5. VICE PRESIDENT

In the absence or disability of the president, the vice presidents, in order of their rank as fixed by the board of directors (or if not ranked, the vice president designated by the board) shall perform all the duties of the president and, when so acting, shall have all the powers of, and be subject to all the restrictions upon, the president. Each vice president shall have such other powers and perform such other duties as may from time to time be prescribed by the board of directors or these bylaws.

SECTION 6. SECRETARY

The secretary shall keep, or cause to be kept, at the principal executive office of the corporation, a book of minutes of all meetings of directors and shareholders. The minutes shall state the time and place of holding of all meetings; whether regular or special, and if special, how called or authorized; the notice thereof given or the waivers of notice received; the names of those present at directors' meetings; the number of shares present or represented at shareholders' meetings; and an account of the proceedings thereof.

The secretary shall keep, or cause to be kept, at the principal executive office of the corporation, or at the office of the corporation's transfer agent, a share register, showing the names of the shareholders and their addresses, the number and classes of shares held by each, the number and date of certificates issued for shares, and the number and date of cancellation of every certificate surrendered for cancellation.

The secretary shall keep, or cause to be kept, at the principal executive office of the corporation, the original or a copy of the bylaws of the corporation, as amended or otherwise altered to date, certified by him or her.

The secretary shall give, or cause to be given, notice of all meetings of shareholders and directors required to be given by law or by the provisions of these bylaws.

The secretary shall have charge of the seal of the corporation and have such other powers and perform such other duties as may from time to time be prescribed by the board or these bylaws.

In the absence or disability of the secretary, the assistant secretaries if any, in order of their rank as fixed by the board of directors (or if not ranked, the assistant secretary designated by the board of directors), shall have all the powers of, and be subject to all the restrictions upon, the secretary. The assistant secretaries, if any, shall have such other powers and perform such other duties as may from time to time be prescribed by the board of directors or these bylaws.

SECTION 7. TREASURER

The treasurer shall be the chief financial officer of the corporation and shall keep and maintain, or cause to be kept and maintained, adequate and correct books and records of accounts of the properties and business transactions of the corporation.

The treasurer shall deposit monies and other valuables in the name and to the credit of the corporation with such depositories as may be designated by the board of directors. He or she shall disburse the funds of the corporation in payment of the just demands against the corporation as authorized by the board of directors; shall render to the president and directors, whenever they request it, an account of all his or her transactions as treasurer and of the financial condition of the corporation; and shall have such other powers and perform such other duties as may from time to time be prescribed by the board of directors or the bylaws.

In the absence or disability of the treasurer, the assistant treasurers, if any, in order of their rank as fixed by the board of directors (or if not ranked, the assistant treasurer designated by the board of directors), shall perform all the duties of the treasurer and, when so acting, shall have all the powers of and be subject to all the restrictions upon the treasurer. The assistant treasurers, if any, shall have such other powers and perform such other duties as may from time to time be prescribed by the board of directors or these bylaws.

SECTION 8. COMPENSATION

The officers of this corporation shall receive such compensation for their services as may be fixed by resolution of the board of directors.

ARTICLE V
EXECUTIVE COMMITTEES

SECTION 1

The board may, by resolution adopted by a majority of the authorized number of directors, designate one or more committees, each consisting of two or more directors, to serve at the pleasure of the board. Any such committee, to the extent provided in the resolution of the board, shall have all the authority of the board, except with respect to:

a. The approval of any action for which the approval of the shareholders or approval of the outstanding shares is also required.

b. The filling of vacancies on the board or in any committee.

c. The fixing of compensation of the directors for serving on the board or on any committee.

d. The amendment or repeal of bylaws or the adoption of new bylaws.

e. The amendment or repeal of any resolution of the board which by its express terms is not so amendable or repealable.

f. A distribution to the shareholders of the corporation, except at a rate or in a periodic amount or within a price range determined by the board.

g. The appointment of other committees of the board or the members thereof.

## ARTICLE VI
## CORPORATE RECORDS AND REPORTS

### SECTION 1. INSPECTION BY SHAREHOLDERS

The share register shall be open to inspection and copying by any shareholder or holder of a voting trust certificate at any time during usual business hours upon written demand on the corporation, for a purpose reasonably related to such holder's interest as a shareholder or holder of a voting trust certificate. Such inspection and copying under this section may be made in person or by agent or attorney.

The accounting books and records of the corporation and the minutes of proceedings of the shareholders and the board and committees of the board shall be open to inspection upon the written demand of the corporation by any shareholder or holder of a voting trust certificate at any reasonable time during usual business hours, for any proper purpose reasonably related to such holder's interests as a shareholder or as the holder of such voting trust certificate. Such inspection by a shareholder or holder of voting trust certificate may be made in person or by agent or attorney, and the right of inspection includes the right to copy and make extracts.

Shareholders shall also have the right to inspect the original or copy of these bylaws, as amended to date and kept at the corporation's principal executive office, at all reasonable times during business hours.

### SECTION 2. INSPECTION BY DIRECTORS

Every director shall have the absolute right at any reasonable time to inspect and copy all books, records, and documents of every kind and to inspect the physical properties of the corporation, domestic or foreign. Such inspection by a director may be made in person or by agent or attorney. The right of inspection includes the right to copy and make extracts.

### SECTION 3. RIGHT TO INSPECT WRITTEN RECORDS

If any record subject to inspection pursuant to this chapter is not maintained in written form, a request for inspection is not complied with unless and until the corporation at its expense makes such record available in written form.

## SECTION 4. WAIVER OF ANNUAL REPORT

The annual report to shareholders, described in Section 1501 of the California Corporations Code is hereby expressly waived, as long as this corporation has less than 100 holders of record of its shares. This waiver shall be subject to any provision of law, including Section 1501(c) of the California Corporations Code, allowing shareholders to request the corporation to furnish financial statements.

## SECTION 5. CONTRACTS, ETC.

The board of directors, except as otherwise provided in the bylaws, may authorize any officer or officers, agent or agents, to enter into any contract or execute any instrument in the name and on behalf of the corporation. Such authority may be general or confined to specific instances. Unless so authorized by the board of directors, no officer, agent, or employee shall have any power or authority to bind the corporation by any contract, or to pledge its credit, or to render it liable for any purpose or to any amount.

## ARTICLE VII
## INDEMNIFICATION AND INSURANCE OF CORPORATE AGENTS

### SECTION 1. INDEMNIFICATION

The directors and officers of the corporation shall be indemnified by the corporation to the fullest extent not prohibited by the California Corporations Code.

### SECTION 2. INSURANCE

The corporation shall have the power to purchase and maintain insurance on behalf of any agent (as defined in Section 317 of the California Corporations Code) against any liability asserted against or incurred by the agent in such capacity or arising out of the agent's status as such, whether or not the corporation would have the power to indemnify the agent against such liability under the provisions of Section 317 of the California Corporations Code.

## ARTICLE VIII
## SHARES

### SECTION 1. CERTIFICATES

The corporation shall issue certificates for its shares when fully paid. Certificates of stock shall be issued in numerical order, and shall state the name of the recordholder of the shares represented thereby; the number, designation, if any, and the class or series of shares represented thereby; and contain any statement or summary required by any applicable provision of the California Corporations Code.

Every certificate for shares shall be signed in the name of the corporation by 1) the chairperson or vice chairperson of the board or the president or a vice president and 2) by the treasurer or the secretary or an assistant secretary.

## SECTION 2. TRANSFER OF SHARES

Upon surrender to the secretary or transfer agent of the corporation of a certificate for shares duly endorsed or accompanied by proper evidence of succession, assignment, or authority to transfer, it shall be the duty of the secretary of the corporation to issue a new certificate to the person entitled thereto, to cancel the old certificate, and to record the transaction upon the share register of the corporation.

## SECTION 3. RECORD DATE

The board of directors may fix a time in the future as a record date for the determination of the shareholders entitled to notice of and to vote at any meeting of shareholders or entitled to receive payment of any dividend or distribution, or any allotment of rights, or to exercise rights in respect to any other lawful action. The record date so fixed shall not be more than sixty (60) days nor less than ten (10) days prior to the date of the meeting nor more than sixty (60) days prior to any other action. When a record date is so fixed, only shareholders of record on that date are entitled to notice of and to vote at the meeting or to receive the dividend, distribution, or allotment of rights, or to exercise the rights as the case may be, notwithstanding any transfer of any shares on the books of the corporation after the record date.

### ARTICLE IX
### AMENDMENT OF BYLAWS

## SECTION 1. BY SHAREHOLDERS

Bylaws may be adopted, amended or repealed by the affirmative vote or by the written consent of holders of a majority of the outstanding shares of the corporation entitled to vote. However, a bylaw amendment which reduces the fixed number of directors to a number less than five (5) shall not be effective if the votes cast against the amendment or the shares not consenting to its adoption are equal to more than 16-2/3 percent of the outstanding shares entitled to vote.

SECTION 2. BY DIRECTORS

Subject to the right of shareholders to adopt, amend or repeal bylaws, the directors may adopt, amend or repeal any bylaw, except that a bylaw amendment changing the authorized number of directors may be adopted by the board of directors only if prior to the issuance of shares.

## CERTIFICATE

This is to certify that the foregoing is a true and correct copy of the Bylaws of the corporation named in the title thereto and that such Bylaws were duly adopted by the board of directors of the corporation on the date set forth below.

Dated: _____          _____

                                                      , Secretary

# WAIVER OF NOTICE AND CONSENT TO HOLDING OF
## FIRST MEETING OF BOARD OF DIRECTORS

of

_____

    We, the undersigned, being all the directors of
_____ ,
a California corporation, hereby waive notice of the first meeting of the
board of directors of the corporation and consent to the holding of said
meeting at _____

_____ ,
on _____ , at _____
and consent to the transaction of any and all business by the directors
at the meeting including, without limitation, the adoption of Bylaws, the
election of officers, the selection of the corporation's accounting
period, the designation of the principal executive office of the
corporation, the selection of the place where the corporation's bank
account will be maintained, and the authorization of the sale and
issuance of the initial shares of stock of the corporation.


    Dated: _____      _____

                                              _____

                                              _____

## MINUTES OF FIRST MEETING
## OF THE BOARD OF DIRECTORS

of

_____

     The board of directors of _____
held its first meeting at _____
on _____, at _____.

     The following directors, marked as present next to their names,
were in attendance at the meeting and constituted a quorum of the full
board:

      _____      [ ] Present   [ ] Absent

      _____      [ ] Present   [ ] Absent

      _____      [ ] Present   [ ] Absent  (

     On motion and by unanimous vote, _____
was elected temporary chairperson and then presided over the meeting.
_____ was elected temporary secretary of the
meeting.

     The chairperson announced that the meeting was held pursuant to
written waiver of notice and consent to holding of the meeting signed by
each of the directors. Upon a motion duly made, seconded, and unanimously
carried, it was resolved that the written waiver of notice and consent to
holding of the meeting be made a part of the minutes of the meeting and
placed in the corporation's minute book.

### ARTICLES OF INCORPORATION

     The chairperson announced that the Articles of Incorporation of the
corporation had been filed with the California Secretary of State's
office on _____ .
The chairperson then presented to the meeting a certified copy of the
Articles showing such filing and the secretary was instructed to insert
this copy in the corporation's minute book.

## BYLAWS

A proposed set of Bylaws of the corporation was then presented to the meeting for adoption. The Bylaws were considered and discussed and, upon motion duly made and seconded, it was unanimously

RESOLVED, that the Bylaws presented to this meeting be and hereby are adopted as the Bylaws of this corporation;

RESOLVED FURTHER, that the secretary of this corporation be and hereby is directed to execute a Certificate of Adoption of the Bylaws, to insert the Bylaws as so certified in the corporation's minute book and to see that a copy of the Bylaws, similarly certified, is kept at the corporation's principal executive office, as required by law.


## ELECTION OF OFFICERS

The chairperson then announced that the next item of business was the election of officers. Upon motion, the following persons were unanimously elected to the following offices, at the annual salaries, if any as determined at the meeting, shown to the right of their names:

President: _____     $ _____

Vice President _____     $ _____

Secretary _____     $ _____

Treasurer _____     $ _____

(Chief Financial Officer)

Each officer who was present accepted his or her office. Thereafter, the President presided at the meeting as chairperson, and the Secretary acted as secretary.


## CORPORATE SEAL

The secretary presented to the meeting for adoption a proposed form of seal of the corporation. Upon motion duly made and seconded, it was

RESOLVED, that the form of the corporate seal presented to this meeting be and hereby is adopted as the corporate seal of this corporation, and the secretary of this corporation is directed to place an impression thereof in the space directly next to this resolution.

## STOCK CERTIFICATE

The secretary then presented to the meeting for adoption a proposed form of stock certificate for the corporation. Upon motion duly made and seconded, it was

RESOLVED, that the form of stock certificate presented to this meeting be and hereby is adopted for use by this corporation, and the secretary of this corporation is directed to annex a copy thereof to the minutes of this meeting.

## ACCOUNTING PERIOD

The chairperson informed the board that the next order of business was the selection of the accounting period of the corporation. After discussion and upon motion duly made and seconded, it was

RESOLVED, that the accounting period of this corporation shall end on _____ of each year.

## PRINCIPAL EXECUTIVE OFFICE

After discussion as to the exact location of the corporation's principal executive office, upon motion duly made and seconded, it was

RESOLVED, that the principal executive office of this corporation shall be located at _____ .

## BANK ACCOUNT

The chairperson recommended that the corporation open a bank account with _____ .
Upon motion duly made and seconded, it was

RESOLVED, that the funds of this corporation shall be deposited with the bank and branch office indicated just above.

RESOLVED FURTHER, that the Treasurer of this corporation is hereby authorized and directed to establish an account with said bank and to deposit the funds of this corporation therein.

RESOLVED FURTHER, that any officer, employee, or agent of this corporation is hereby authorized to endorse checks, drafts, or other evidences of indebtedness made payable to this corporation, but only for the purpose of deposit.

RESOLVED FURTHER, that all checks, drafts, and other instruments obligating this corporation to pay money shall be signed on behalf of this corporation by any _____ of the following:

_____

_____

_____

_____

_____

RESOLVED FURTHER, that said bank is hereby authorized to honor and pay any and all checks and drafts of this corporation signed as provided herein.

RESOLVED FURTHER, that the authority hereby conferred shall remain in force until revoked by the board of directors of this corporation and until written notice of such revocation shall have been received by said bank.

RESOLVED FURTHER, that the secretary of this corporation be and is hereby authorized to certify as to the continuing authority of these resolutions, the persons authorized to sign on behalf of this corporation, and the adoption of said bank's standard form of resolution, provided that said form does not vary materially from the terms of the foregoing resolutions.

## PAYMENT AND DEDUCTION OF ORGANIZATIONAL EXPENSES

The board next considered the question of paying the expenses incurred in the formation of this corporation. A motion was made, seconded and unanimously approved, and it was

RESOLVED, that the President and the Treasurer of this corporation are authorized and empowered to pay all reasonable and proper expenses incurred in connection with the organization of the corporation, including, among others, filing, licensing, and attorney's and accountant's fees, and to reimburse any persons making any such disbursements for the corporation, and it was

FURTHER RESOLVED, that the Treasurer is authorized to elect to deduct on the first federal income tax return of the corporation the foregoing expenditures ratably over a sixty-month period starting in the month the corporation begins its business, pursuant to, and to the extent permitted by, Section 248 of the Internal Revenue Code of 1986, as amended.

## FEDERAL S CORPORATION TAX TREATMENT

The board of directors next considered the advantages of electing to be taxed under the provisions of Subchapter S of the Internal Revenue Code of 1986, as amended. After discussion, upon motion duly made and seconded, it was unanimously

RESOLVED, that this corporation hereby elects to be treated as a Small Business Corporation for federal income tax purposes under Subchapter S of the Internal Revenue Code of 1986, as amended.

RESOLVED FURTHER, that the officers of this corporation take all actions necessary and proper to effectuate the foregoing resolution, including, among other things, obtaining the requisite consents from the shareholders of this corporation and executing and filing the appropriate forms with the Internal Revenue Service within the time limits specified by law.

## QUALIFICATION OF STOCK AS SECTION 1244 STOCK

The board next considered the advisability of qualifying the stock of this corporation as Section 1244 Stock as defined in Section 1244 of the Internal Revenue Code of 1986, as amended, and of organizing and managing the corporation so that it is a Small Business Corporation as defined in that section. Upon motion duly made and seconded, it was unanimously

RESOLVED, that the proper officers of the corporation are, subject to the requirements and restrictions of federal, California and any other applicable securities laws, authorized to sell and issue shares of stock in return for the receipt of an aggregate amount of money and other property, as a contribution to capital and as paid-in surplus, which does not exceed $1,000,000.

RESOLVED FURTHER, that the sale and issuance of shares shall be conducted in compliance with Section 1244 so that the corporation and its shareholders may obtain the benefits of that section.

RESOLVED FURTHER, that the proper officers of the corporation are directed to maintain such records as are necessary pursuant to Section 1244 so that any shareholder who experiences a loss on the transfer of shares of stock of the corporation may determine whether he or she qualifies for ordinary loss deduction treatment on his or her individual income tax return.

## AUTHORIZATION OF ISSUANCE OF SHARES

The board of directors next took up the matter of the sale and issuance of stock to provide capital for the corporation. Upon motion duly made and seconded, it was unanimously

RESOLVED, that the corporation sell and issue the following number of its authorized common shares to the following persons, in the amounts and for the consideration set forth under their names below. The board also hereby determines that the fair value to the corporation of any consideration for such shares issued other than for money is as set forth below:

| Name | Number of Shares | Consideration | Fair Value |
|------|------------------|---------------|------------|
| _____ | _____ | _____ | $_____ |
| _____ | _____ | _____ | $_____ |
| _____ | _____ | _____ | $_____ |
| _____ | _____ | _____ | $_____ |
| _____ | _____ | _____ | $_____ |
| _____ | _____ | _____ | $_____ |
| _____ | _____ | _____ | $_____ |
| _____ | _____ | _____ | $_____ |
| _____ | _____ | _____ | $_____ |
| _____ | _____ | _____ | $_____ |

RESOLVED FURTHER, that these shares shall be sold and issued by this corporation strictly in accordance with the terms of the exemption from qualification of these shares as provided for in Section 25102(f) of the California Corporations Code.

RESOLVED FURTHER, that the appropriate officers of this corporation are hereby authorized and directed to take such actions and execute such documents as they may deem necessary or appropriate to effectuate the sale and issuance of such shares for such consideration.

Since there was no further business to come before the meeting, upon motion duly made and seconded, the meeting was adjourned.

_____

, Secretary

# SHAREHOLDER REPRESENTATION LETTER

To: _____

_____

_____

I, _____ in connection with
my purchase of a/an _____ interest in
_____ common shares of the corporation
named above, hereby make the following representations:

A. I am a suitable purchaser of these shares under the California limited offering exemption because:

1. [  ] I am a director, officer or promoter of the corporation, or because I occupy a position with the corporation with duties and authority substantially similar to those of an executive officer of the corporation.

2. [  ] I have a pre-existing personal and/or business relationship with the corporation, or one or more of its directors, officers or controlling persons, consisting of personal or business contacts of a nature and duration which enables me to be aware of the character, business acumen and general business and financial circumstances of the person (including the corporation) with whom such relationship exists.

3. [  ] I have the capacity to protect my own interests in connection with my purchase of the above shares by reason of my own business and/or financial experience.

4. [  ] I meet one of the investment, net worth or individual income requirements provided for in Sections 260.102.13(e) and 260.102.13(g) of Title 10 of the California Code of Regulations and I meet one of the additional requirements provided for in Sections 260.102.13(e)(1)-(3) of this Title.

5(a).  [  ]  I have the capacity to protect my own interests in connection with my purchase of the above shares by reason of the business and/or financial experience of _____ , whom I have engaged and hereby designate as my professional advisor in connection with my purchase of the above shares.

    5(b).  REPRESENTATION OF PROFESSIONAL ADVISOR

_____ hereby represents:

    (1) I have been engaged as the professional advisor of
_____ and have provided him or her with investment advice in connection with the purchase of _____ common shares in _____ .

    (2) As a regular part of my business as a/an _____
_____ I am customarily relied upon by others for investment recommendations or decisions and I am customarily compensated for such services, either specifically or by way of compensation for related professional services.

    (3) I am unaffiliated with and am not compensated by the corporation or any affiliate or selling agent of the corporation, directly or indirectly. I do not have, nor will I have (a) a relationship of employment with the corporation, either as an employee, employer, independent contractor or principal; (b) the beneficial ownership of securities of the corporation, its affiliates or selling agents, in excess of 1% of the its securities; or (c) a relationship with the corporation such that I control, am controlled by, or am under common control with the corporation, and, more specifically, a relationship by which I possess, directly or indirectly, the power to direct, or cause the direction, of the management, policies or actions of the corporation.


    Dated: _____     _____
                                                 , Professional Advisor

6. [ ] I am the spouse, relative, or relative of the spouse of another purchaser of shares and I have the same principal residence as this purchaser.

B. I represent that I am purchasing these shares for investment for my own account and not with a view to, or for, sale in connection with any distribution of the shares. I understand that these shares have not been qualified or registered under any state or federal securities law and that they may not be transferred or otherwise disposed of without such qualification or registration pursuant to such laws or an opinion of legal counsel satisfactory to the corporation that such qualification or registration is not required.

C. I have not received any advertisement or general solicitation with respect to the sale of the shares of the above named corporation.

D. I represent that, before signing this document, I have been provided access to, or been given, all material facts relevant to the purchase of my shares, including all financial and written information about the corporation and the terms and conditions of the stock offering and that I have been given the opportunity to ask questions and receive answers concerning any additional terms and conditions of the stock offering or other information which I, or my professional advisor if I have designated one, felt necessary to protect my interests in connection with the stock purchase transaction.

Dated: _____      _____

# BILL OF SALE FOR ASSETS OF A BUSINESS

This is an agreement between:

_____

_____

_____

herein called "transferor(s)," and _____

_____ ,

a California corporation, herein called "the corporation."

In return for the issuance of _____
shares of stock of the corporation, transferor(s) hereby sell(s),
assign(s), and transfer(s) to the corporation all right, title, and
interest in the following property:

All the tangible assets listed on the inventory attached to this
Bill of Sale and all stock in trade, goodwill, leasehold interests, trade
names, and other intangible assets except _____

_____

_____

_____

_____

of _____ , located at

_____ .

In return for the transfer of the above property to it, the
corporation hereby agrees to assume, pay, and discharge all debts,
duties, and obligations that appear on the date of this agreement on
the books and owed on account of said business except _____

_____

_____

_____

_____ .

The corporation agrees to indemnify and hold the transferor(s) of said
business and their property free from any liability for any such debt,
duty, or obligation and from any suits, actions, or legal proceedings
brought to enforce or collect any such debt, duty, or obligation.

The transferor(s) hereby appoint(s) the corporation as
representative to demand, receive, and collect for itself any and all
debts and obligations now owing to said business and hereby assumed by
the corporation. The transferor(s) further authorize(s) the corporation

to do all things allowed by law to recover and collect any such debts and obligations and to use the transferor's(s') name(s) in such manner as it considers necessary for the collection and recovery of such debts and obligations, provided, however, without cost, expense, or damage to the transferor(s).

Dated: _____        _____
                                                        , Transferor
                              _____
                                                        , Transferor
                              _____
                                                        , Transferor

Dated: _____        _____

                  By: _____
                                                        , President
                              _____
                                                        , Treasurer

RECEIPT FOR CASH PAYMENT

Receipt of $ _____ from

_____ ,

representing payment in full for shares of the stock of this corporation
is hereby acknowledged.


Dated: _____        _____

                              Name of Corporation

                   By: _____

                                           , Treasurer

## FORM FOR CANCELLATION OF INDEBTEDNESS

The receipt of _____ shares of this corporation to

_____

for the cancellation by _____

of a current loan outstanding to this corporation, dated _____ ,

with a remaining unpaid principal amount and unpaid accrued interest, if

any, totalling $ _____ is hereby acknowledged.


Dated: _____        _____

## BILL OF SALE FOR ITEMS OF PROPERTY

In consideration of the issuance of _____

shares of stock in and by _____ ,

_____

hereby sells, assigns, conveys, transfers, and delivers to the

corporation all right, title and interest in and to the following

property:

Dated: _____     _____

                                                        , Transferor

# RECEIPT FOR SERVICES RENDERED

In consideration of the performance of the following services actually rendered to, or labor done for _____ ,

_____ ,

the provider of such services or labor done, hereby acknowledges the

receipt of _____

shares of stock in _____

as payment in full for these services:

Dated: _____     _____

(Department of Corporations Use Only)          Department of Corporations File No., if any
Fee Paid $ _____     _____
Receipt No. _____      (Insert File Number(s) of Previous Filings
                                                Before the Department, if any)

FEE:   $25.00   $35.00   $50.00   $150.00   $300.00
(Circle the appropriate amount of fee.
See Corp. Code Section 25608(c))

COMMISSIONER OF CORPORATIONS
STATE OF CALIFORNIA

NOTICE OF TRANSACTION PURSUANT TO CORPORATIONS CODE SECTION 25102(f)

A. Check one:  Transaction under [ ] Section 25102(f)    ( ) Rule 260.103.

1.  Name of Issuer: _____
2.  Address of Issuer: _____
                              Street          City        State        ZIP

    Mailing Address: _____
                              Street          City        State        ZIP
3.  Area Code and Telephone Number: _____
4.  Issuer's state (or other jurisdiction) of incorporation or organization: _____
_____
5.  Title of class or classes of securities sold in transaction: _____
_____
6.  The value of the securities sold or proposed to be sold in the transaction,
determined in accordance with Corp. Code Sec. 25608(g) in connection with the fee
required upon filing this notice, is (fee based on amount shown in line (iii) under
"Total Offering"):

                                              California         Total Offering

    (a) (i)  in money                         $_____        $_____

        (ii) in consideration other than money $_____       $_____

        (iii) total of (i) and (ii)           $_____        $_____

    (b)       ( ) Change in rights, preferences, privileges or restrictions of or
                  on outstanding securities. ($25.00 fee)   (See Rule 260.103)
7.  Type of filing under Securities Act of 1933, if applicable: _____
_____

8.  Date of Notice: _____     _____
                                                              Issuer

( ) Check if issuer already has a            _____
    consent to service of process            Authorized Signature on behalf of issuer
    on file with the Commissioner.
                                             _____
                                             Print name and title of signatory
Name, Address and Phone number of contact person:
_____
_____
_____

Instruction: Each issuer (other than a California corporation) filing a notice under
Section 25102(f) must file a consent to service of process (Form 260.165), unless it
already has a consent to service on file with the Commissioner.


260.102.14(c)   (10/84)

From Whom Transferred

Dated _____ 19 ___

| No. Original Shares | No. Original Certificate | No. of Shares Transferred |
|---|---|---|

Received Certificate Number _____

For _____ Shares

This _____ day of _____ 19 ___

_____
SIGNATURE

---

NUMBER _____

SHARES _____

INCORPORATED UNDER THE LAWS OF CALIFORNIA

Common Shares

**THE SHARES REPRESENTED BY THIS CERTIFICATE HAVE NOT BEEN REGISTERED OR QUALIFIED UNDER ANY FEDERAL OR STATE SECURITIES LAW. THEY HAVE BEEN ACQUIRED FOR INVESTMENT PURPOSES AND NOT WITH A VIEW TOWARD RESALE AND MAY NOT BE OFFERED FOR SALE, SOLD, TRANSFERRED, OR PLEDGED WITHOUT REGISTRATION AND QUALIFICATION PURSUANT TO SUCH LAWS OR AN OPINION OF LEGAL COUNSEL SATISFACTORY TO THE CORPORATION THAT SUCH REGISTRATION AND QUALIFICATION IS NOT REQUIRED.**

*This Certifies that* _____ *is the owner of* _____ *fully paid and non-assessable Shares of the above Corporation transferable only on the books of the Corporation by the holder hereof in person or by duly authorized Attorney upon surrender of this Certificate properly endorsed.*

*In Witness Whereof, the Corporation has caused this Certificate to be signed by its duly authorized officers and to be sealed with the Seal of the Corporation.*

*Dated* _____

_____, *President*

_____, *Secretary*

*For value received, the undersigned hereby sells, assigns and*

*transfers to* _____

PRINT OR TYPE NAME AND ADDRESS OF ASSIGNEE

_____

_____ *Shares*

*represented by the within Certificate, and does hereby irrevocably*

*constitute and appoint* _____

*Attorney to transfer the said shares on the books of the within-*

*named Corporation with full power of substitution in the premises.*

*Dated:* _____

                 *In presence of* _____

_____

**NOTICE:** The signature to this assignment must correspond with the name as written upon the face of this certificate in every particular without alteration or enlargement, or any change whatever.

## Certificate Number _____

### Issued To:

For _____ Shares

Dated _____ 19___

---

## From Whom Transferred

Dated _____ 19___

| No. Original Shares | No. Original Certificate | No. of Shares Transferred |
|---|---|---|
| | | |

---

## Received Certificate Number _____

For _____ Shares

This _____ day of _____ 19___

SIGNATURE _____

---

NUMBER _____                                                    SHARES _____

## INCORPORATED UNDER THE LAWS OF CALIFORNIA
### Common Shares

THE SHARES REPRESENTED BY THIS CERTIFICATE HAVE NOT BEEN REGISTERED OR QUALIFIED UNDER ANY FEDERAL OR STATE SECURITIES LAW. THEY HAVE BEEN ACQUIRED FOR INVESTMENT PURPOSES AND NOT WITH A VIEW TOWARD RESALE AND MAY NOT BE OFFERED FOR SALE, SOLD, TRANSFERRED, OR PLEDGED WITHOUT REGISTRATION AND QUALIFICATION PURSUANT TO SUCH LAWS OR AN OPINION OF LEGAL COUNSEL SATISFACTORY TO THE CORPORATION THAT SUCH REGISTRATION AND QUALIFICATION IS NOT REQUIRED.

*This Certifies that* _____ *is the owner of* _____ *fully paid and non-assessable Shares of the above Corporation transferable only on the books of the Corporation by the holder hereof in person or by duly authorized Attorney upon surrender of this Certificate properly endorsed.*

*In Witness Whereof, the Corporation has caused this Certificate to be signed by its duly authorized officers and to be sealed with the Seal of the Corporation.*

*Dated* _____

_____, *President*

_____, *Secretary*

*For value received, the undersigned hereby sells, assigns and transfers to* _____

_____

_____ *Shares*

*represented by the within Certificate, and does hereby irrevocably constitute and appoint* _____

*Attorney to transfer the said shares on the books of the within-named Corporation with full power of substitution in the premises.*

*Dated:* _____

*In presence of* _____

_____

**NOTICE:** The signature to this assignment must correspond with the name as written upon the face of this certificate in every particular without alteration or enlargement, or any change whatever.

## Left stub (transfer record)

Certificate Number _____

For _____ Shares

Issued To:

_____

Dated _____ 19___

From Whom Transferred

Dated _____ 19___

| No. Original Shares | No. Original Certificate | No. of Shares Transferred |
| --- | --- | --- |
| _____ | _____ | _____ |

Received Certificate Number _____

For _____ Shares

This _____ day of _____ 19___

_____
SIGNATURE

## Certificate face

NUMBER _____

SHARES _____

### INCORPORATED UNDER THE LAWS OF CALIFORNIA

Common Shares

THE SHARES REPRESENTED BY THIS CERTIFICATE HAVE NOT BEEN REGISTERED OR QUALIFIED UNDER ANY FEDERAL OR STATE SECURITIES LAW. THEY HAVE BEEN ACQUIRED FOR INVESTMENT PURPOSES AND NOT WITH A VIEW TOWARD RESALE AND MAY NOT BE OFFERED FOR SALE, SOLD, TRANSFERRED, OR PLEDGED WITHOUT REGISTRATION AND QUALIFICATION PURSUANT TO SUCH LAWS OR AN OPINION OF LEGAL COUNSEL SATISFACTORY TO THE CORPORATION THAT SUCH REGISTRATION AND QUALIFICATION IS NOT REQUIRED.

*This Certifies that* _____ *is the owner of* _____ *fully paid and non-assessable Shares of the above Corporation transferable only on the books of the Corporation by the holder hereof in person or by duly authorized Attorney upon surrender of this Certificate properly endorsed.*

*In Witness Whereof, the Corporation has caused this Certificate to be signed by its duly authorized officers and to be sealed with the Seal of the Corporation.*

*Dated* _____

_____ , *President*

_____ , *Secretary*

*For value received, the undersigned hereby sells, assigns and transfers to* _____

PRINT OR TYPE NAME AND ADDRESS OF ASSIGNEE

_____

_____ *Shares*

*represented by the within Certificate, and does hereby irrevocably constitute and appoint* _____

*Attorney to transfer the said shares on the books of the within-named Corporation with full power of substitution in the premises.*

*Dated:* _____

*In presence of* _____

_____

**NOTICE:** The signature to this assignment must correspond with the name as written upon the face of this certificate in every particular without alteration or enlargement, or any change whatever.

NUMBER _____

INCORPORATED UNDER THE LAWS OF CALIFORNIA

Common Shares

SHARES _____

THE SHARES REPRESENTED BY THIS CERTIFICATE HAVE NOT BEEN REGISTERED OR QUALIFIED UNDER ANY FEDERAL OR STATE SECURITIES LAW. THEY HAVE BEEN ACQUIRED FOR INVESTMENT PURPOSES AND NOT WITH A VIEW TOWARD RESALE AND MAY NOT BE OFFERED FOR SALE, SOLD, TRANSFERRED, OR PLEDGED WITHOUT REGISTRATION AND QUALIFICATION PURSUANT TO SUCH LAWS OR AN OPINION OF LEGAL COUNSEL SATISFACTORY TO THE CORPORATION THAT SUCH REGISTRATION AND QUALIFICATION IS NOT REQUIRED.

*This Certifies that* _____ *is the owner of* _____ *fully paid and non-assessable Shares of the above Corporation transferable only on the books of the Corporation by the holder hereof in person or by duly authorized Attorney upon surrender of this Certificate properly endorsed.*

*In Witness Whereof, the Corporation has caused this Certificate to be signed by its duly authorized officers and to be sealed with the Seal of the Corporation.*

*Dated* _____

_____ *, President*

_____ *, Secretary*

*For value received, the undersigned hereby sells, assigns and transfers to* _____

PRINT OR TYPE NAME AND ADDRESS OF ASSIGNEE

_____

_____ *Shares*

*represented by the within Certificate, and does hereby irrevocably constitute and appoint* _____

*Attorney to transfer the said shares on the books of the within-named Corporation with full power of substitution in the premises.*

*Dated:* _____

*In presence of* _____

_____

**NOTICE:** The signature to this assignment must correspond with the name as written upon the face of this certificate in every particular without alteration or enlargement, or any change whatever.

## INCORPORATED UNDER THE LAWS OF CALIFORNIA
### Common Shares

NUMBER _____

SHARES _____

THE SHARES REPRESENTED BY THIS CERTIFICATE HAVE NOT BEEN REGISTERED OR QUALIFIED UNDER ANY FEDERAL OR STATE SECURITIES LAW. THEY HAVE BEEN ACQUIRED FOR INVESTMENT PURPOSES AND NOT WITH A VIEW TOWARD RESALE AND MAY NOT BE OFFERED FOR SALE, SOLD, TRANSFERRED, OR PLEDGED WITHOUT REGISTRATION AND QUALIFICATION PURSUANT TO SUCH LAWS OR AN OPINION OF LEGAL COUNSEL SATISFACTORY TO THE CORPORATION THAT SUCH REGISTRATION AND QUALIFICATION IS NOT REQUIRED.

This Certifies that _____ is the owner of _____ fully paid and non-assessable Shares of the above Corporation transferable only on the books of the Corporation by the holder hereof in person or by duly authorized Attorney upon surrender of this Certificate properly endorsed.

In Witness Whereof, the Corporation has caused this Certificate to be signed by its duly authorized officers and to be sealed with the Seal of the Corporation.

Dated _____

_____ , President

_____ , Secretary

---

Certificate Number _____

For _____ Shares

Issued To: _____

Dated _____ 19 _____

From Whom Transferred

Dated _____ 19 _____

| No. Original Shares | No. Original Certificate | No. of Shares Transferred |
|---|---|---|
| | | |

Received Certificate Number _____

For _____ Shares

This _____ day of _____ 19 _____

_____
SIGNATURE

*For value received, the undersigned hereby sells, assigns and*
*transfers to* _____

PRINT OR TYPE NAME AND ADDRESS OF ASSIGNEE

_____

_____ *Shares*

*represented by the within Certificate, and does hereby irrevocably*
*constitute and appoint* _____
*Attorney to transfer the said shares on the books of the within-*
*named Corporation with full power of substitution in the premises.*
*Dated:* _____

*In presence of* _____

_____

**NOTICE: The signature to this assignment must correspond with the
name as written upon the face of this certificate in every particular
without alteration or enlargement, or any change whatever.**

NUMBER _____

SHARES _____

INCORPORATED UNDER THE LAWS OF CALIFORNIA

Common Shares

THE SHARES REPRESENTED BY THIS CERTIFICATE HAVE NOT BEEN REGISTERED OR QUALIFIED UNDER ANY FEDERAL OR STATE SECURITIES LAW. THEY HAVE BEEN ACQUIRED FOR INVESTMENT PURPOSES AND NOT WITH A VIEW TOWARD RESALE AND MAY NOT BE OFFERED FOR SALE, SOLD, TRANSFERRED, OR PLEDGED WITHOUT REGISTRATION AND QUALIFICATION PURSUANT TO SUCH LAWS OR AN OPINION OF LEGAL COUNSEL SATISFACTORY TO THE CORPORATION THAT SUCH REGISTRATION AND QUALIFICATION IS NOT REQUIRED.

This Certifies that _____ is the owner of _____ fully paid and non-assessable Shares of the above Corporation transferable only on the books of the Corporation by the holder hereof in person or by duly authorized Attorney upon surrender of this Certificate properly endorsed.

In Witness Whereof, the Corporation has caused this Certificate to be signed by its duly authorized officers and to be sealed with the Seal of the Corporation.

Dated _____

_____ , President

_____ , Secretary

*For value received, the undersigned hereby sells, assigns and*

*transfers to* _____

PRINT OR TYPE NAME AND ADDRESS OF ASSIGNEE

_____

_____ *Shares*

*represented by the within Certificate, and does hereby irrevocably*

*constitute and appoint* _____

*Attorney to transfer the said shares on the books of the within-*

*named Corporation with full power of substitution in the premises.*

*Dated:* _____

*In presence of* _____

_____

NOTICE: The signature to this assignment must correspond with the
name as written upon the face of this certificate in every particular
without alteration or enlargement, or any change whatever.

NUMBER _____

SHARES _____

## INCORPORATED UNDER THE LAWS OF CALIFORNIA

### Common Shares

THE SHARES REPRESENTED BY THIS CERTIFICATE HAVE NOT BEEN REGISTERED OR QUALIFIED UNDER ANY FEDERAL OR STATE SECURITIES LAW. THEY HAVE BEEN ACQUIRED FOR INVESTMENT PURPOSES AND NOT WITH A VIEW TOWARD RESALE AND MAY NOT BE OFFERED FOR SALE, SOLD, TRANSFERRED, OR PLEDGED WITHOUT REGISTRATION AND QUALIFICATION PURSUANT TO SUCH LAWS OR AN OPINION OF LEGAL COUNSEL SATISFACTORY TO THE CORPORATION THAT SUCH REGISTRATION AND QUALIFICATION IS NOT REQUIRED.

*This Certifies that* _____ *is the owner of* _____ *fully paid and non-assessable Shares of the above Corporation transferable only on the books of the Corporation by the holder hereof in person or by duly authorized Attorney upon surrender of this Certificate properly endorsed.*

*In Witness Whereof, the Corporation has caused this Certificate to be signed by its duly authorized officers and to be sealed with the Seal of the Corporation.*

*Dated* _____

_____ , *President*

_____ , *Secretary*

*For value received, the undersigned hereby sells, assigns and transfers to* _____

PRINT OR TYPE NAME AND ADDRESS OF ASSIGNEE

_____

_____ *Shares*

*represented by the within Certificate, and does hereby irrevocably constitute and appoint* _____

*Attorney to transfer the said shares on the books of the within-named Corporation with full power of substitution in the premises.*

*Dated:* _____

*In presence of* _____

_____

**NOTICE:** The signature to this assignment must correspond with the name as written upon the face of this certificate in every particular without alteration or enlargement, or any change whatever.

---

NUMBER _____

SHARES _____

## INCORPORATED UNDER THE LAWS OF CALIFORNIA
### Common Shares

THE SHARES REPRESENTED BY THIS CERTIFICATE HAVE NOT BEEN REGISTERED OR QUALIFIED UNDER ANY FEDERAL OR STATE SECURITIES LAW. THEY HAVE BEEN ACQUIRED FOR INVESTMENT PURPOSES AND NOT WITH A VIEW TOWARD RESALE AND MAY NOT BE OFFERED FOR SALE, SOLD, TRANSFERRED, OR PLEDGED WITHOUT REGISTRATION AND QUALIFICATION PURSUANT TO SUCH LAWS OR AN OPINION OF LEGAL COUNSEL SATISFACTORY TO THE CORPORATION THAT SUCH REGISTRATION AND QUALIFICATION IS NOT REQUIRED.

*This Certifies that* _____ *is the owner of* _____ *fully paid and non-assessable Shares of the above Corporation transferable only on the books of the Corporation by the holder hereof in person or by duly authorized Attorney upon surrender of this Certificate properly endorsed.*

*In Witness Whereof, the Corporation has caused this Certificate to be signed by its duly authorized officers and to be sealed with the Seal of the Corporation.*

*Dated* _____

_____ *, President*

_____ *, Secretary*

*For value received, the undersigned hereby sells, assigns and*
*transfers to* _____

PRINT OR TYPE NAME AND ADDRESS OF ASSIGNEE

_____

_____ *Shares*

*represented by the within Certificate, and does hereby irrevocably*
*constitute and appoint* _____

*Attorney to transfer the said shares on the books of the within-*
*named Corporation with full power of substitution in the premises.*

*Dated:* _____

   *In presence of* _____

_____

NOTICE: The signature to this assignment must correspond with the
name as written upon the face of this certificate in every particular
without alteration or enlargement, or any change whatever.

NUMBER _____

SHARES _____

INCORPORATED UNDER THE LAWS OF CALIFORNIA

Common Shares

THE SHARES REPRESENTED BY THIS CERTIFICATE HAVE NOT BEEN REGISTERED OR QUALIFIED UNDER ANY FEDERAL OR STATE SECURITIES LAW. THEY HAVE BEEN ACQUIRED FOR INVESTMENT PURPOSES AND NOT WITH A VIEW TOWARD RESALE AND MAY NOT BE OFFERED FOR SALE, SOLD, TRANSFERRED, OR PLEDGED WITHOUT REGISTRATION AND QUALIFICATION PURSUANT TO SUCH LAWS OR AN OPINION OF LEGAL COUNSEL SATISFACTORY TO THE CORPORATION THAT SUCH REGISTRATION AND QUALIFICATION IS NOT REQUIRED.

*This Certifies that* _____ *is the owner of* _____ *fully paid and non-assessable Shares of the above Corporation transferable only on the books of the Corporation by the holder hereof in person or by duly authorized Attorney upon surrender of this Certificate properly endorsed.*

*In Witness Whereof, the Corporation has caused this Certificate to be signed by its duly authorized officers and to be sealed with the Seal of the Corporation.*

*Dated* _____

_____ , *President*

_____ , *Secretary*

*For value received, the undersigned hereby sells, assigns and*
*transfers to* _____

_____

_____ *Shares*

*represented by the within Certificate, and does hereby irrevocably*
*constitute and appoint* _____

*Attorney to transfer the said shares on the books of the within-*
*named Corporation with full power of substitution in the premises.*

*Dated:* _____

*In presence of* _____

_____

**NOTICE: The signature to this assignment must correspond with the
name as written upon the face of this certificate in every particular
without alteration or enlargement, or any change whatever.**

NUMBER _____

INCORPORATED UNDER THE LAWS OF CALIFORNIA

Common Shares

SHARES _____

THE SHARES REPRESENTED BY THIS CERTIFICATE HAVE NOT BEEN REGISTERED OR QUALIFIED UNDER ANY FEDERAL OR STATE SECURITIES LAW. THEY HAVE BEEN ACQUIRED FOR INVESTMENT PURPOSES AND NOT WITH A VIEW TOWARD RESALE AND MAY NOT BE OFFERED FOR SALE, SOLD, TRANSFERRED, OR PLEDGED WITHOUT REGISTRATION AND QUALIFICATION PURSUANT TO SUCH LAWS OR AN OPINION OF LEGAL COUNSEL SATISFACTORY TO THE CORPORATION THAT SUCH REGISTRATION AND QUALIFICATION IS NOT REQUIRED.

This Certifies that _____ is the owner of _____ fully paid and non-assessable Shares of the above Corporation transferable only on the books of the Corporation by the holder hereof in person or by duly authorized Attorney upon surrender of this Certificate properly endorsed.

In Witness Whereof, the Corporation has caused this Certificate to be signed by its duly authorized officers and to be sealed with the Seal of the Corporation.

Dated _____

_____, President

_____, Secretary

*For value received, the undersigned hereby sells, assigns and transfers to* _____

_____

_____ *Shares*

*represented by the within Certificate, and does hereby irrevocably constitute and appoint* _____

*Attorney to transfer the said shares on the books of the within-named Corporation with full power of substitution in the premises.*

*Dated:* _____

        *In presence of* _____

_____

**NOTICE: The signature to this assignment must correspond with the name as written upon the face of this certificate in every particular without alteration or enlargement, or any change whatever.**

# Index

# T

# CORPORATE KITS

Nolo Press, in cooperation with Julius Blumberg, Inc. offers two superior corporate kits: the Ex Libris®, and Portfolio corporate kits. These kits are fully described in Chapter 5, Step 3B.

The Ex Libris uses a high quality brown vinyl three-ring binder with an integrated slipcase with your corporate name embossed on the spine. The Portfolio features a handcrafted, red and black simulated leather corporate records book with your corporate name embossed in gold on the spine. EACH KIT INCLUDES:

**A Corporate Records Book.** The primary differences between the two books are described above.

**A Share Register & Stock Transfer Ledger, Minute Paper and Index Dividers** for Articles, Bylaws, Minutes, and Stock Certificates.

20 numbered, lithographed green and black **Stock Certificates** with your corporate name printed on the face of each certificate.

**A Corporate Seal.** This is a solid metal tool designed to imprint the name of your corporation on corporate documents.

Ex Libris is a registered trademark of Julius Blumberg, Inc. Portfolio is our name for the Syndicate® Kit, a registered trademark of Julius Blumberg, Inc.

- - - - - - - - - - - - - - - - - - - - - - - - - - - - - - - - - - - - -

## ORDER COUPON

*How to Form Your Own California Corporation*
California Profit Corporations—For Common Shares with 5C Clause

Name of Corporation (print exactly as on Articles of Incorporation). Put one character per space (including punctuation and spaces). BE SURE CAPITAL AND LOWER CASE LETTERS ARE CLEAR AND SPELLING IS ACCURATE. CORPORATE KITS ARE NONREFUNDABLE.

[ ][ ][ ][ ][ ][ ][ ][ ][ ][ ][ ][ ][ ][ ][ ][ ][ ][ ][ ][ ][ ][ ][ ][ ][ ][ ][ ][ ][ ][ ][ ][ ][ ][ ][ ][ ][ ][ ][ ][ ][ ][ ][ ][ ][ ]  45
[ ][ ][ ][ ][ ][ ][ ][ ][ ][ ][ ][ ][ ][ ][ ][ ][ ][ ][ ][ ][ ][ ][ ][ ][ ][ ][ ][ ][ ][ ][ ][ ][ ][ ][ ][ ][ ][ ][ ][ ][ ][ ][ ][ ][ ]

Year of Incorporation: _____, CA

☐ Ex Libris Kit $68.00     ☐ Portfolio Kit $84.00 ............................................................... $ _____

Long corporate names (over 45 characters) cost an additional $8.00 .......................................... $ _____

Shipping Charges    ☐ $5.00  *or*  ☐ $10.00  *or*  ☐ $25.00 ........................................ $ _____

Regular delivery by UPS costs $5.00 and is within 3 weeks
10-12 day expedited delivery costs $10.00
Air Courier (within 4 days) costs $25.00*

Add California Sales Tax—8.25% ................................................................................. $ _____

**TOTAL** ...................................................................................................................... $ _____

METHOD OF PAYMENT  ☐ Check enclosed   ☐ VISA  ☐ Mastercard  ☐ Discover Card  ☐ American Express

NAME _____

STREET ADDRESS (NO PO BOXES) _____

CITY _____ STATE _____ ZIP _____ PHONE _____

SIGNATURE _____ ACCOUNT # _____ EXP. DATE _____

EXTRA STOCK CERTIFICATES:    25¢ for each additional certificate.
*If ordering separately,* $28.50 for 20 certificates, plus half the corporate kit shipping cost.
Please indicate the numbers to be printed on the stock certificates.

CORPORATE SEAL ONLY:    $25 each plus half the corporate kit shipping cost.

*All delivery dates are calculated from the day we receive your order. Sorry, we do not accept telephone orders for corporate kits.
Prices are subject to change without notice.

## SEND TO: NOLO PRESS/FOLK LAW, INC. 950 PARKER STREET, BERKELEY CA 94710

# NOLO'S CORPORATE FORMS TYPING SERVICE

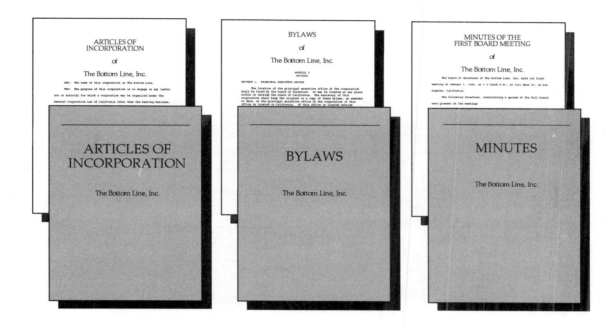

The NOLO PRESS TYPING SERVICE will prepare personalized Articles of Incorporation, Bylaws and Minutes of the First Board Meeting for your corporation according to the information which you provide in the blanks on the order form. The cover pages as well as the first page of each document will be custom printed with your corporate name. Cover pages are printed on grey bond. The remaining pages are printed on quality 20-pound rag bond. Depending on how many minute resolutions you choose to include, the total number of pages you will receive will be between 30 and 35. Your forms will be completed within seven working days and sent to you by first class mail.

Please realize that this is a forms preparation service only and a lawyer will not review your papers. We will prepare your forms to include the exact information which you provide, and we will not be able to check for accuracy in substance or form. Of necessity, we must leave this responsibility to you. Please refer to the special instructions in Chapter 5 of this book when filling in the blanks on the order form.

**PLEASE REVIEW YOUR ORDER FORM TO BE SURE YOU HAVE RESPONDED TO ALL OF THE QUESTIONS—ANY ITEMS LEFT BLANK WILL ALSO BE LEFT BLANK ON YOUR FORMS.**

*Send $70.00 + $2.00 postage and handling to:*   NOLO PRESS TYPING SERVICE
950 Parker Street
Berkeley CA 94710

*Ship Corporate Documents to:*

NAME

ADDRESS

DAYTIME PHONE NUMBER

# TYPING SERVICE ORDER FORM

**TO AVOID CONFUSION AND DELAY IN PROCESSING, PLEASE CAREFULLY TYPE IN YOUR RESPONSES**

## Articles of Incorporation   Refer to the Special Instructions in Chapter 5, Step 2 as indicated.

1. Name of corporation: _____ (Special Instruction 1)

2. Name and address of initial agent for service of process (Special Instruction 2): _____
   _____

3. Total number of authorized shares: _____ (Special Instruction 3)

4. Name and address of each initial director (Special Instruction 4):

   _____          _____
   _____          _____
   _____          _____

## Bylaws   Refer to the Special Instructions in Chapter 5, Step 4 as indicated.

5. Date and time of the annual shareholders' meeting (Special Instruction 2): _____

6. Authorized number of Directors (Special Instruction 3): _____

7. Number or Percentage of Directors for a quorum of the Board (Special Instruction 4): _____

## Minutes   Refer to the Special Instructions in Chapter 5, Step 5 as indicated.

8. Address where first meeting will be held (Special Instruction 2): _____

9  Date and time of first meeting (Special Instruction 2): _____

10. Names of Directors present at meeting (Special Instruction 4): _____

11. Names of Directors absent (Special Instruction 4): _____

12. Name of temporary Chairperson (Special Instruction 5): _____

13. Name of temporary Secretary (Special Instruction 5): _____

14. Date of filing of the Articles of Incorporation (Special Instruction 6): (If your Articles haven't been filed, leave this line blank.)

    _____

15. Indicate the names, titles and, if applicable, annual salaries of corporate officers (Special Instruction 7):

    President          _____          $ _____
    Vice President     _____          $ _____
    Secretary          _____          $ _____
    Treasurer          _____          $ _____
    (Chief Financial Officer)

16. Accounting period shall end on (Special Instruction 9): _____

17. The street address, city and county where the principal executive office of the corporation is located
    (Special Instruction 10): _____

18. Name of bank(s) and city of branch office(s) (Special Instruction 11): _____

19. Number of people who must sign checks (Special Instruction 12): _____

20. Names of people who may sign checks (Special Instruction 13): _____

21. Do you wish to include thr Payment and Deduction of Expenses Resolution in your Minutes? (Special Instruction 14) _____

22. Do you wish to include the Federal S Corporation Tax Treatment Resolution in your Minutes? Special Instruction 15) _____

23. Do you wish to include the Section 1244 Stock Resolution in your Minutes? (Special Instruction 16) _____

24. Provide the following information for each of your proposed shareholders (Special Instruction 17):

| NAME | NUMBER OF SHARES | CONSIDERATION | FAIR VALUE |
|---|---|---|---|
| _____ | _____ | _____ | $ _____ |
| _____ | _____ | _____ | $ _____ |
| _____ | _____ | _____ | $ _____ |
| _____ | _____ | _____ | $ _____ |
| _____ | _____ | _____ | $ _____ |

(please keep "consideration" description brief and refer to an attachment if necessary)

**PLEASE REVIEW YOUR ORDER FORM TO BE SURE YOU HAVE RESPONDED TO ALL OF THE QUESTIONS—ANY ITEMS LEFT BLANK WILL ALSO BE LEFT BLANK ON YOUR FORMS.**

# ... more books from Nolo Press

## BUSINESS & WORKPLACE

| | | | | |
|---|---|---|---|---|
| 💾 Taking Care of Your Corporation, Mancuso | 1st Ed | $26.95 | CORK |
| 💾 Software Development: A Legal Guide, Fishman | 1st Ed | $44.95 | SFT |
| The Legal Guide for Starting & Running a Small Business, Steingold | 1st Ed | $22.95 | RUNS |
| Sexual Harassment on the Job, Petrocelli & Repa | 1st Ed | $14.95 | HARS |
| Your Rights in the Workplace, Repa | 2nd Ed | $15.95 | YRW |
| How to Write a Business Plan, McKeever | 4th Ed | $19.95 | SBS |
| Marketing Without Advertising, Phillips & Rasberry | 1st Ed | $14.00 | MWAD |
| The Partnership Book, Clifford & Warner | 4th Ed | $24.95 | PART` |
| The California Nonprofit Corporation Handbook, Mancuso | 6th Ed | $29.95 | NON |
| 💾 The California Nonprofit Corporation Handbook, Mancuso | DOS | $39.95 | NPI |
| | MAC | $39.95 | NPM |
| How to Form Your Own California Corporation, Mancuso | 7th Ed | $29.95 | CCOR |
| The California Professional Corporation Handbook, Mancuso | 5th Ed | $34.95 | PROF |
| The Independent Paralegal's Handbook, Warner | 2nd Ed | $24.95 | PARA |
| Getting Started as an Independent Paralegal (audio cassette), Warner | 2nd Ed | $44.95 | GSIP |
| How To Start Your Own Business: Small Business Law (audio cassette), Warner & Greene | 1st Ed | $14.95 | TBUS |

## ESTATE PLANNING & PROBATE

| | | | | |
|---|---|---|---|---|
| Make Your OwnLiving Trust, Clifford | 1st Ed | $19.95 | LITR |
| Plan Your Estate With a Living Trust, Clifford | 2nd Ed | $19.95 | NEST |
| Nolo's Simple Will Book, Clifford | 2nd Ed | $17.95 | SWIL |
| Who Will Handle Your Finances If You Can't?, Clifford & Randolph | 1st Ed | $19.95 | FINA |
| The Conservatorship Book, Goldoftas & Farren | 1st Ed | $24.95 | CNSV |
| How to Probate an Estate, Nissley | 7th Ed | $34.95 | PAE |
| Nolo's Law Form Kit: Wills, Clifford & Goldoftas | 1st Ed | $14.95 | KWL |
| Write Your Will (audio cassette), Warner & Greene | 1st Ed | $14.95 | TWYW |
| 5 Ways to Avoid Probate (audio cassette), Warner & Greene | 1st Ed | $14.95 | TPRO |

## GOING TO COURT

| | | | | |
|---|---|---|---|---|
| Represent Yourself in Court, Bergman & Berman-Barrett | 1st Ed | $29.95 | RYC |
| Everybody's Guide to Municipal Court, Duncan | 1st Ed | $29.95 | MUNI |
| Everybody's Guide to Small Claims Court, Warner | 11th Ed | $16.95 | CSCC |
| Fight Your Ticket, Brown | 5th Ed | $18.95 | FYT |
| Collect Your Court Judgment, Scott, Elias & Goldoftas | 2nd Ed | $19.95 | JUDG |
| How to Change Your Name, Loeb & Brown | 5th Ed | $19.95 | NAME |
| The Criminal Records Book, Siegel | 3rd Ed | $19.95 | CRIM |
| Winning in Small Claims Court (audio cassette), Warner & Greene | 1st Ed | $14.95 | TWIN |

## LEGAL REFORM

| | | | | |
|---|---|---|---|---|
| Legal Breakdown: 40 Ways to Fix Our Legal System, Nolo Press | 1st Ed | $8.95 | LEG |

## THE NEIGHBORHOOD

| | | | | |
|---|---|---|---|---|
| Neighbor Law: Fences, Trees, Boundaries & Noise, Jordan | 1st Ed | $14.95 | NEI |
| Safe Home, Safe Neighborhoods: Stopping Crime Where You Live, Mann & Blakeman | 1st Ed | $14.95 | SAFE |
| Dog Law, Randolph | 2nd Ed | $12.95 | DOG |

## MONEY MATTERS

| | | | | |
|---|---|---|---|---|
| Stand Up to the IRS, Daily | 2nd Ed | $21.95 | SIRS |
| Money Troubles: Legal Strategies to Cope With Your Debts, Leonard | 2nd Ed | $16.95 | MT |
| How to File for Bankruptcy, Elias, Renauer & Leonard | 4th Ed | $25.95 | HFB |
| Simple Contracts for Personal Use, Elias & Stewart | 2nd Ed | $16.95 | CONT |
| Nolo's Law Form Kit: Power of Attorney, Clifford, Randolph & Goldoftas | 1st Ed | $14.95 | KPA |
| Nolo's Law Form Kit: Personal Bankruptcy, Elias, Renauer, Leonard & Goldoftas | 1st Ed | $14.95 | KBNK |
| Nolo's Law Form Kit: Rebuild Your Credit, Leonard & Goldoftas | 1st Ed | $14.95 | KCRD |
| Nolo's Law Form Kit: Loan Agreements, Stewart & Goldoftas | 1st Ed | $14.95 | KLOAN |
| Nolo's Law Form Kit: Buy & Sell Contracts, Elias, Stewart & Goldoftas | 1st Ed | $9.95 | KCONT |

## FAMILY MATTERS

| | | | | |
|---|---|---|---|---|
| How To Raise or Lower Child Support In California, Duncan & Siegal | 2nd Ed | $17.95 | CHLD |
| Divorce & Money, Woodhouse & Felton-Collins with Blakeman | 2nd Ed | $21.95 | DIMO |
| The Living Together Kit, Ihara & Warner | 6th Ed | $17.95 | LTK |
| The Guardianship Book, Goldoftas & Brown | 1st Ed | $19.95 | GB |
| A Legal Guide for Lesbian and Gay Couples, Curry & Clifford | 7th Ed | $21.95 | LG |
| How to Do Your Own Divorce, Sherman | 19th Ed | $21.95 | CDIV |
| Practical Divorce Solutions, Sherman | 1st Ed | $14.95 | PDS |
| How to Adopt Your Stepchild in California, Zagone & Randolph | 4th Ed | $22.95 | ADOP |
| Nolo's Pocket Guide to Family Law, Leonard & Elias | 3rd Ed | $14.95 | FLD |

## JUST FOR FUN

| | | | | |
|---|---|---|---|---|
| 29 Reasons Not to Go to Law School, Warner & Ihara | 3rd Ed | $9.95 | 29R |
| Devil's Advocates, Roth & Roth | 1st Ed | $12.95 | DA |
| Poetic Justice, Roth & Roth | 1st Ed | $8.95 | PJ |

## PATENT, COPYRIGHT & TRADEMARK

| | | | | |
|---|---|---|---|---|
| Trademark: How To Name Your Business & Product, McGrath & Elias, with Shena | 1st Ed | $29.95 | TRD |
| Patent It Yourself, Pressman | 3rd Ed | $36.95 | PAT |
| The Inventor's Notebook, Grissom & Pressman | 1st Ed | $19.95 | INOT |
| The Copyright Handbook, Fishman | 2nd Ed | $24.95 | COHA |

## LANDLORDS & TENANTS

| | | | | |
|---|---|---|---|---|
| The Landlord's Law Book, Vol. 1: Rights & Responsibilities, Brown & Warner | 4th Ed | $32.95 | LBRT |
| The Landlord's Law Book, Vol. 2: Evictions, Brown | 4th Ed | $32.95 | LBEV |
| Tenants' Rights, Moskovitz & Warner | 11th Ed | $15.95 | CTEN |
| Nolo's Law Form Kit: Leases & Rental Agreements, Warner & Stewart | 1st Ed | $14.95 | KLEAS |

💾 = Books With Disk

## TO ORDER CALL 800-995-4775

## HOMEOWNERS

| | | | |
|---|---|---|---|
| How to Buy a House in California, Warner, Serkes & Devine | 2nd Ed | $19.95 | BHCA |
| For Sale By Owner, Devine | 2nd Ed | $24.95 | FSBO |
| Homestead Your House, Warner, Sherman & Ihara | 8th Ed | $9.95 | HOME |
| The Deeds Book, Randolph | 2nd Ed | $15.95 | DEED |

## OLDER AMERICANS

| | | | |
|---|---|---|---|
| Beat the Nursing Home Trap: A Consumer's Guide to Choosing & Financing Long Term Care, Matthews | 2nd Ed | $18.95 | ELD |
| Social Security, Medicare & Pensions, Matthews with Berman | 5th Ed | $15.95 | SOA |

## RESEARCH/REFERENCE

| | | | |
|---|---|---|---|
| Legal Research, Elias & Levinkind | 3rd Ed | $19.95 | LRES |
| Legal Research Made Easy: A Roadmap Through the Law Library Maze (2-1/2 hr videotape & manual), Nolo & Legal Star | 1st Ed | $89.95 | LRME |

## CONSUMER

| | | | |
|---|---|---|---|
| How to Get A Green Card: Legal Ways To Stay In The U.S.A., Nicolas Lewis | 1st Ed | $19.95 | GRN |
| How to Win Your Personal Injury Claim, Matthews | 1st Ed | $24.95 | PICL |
| Nolo's Pocket Guide to California Law, Guerin & Nolo Press Editors | 2nd Ed | $10.95 | CLAW |
| Nolo's Pocket Guide to California Law on Disk, Guerin & Nolo Press Editors | Windows | $24.95 | CLW |
| | MAC | $24.95 | CLM |
| Nolo's Law Form Kit: Hiring Child Care & Household Help, Repa & Goldoftas | 1st Ed | $14.95 | KCHLD |
| Nolo's Pocket Guide to Consumer Rights, Kaufman | 2nd Ed | $12.95 | CAG |

## SOFTWARE

| | | | |
|---|---|---|---|
| WillMaker 5.0, Nolo Press | Windows | $69.95 | WIW5 |
| | DOS | $69.95 | WI5 |
| | MAC | $69.95 | WM5 |
| Nolo's Personal RecordKeeper 3.0, Pladsen & Warner | DOS | $49.95 | FRI3 |
| | MAC | $49.95 | FRM3 |
| Nolo's Living Trust 1.0, Randolph | MAC | $79.95 | LTM1 |
| Nolo's Partnership Maker 1.0, Mancuso & Radtke | DOS | $129.95 | PAGI1 |
| California Incorporator 1.0, Mancuso | DOS | $129.00 | INCI |
| Patent It Yourself 1.0, Pressman | Windows | $229.00 | PYW1 |

### RECYCLE YOUR OUT-OF-DATE BOOKS & GET 25% OFF YOUR NEXT PURCHASE

It's important to have the most current legal information. Because laws and legal procedures change often, we update our books regularly. To help keep you up-to-date we are extending this special offer. Cut out and mail the title portion of the cover of any old Nolo book with your next order and we'll give you a 25% discount off the retail price of ANY new Nolo book you purchase directly from us. For current prices and editions call us at 1 (800) 992-6656.

This offer is to individuals only. Prices subject to change.

### VISIT OUR STORE

If you live in the Bay Area, be sure to visit the Nolo Press Bookstore on the corner of 9th & Parker Streets in west Berkeley. You'll find our complete line of books and software—all at a discount. CALL 1-510-704-2248 for hours.

---

---